Readers in Social Problems

DONALD R. CRESSEY, CONSULTING EDITOR

UNIVERSITY OF CALIFORNIA, SANTA BARBARA

VIOLENCE
AND THE MASS M

VIOLENCE
AND THE
MASS MEDIA

EDITED BY

OTTO N. LARSEN

UNIVERSITY OF WASHINGTON

J. & J. HARPER EDITIONS

HARPER & ROW, PUBLISHERS

NEW YORK AND EVANSTON

TO

PAUL, LORI, CHRIS, AND JOHN

WHO PROVIDE REASON ENOUGH

TO BE CONCERNED WITH THE QUESTION

FIRST J. & J. HARPER EDITION 1969
Printed on long-life, acid-free paper, with reinforced bindings

LIBRARY OF CONGRESS CATALOG CARD NUMBER: 68-11718

CONTENTS

v

PART IV / EFFECTS OF MASS MEDIA VIOLENCE: EMPIRICAL STUDIES

PART V / REGULATION AND CONTROL: PUBLIC PARTICIPATION

PART VI / REGULATION AND CONTROL: GOVERNMENTAL PARTICIPATION

PART VII / REGULATION AND CONTROL: MEDIA PARTICIPATION

PART VIII / EPILOGUE

PREFACE

WHAT ARE the *effects* of the portrayal of violence in the media of mass communication? Many people have asked this question, but it means different things to different people in different contexts. Since it encompasses a bundle of curiosities, each article in this book is in some way responsive to it. Furthermore, the total presentation of this book addresses the question on a broad analytic level designed to clarify the dynamics of issue formation and resolution generally. This is possible because, sociologically, one of the major effects of mass media violence is to generate controversy over what mass media material might do to make people more violent in their relations with other persons and to generate controversy over what controls, if any, should or could be instituted as a consequence. In the introductions to the several parts of this book, I have attempted to trace, stage by stage, how social problems emerge by treating aspects of the genesis, development, and implications of these on-going controversies. Within this framework, there is specific material on the individual and social effects of media violence, on the history, scope, and character of violent content in mass communication, on methodological problems in studying effects, on the mechanisms of local and national protest that lead to control efforts, and on the nature and impact of various forms of censorship.

To edit a volume of this sort is to embrace a wide-range of obligations and debts. First, I am grateful to the authors and publishers who have granted permission to take their words out of one context to restage them here for the purpose of illuminating factors and forces that shape our subject matter into a problem of both public and academic concern. I am also indebted to a number of graduate students, particularly to Shirley Olafson and Sandra Ball, who labored with me to seek and sort out materials to fit the framework of this presentation. Their critical insights brought many refinements to the final organization and content of the text.

Finally, to Ruth Berndahl, and her efficient secretarial staff in the Washington Institute for Sociological Research, I am beholden for generous aid in preparing the manuscript.

OTTO N. LARSEN

Seattle, Washington

PART I

The Context of Controversy

> The effect of television on children is controversial
> not because some people are against crime and
> others for it; it is controversial because so little is
> known that anyone can inject his prejudices or his
> views into the debate without being proven wrong.
>   PAUL F. LAZARSFELD

IT IS impossible to prove that man is becoming more violent
or that we live in a more violent world today than that experienced by our ancestors. It is probably true, however, that
this generation *believes* that never has there been so much
violence and, indeed, that we are experiencing a rising tide
of antisocial violence in modern life. Moreover, since the
onset of the mass media it is certainly true that more people
witness portrayals of real and fantasy violence more frequently than ever before in human history.

These estimates contain several distinguishable elements:
(1) The performance of real violence in the real world (e.g.,
war, murder, assault, etc.); (2) the direct experience of real
violence; (3) media portrayal of real violence; (4) media
portrayal of fantasy violence; and (5) audience perception
of the media portrayal of real and fantasy violence.

This book is concerned with the question of linkages
among these elements. In particular, we draw upon the
works of researchers and commentators who have been interested in what the mass media portrayal of fantasy violence has to do with the performance of real violence in the
real world. This is a specialized focus. It means limiting
attention to the "entertainment" content of mass communication and largely ignoring news and informational aspects.
It also means touching only incidentally on a larger literature that approaches the question of violence in society from
broad assumptions about human nature, national character,
or social conflict as these premises give rise to inquiries that
trace violence to such factors as the breakdown of social
institutions, or sexual frustration, or growing moral laxity,
or economic deprivation, or population pressure.

While the specialized topic of this text evokes broad interest, it cannot be claimed that the subject matter has become
the focus of any one discipline or, indeed, that it has been
subject to anything resembling systematic inquiry in any
combination of disciplines. This being the case, the challenge

in editing this volume became one of gathering disparate materials from a variety of sources and assembling them in a framework that would integrate specialized efforts, stake out larger issues allied with the central topic, and suggest that we are dealing with a dynamic problem that calls for continuing surveillance and analysis.

Taken individually, nearly every article in this book in some manner treats the question of how the nature and incidence of real violence might be affected by exposure to mass media violence. Joined together in the present framework, the articles also reveal a patterned social response that can be used to illuminate general processes of opinion formation and social control in a democratic society.

The selection and organization of materials for this book involved a pursuit of the following kinds of questions: How does mass media violence emerge as a public issue? To whom does the condition appear troublesome? What social mechanisms operate to force the issue to points of policy decision? What possible solutions are available? How are they initiated and processed? What actions have been taken? How are they sustained after the public loses interest? What other consequences do institutionalized controls have beyond affecting the portrayal of media violence?

In dealing with such questions, this book attempts to identify in action terms how public opinion is generated, molded, expressed, and impressed on policy decisions concerning the presentation of violence by the mass media. Several articles locate the key points at which influence is operative in the social structures and processes that produce the problem. This helps to clarify the conditions under which public opinion commences to form through various exploratory ventures in collective behavior before it is registered in rational commitments to action. Knowledge of this order is requisite to a full understanding of media violence as a social problem over which society could come to exercise whatever it deems to be appropriate control.

Thus to be concerned with mass media violence is to be concerned with two major areas of interest to students of social problems: (1) The impact of media violence on the form and levels of actual violence in society, and (2) the relationship between mass communication and public opinion as it bears on matters of public policy—in this case, a policy to define the social responsibility of the media themselves.

The simultaneous pursuit of these two interests brings the case materials of this book directly into the province of the sociological analysis of social problems. Violence in the mass media can be established by verifiable procedures as an objective condition in society. But a set of objective conditions does not in and of itself constitute a social problem. An objective condition becomes a social problem when it is widely perceived as a threat to cherished values and thus impels collective action to do something about it. Since perceptions of threat and definitions of action may vary significantly according to social location, the objective condition evolves through social definition to take various problematic forms before a resolution can be reached and can be sustained.

Social problems, then, do not arise automatically from objective conditions, but may be seen to emerge in a context of controversy in which opposing views are projected, persuasion processes are activated, organization is mobilized, and attempts are made to institutionalize power and authority to manage the condition in accord with preferred values.

Few would dispute that American mass communication media dispense large doses of violence to audiences ever growing in size. What does this mean? So far, it means controversy over two related issues, the question of effects and the question of control of violent media content. This book, organized into eight parts, centers on these controversies. The first article of Part I sketches what the following six parts will elaborate: Critics play a vital role in defining discontent by identifying what is deemed "undesirable" (Part II) and directing attention to the substance of violent media content (Part III). An inventory of relevant research is inconclusive about effects, partly because of varying conceptions of what constitutes evidence (Part IV). A dynamic opinion process involving a network of voluntary associations (Part V) leads to control efforts by governmental agencies (Part VI). The mass media respond to controversy and threat of censorship with systems of self-regulation (Part VII). In American society, systems of regulation and control grow out of public opinion and are sustained by it in a delicate balance of social, political, and economic forces linked to some degree to developing knowledge of the effects of violence. (Part VIII summarizes the opinions of four professionals concerned with the problem.)

Mass communication to most people simply means radio, television, newspapers, magazines, books, and motion pictures. Reaction to these media is often based on the assumption that their content, like some poison gas or radioactive fallout, is being poured over a large population in a ubiquitous and inescapable deluge. To evaluate this and other conceptions of mass media effects, it is useful to specify in general terms how mass communication works. The second article in Part I by Professor De Fleur is designed to meet this need.

Defined in general terms, mass communication refers to the relatively simultaneous exposure of a large, scattered, and heterogeneous audience to stimuli transmitted by impersonal means from an organized source for whom the audience members are anonymous. Sociological interest penetrates this phenomenon at several points. The greatest concern is directed toward the social effects of mass communication. This means examining how consumers use and respond to mass media material, including that which deals with violence. But, as De Fleur's paper indicates, sociological analysis can also illuminate prior considerations—the social influences operating in the production and distribution of violent content in a mass media system.

At one end of a mass communication chain is the *source* of information, a complex organization, itself a product as well as a potential molder of social forces. At the other end are the *receivers* of information. Taken as a whole, these receivers constitute a "mass," large numbers of anonymous persons coming from all walks of life. But seen in terms of the ways they sense, interpret, and act on information about violence, the audience members, though anonymous to the communicator, are embedded in a network of primary and secondary groupings, and these are highly relevant for our understanding of how media violence is perceived and acted upon.

The source and the receivers of mass media material are brought together by impersonal transmission mechanisms, but even the operation of these *distribution systems* is influenced by social contexts. Furthermore, since this chain is forged in the culture of a particular society, sociologists can contribute some understandings of its form and functioning from this broad perspective. Sociological interest in the mass communication of violence does not confine itself simply to asking *what* men do, or even *why* they do it; it is also concerned with the problem of why men *must* do what they do. In other words, sociologists are interested in getting at underlying factors which impose structural opportunities and constraints on mass communication with respect to the portrayal of violence.

The central task of mass communication organization is to formulate the content that is transmitted to the audience. De Fleur's discussion of the media as a social system, along with his diagram of the elements in that system, makes it clear that many roles interlock in this effort. Since there are always alternative ways in which content involving violence can be presented, if it is to be presented at all, and since the mass communicator is usually under considerable time pressure, the decision-making process is not a simple one. By grasping the elements of this process, we are in a better position to understand the responsibilities involved in bringing expressions of violence to media audiences. As will be seen, these responsibilities can be shared to some degree by many, by mass communicators, critics, government agencies, citizen groups, and by the audience itself. Viewed sociologically, violence in the mass media is a product of social forces flowing through intersecting channels that eddy around many persons, groups, and values in the total society.

Controversy over violence in the mass media can be useful if it leads to clarification of issues and if it poses realistic alternatives for the solution of problems. This book is designed to clarify issues connected with media violence so that we may cope with old controversies on a more fruitful level and generate new ones that are capable of resolution.

CONTROVERSIES ABOUT THE
MASS COMMUNICATION OF VIOLENCE

Otto N. Larsen

ON DECEMBER 12, 1963, the following brief letter appeared in *The New York Times,* sent by a man from Nazareth, Pennsylvania:

> The shooting of President Kennedy was the normal method of dealing with an opponent as taught by countless television programs. This tragedy is one of the results of the corruption of peoples minds and hearts by the violence of commercial television. It must not continue.

This terse statement, perhaps cogent to some because it offers an "explanation" for an otherwise unfathomable event, is typical of an indictment frequently directed toward the media of mass communication in American society, not only by letter-writers but by men of letters from many disciplines. It says, in effect, that violence is a dominant mode of mass media content. It adds that such content affects behavior. And it concludes that this calls for regulation and control. In the American system of mass communication, such indictments can have a significant social force of their own. They sensitize audience perception, generate public opinion, marshal pressures by special-interest groups, stimulate governmental investigation, and induce counteraction by the agencies of mass communication. They also raise questions of fact, problems of evidence, and matters of judgment concerning values and alternative social mechanisms for their implementation.

For these reasons, this paper attempts to assay the present state of knowledge concerning mass media violence in a context stressing the process of public indictment of the media

Reprinted with the permission of the publisher from *The Annals of the American Academy of Political and Social Science,* March, 1966, pp. 37–49.

All sources cited in readings are given in full in the Notes and References section at the end of this book.

for presenting such materials. Two concurrent but not perfectly correlated controversies will be explored: (1) the controversy over the effects of media violence and the evidence concerning such effects and (2) the controversy over the control of the portrayal of such violence.

The repeated portrayal of violence by the mass media could have many effects. One of the immediate results is the polarization of concern about such content. Thus, the body of relevant literature is mainly a compendium of lines of protest and defense, claims and counterclaims, charges and denials. To register this observation is to note more than a paucity of research. It means the presence of a public dialogue over effects and control repeated in broad form for each medium as it gains prominence and confronts decisions concerning the portrayal of violence. The pattern of this dialogue is, for the present at least, as important as the content of the competing claims. It may be said to signify the search that man is making for control mechanisms to contain the new scale that is introduced into personal and social life by the impressive technology of mass communication. In the process of examining this feature we shall naturally review conventional concerns with effects such as the alleged imprint that violent media content makes on personality, delinquency, and the like. The total effort may enhance our understanding of the functioning of mass communication in modern society generally. This, I believe, must ultimately come from continued efforts to penetrate the complexities of the reciprocal relationship between public opinion and mass communication (e.g., Gans, 1957).

CONTROVERSY OVER EFFECTS

I have recently had occasion to review the extensive literature on the general social effects of mass communication (Larsen, 1964). Rather than repeat a version of that exercise, here directed toward the specific question of the effects of violence, I shall attempt an approach employed by television when it meshes interviews with two or more public figures to simulate direct debate between them; thus I shall borrow a mass media technique to draw together the diverse appraisals of the mass media. . . . The manner of selection below does not warrant generalization about either the views of a given person or the discipline in which he happens to be working. The dialogue is designed merely to project significant views extant in the controversy.

The following presentation was initially developed by abstracting statements from a single publication of each of three men who have particular competence in the area: (1) Joseph T. Klapper (1960), a Ph.D. in sociology, currently directing research for the Columbia Broadcasting System, (2) Fredric Wertham (1962), a New York psychiatrist, and (3) Dallas W. Smythe (1955), a Ph.D. in economics, formerly Chief Economist for the Federal Communications Commission and now a professor of economics. Material from their publications is connected in dialogue form, with adaptations and additions to meet the requirements of this style. While the authors cite each other in their work, they by no means address each other in the manner imagined below. Accordingly, this presentation is not a stipulation of fact according to their choosing but a composite of perceived truth for our purposes. For further convenience, the dialogue will be presented as a conversation between a media-sociologist, a media-psychiatrist, and a media-economist.

MEDIA-SOCIOLOGIST: The fear regarding the effects of mass media content is more frequently expressed by parents, educators, and freelance witers than by disciplined communication researchers. True, there can be no doubt that violence is frequently depicted in the media. However, the statistics of violence shine conspicuously in a standardless void. Their increasing size may attest a trend in media content, but it does not indicate that any particular effects are therefore more or less likely to occur. Actually, nothing is known about the relationship, if any, between the incidence of violence in media programs and the likelihood that it will produce effects.

MEDIA-PSYCHIATRIST: If, as you say, there is nothing known, we are scientifically in a bad way indeed. As I see it, we are confronted in the mass media with a display to children of brutality, sadism, and violence such as the world has never seen. At the same time there is such a rise of violence among our youth that no peace corps abroad can make up for the violence corps at home. Social scientists say that the test of science is prediction, and I predicted fifteen years ago that more and more brutal violence would be committed by younger and younger age groups. Now it is a matter of common knowledge.

MEDIA-ECONOMIST: Can it be proved that particular television programs or comic books are prime causes of delinquency? The problem children you have studied appear to be media addicts who are affected by the cumulation of media violence. However, your book also seems to indicate that delinquency arises from a complex of factors, including the economic and social conditions of the environment.

MEDIA-PSYCHIATRIST: It makes no difference in our stage of knowledge if a cause is not "immediate" but remote, not "primary" but secondary, not "direct" but indirect. What is important is that without this contributing factor the harmful effect would not have taken place, or at least not in that form. In mental life, all contributory factors have to be regarded as causal. My clinical studies of over two hundred unselected cases lead to the conclusion that children are getting more and more tele-directed. As a result there is a loss of emotional spontaneity and a distortion of natural attitudes in the direction of cynicism, greed, hostility, callousness, and insensitivity expressed in overt acts, in fantasy, and in dreams.

MEDIA-SOCIOLOGIST: You mention only a few of the specific fears about media effects; some of those who fear the effects of violence seem unsure of what specific consequences might follow, only that they are undesirable. Others fear that such material elicits direct, imitative behavior—that an otherwise normal child may commit crimes after seeing them on television.

MEDIA-PSYCHIATRIST: I have seen it in my clinical studies.

MEDIA-SOCIOLOGIST: This presupposes that the media have a kind of direct, "hypodermic needle" effect. Research would not support this. Others say that media depictions of violence constitute a school for delinquency, teaching methods of crime, or that the media will have a kind of trigger effect which operates in situations of reduced moral resistance. Finally, there are even those who believe that media violence has beneficial effects by providing a kind of catharsis of antisocial drives.

MEDIA-ECONOMIST: To my knowledge there is no research evidence to support any of these charges, but my hunch would be that no child, exposed to mass media content in large doses, is unaffected by it. Certainly, from our content analysis of television programs, one can conclude that, except for doctors and the unemployed, characters are highly stereotyped, with some of the stereotypes being presumptively dangerous if taken as models for viewer behavior.

MEDIA-PSYCHIATRIST: I might point out here that although your empirical research may not prove that there are effects, neither does it prove that there are not. At the present time, a number of books are appearing which minimize or deny media effects and confuse the issue. So the home, which in pre-electronic times afforded the child protection, is now invaded on two fronts: by bad television programs which influence the children and by slanted books about them which influence the parents.

MEDIA-SOCIOLOGIST: Let us discuss one of these books. It seems to me that *Television and the Child* by Hilde Himmelweit and associates (1958) gives evidence on some of the charges we have been talking about. They studied 1,854 children in England divided into viewers and nonviewers and matched by age, sex, intelligence, social background, and other factors to determine whether observed differences were the product of viewing or were pre-existing.

MEDIA-PSYCHIATRIST: The children were not examined. They just filled out formal questionnaires. Furthermore, when this report appeared it was already out-of-date; the British screen had not yet become littered with dead cowboys. Moreover, it does not apply, then or now, to American children who are exposed to much more and worse screen mayhem. It is also a fallacy to think that findings are not scientific unless they can be expressed in a graph and in very large numbers. There is no substitute for a thorough clinical psychiatric examination of actual cases.

MEDIA-ECONOMIST: You are saying that you don't believe that they can generalize their findings from a large sample to the individual, but that you can generalize your results working with an individual to the larger group.

MEDIA-SOCIOLOGIST: Despite your objections, let's look at some of their findings; we may even find some support for your conclusions. First, they do find that some content may be frightening, on radio as well as television.

MEDIA-ECONOMIST: We must not forget the violence in

documentaries, on news broadcasts, and perhaps even in sports programs.

MEDIA-SOCIOLOGIST: True. However, Himmelweit did find that real violence is less likely to frighten children than is violence in fictional programs, but, on the other hand, real violence is more widely disliked. Virtually nothing is known regarding the duration of such fright or the ways, if any, in which it may affect children's concepts or behavior. The alleged effect on disturbed sleep, nightmares, and the like would appear to be evanescent.

MEDIA-PSYCHIATRIST: Case histories in psychiatric literature. . . .

MEDIA-SOCIOLOGIST: Let me complete the summary. Himmelweit did find that the degree to which children are disturbed appears to be related to the means by which injury is done. Shooting is not disturbing, but a knife attack may be. Violence which follows a conventional pattern, the outcome of which is predictable, such as is found in Westerns, apparently disturbs few children.

MEDIA-PSYCHIATRIST: That pronouncement indicates the difference between the adult's offhand acceptance of what he *thinks* the child gets from television and the actual reaction of the child. It is a typical adult response, and is not how children see it. For example, the report states that if the victim who has been shot clutches at his stomach, that merely means to the child that he has been shot from the front! Many children have told me what it means to *them:* that the man is shot in the stomach because that is one of the places where it hurts most.

MEDIA-SOCIOLOGIST: However, the study shows that children are apparently more sensitive to acts of verbal aggression than to actual physical violence. Sound effects are about equally as frightening as visual effects, and the child is more likely to be frightened viewing alone or with children his own age than when viewing with adults present. They also found that there was no more aggressive, maladjusted, or delinquent behavior among viewers than among nonviewers.

MEDIA-PSYCHIATRIST: As far as negative effects are concerned, this report centers on what is frightening or disturbing to the child. From a mental health point of view, these are neither the only nor even the most important bad effects.

Furthermore, the study relies on statistics based on individual answers to questions, without considering the whole child.

MEDIA-SOCIOLOGIST: In general, while the media do not appear to be a crucial or primary determinant of behavioral tendencies, there are indications that violent fare may serve special functions for those who are already socially maladjusted.

MEDIA-PSYCHIATRIST: The normal child is alleged to be invulnerable, the abnormal child vulnerable. It is not only the abnormal child, however, who can learn—and be seduced. Normal children are not inaccessible.

MEDIA-ECONOMIST: Certainly there have been studies, by Albert Bandura and others, which have shown that children in laboratory experiments exhibited greater aggression and inflicted greater punishments on others after seeing a film with violent content than control subjects who had seen a neutral film. Does this not cast doubt on the catharsis principle?

MEDIA-SOCIOLOGIST: Perhaps. And while we all follow with interest the newer laboratory studies, we will also continue to be curious about what happens when laboratory studies are translated into real-life situations where influences such as social norms and parental sanctions operate. Certainly we need to know more about the duration of any immediate effects that have been observed.

MEDIA-ECONOMIST: I wonder if television crime programs and crime comics are being made scapegoats?

MEDIA-PSYCHIATRIST: How do you mean?

MEDIA-ECONOMIST: Any review of the history of technological innovation would show that where such innovations bear on the public, they tend to become blamed for current social ills. Could it be that we are really fighting the threat to individual integrity of a technologically oriented society? Our mass media have the aspect of a one-way conveyer belt. In work, the individual has become a narrow specialist. In leisure time with the mass media he seems to become more a passive, receiving automaton. If the adult senses that political apathy and a feeling of anomie are somehow related to these threats to his autonomy, small wonder that he protests that passively sitting and watching television crime programs is not good for his child. Couldn't mass media violence also be a symptom of our general social life and not a cause?

MEDIA-PSYCHIATRIST: Something may very well be a symptom and at the same time a cause. This is no argument. Socially, mass media violence is a symptom; individually, it may be an operative cause.

MEDIA-ECONOMIST: Possibly our concern over television and children would lead to more significant results if it were focused on the effects which are precluded because certain kinds of cultural experience, being outside the orbit of cultural industry, are not being made available to children.

MEDIA-SOCIOLOGIST: Himmelweit points out that since violence programs take up a disproportionate amount of viewing time, this prevents the showing of more varied fare that could offer children a broader view of life.

MEDIA-ECONOMIST: What do we actually find on television? Do we find a world where men and women enjoy self-respect and freely accord it to others? Or does it present a world which is peopled with characters so stereotyped as to lack diversity and portrayed merely as all good or all bad? We don't know, but perhaps the intuition of sensitive laymen—such as found in Parent-Teacher Association (PTA) groups—may not be too far wide of the mark.

MEDIA-PSYCHIATRIST: Hear! Hear!

MEDIA-SOCIOLOGIST: I rest my case with need for further research. Thus far, there is little evidence that media violence is a prime mover of behavior. The content seems rather to reinforce or implement existing and otherwise induced behavioral tendencies. For the well-adjusted, it appears to be innocuous or even to be selectively perceived as socially useful. For the maladjusted, particularly the aggressively inclined and the frustrated, it appears to serve, at the very least, as a stimulant to escapist and possibly aggressive fantasy and probably to serve other functions as yet unidentified. I would also add that further information on the role of mass communication in the development of delinquency is more likely to come from the study of delinquency than from the study of mass communication.

MEDIA-PSYCHIATRIST: We are asked to eradicate from our thinking the stereotype of the Big Media and the Little Me. This is far from being a wrong stereotype; the contrast between the immensely powerful mass media and the individual family and child is one of the most essential facts of our present existence.

The dialogue could go on, but *its inconclusiveness is enough to indicate contrasting estimates of what is known, what needs to be known, and what constitutes knowing* about the effects of mass media violence. In the face of such circumstances when confronted with the problem of selecting from alternative control mechanisms, it is prudent to subscribe to Charles Winick's (1961, p. 119) conclusion that

social scientists have generally felt that their knowledge of the effects of media is not substantial enough to permit recommendation of what ought to be proscribed, even assuming the existence of a censorship apparatus.

Research is a continuous activity, and the above conclusion will not be taken as the final word in the research-policy relationship. Some additional cautions should be posted here, however. More recent and more rigorous research than that referred to above is in the direction indicating that exposure to mass media violence can directly induce aggressive behavior in both children and adults (e.g., Berkowitz, 1963). But even if future efforts substantiated such research, further work would be required to establish the social implications of such findings. The debate so far has tacitly assumed that aggressiveness of the individual is socially dysfunctional. This may be, but do we know that it is? Researchers need to consider this question.

Furthermore, in the history of each medium of mass communication, there is little evidence to support the logic that if the controversy over effects could be resolved, the problem over control might readily be solved. Indeed, folk-experience does not wait passively for technical knowledge to emerge to solve problems, but proceeds under a dynamic of its own to search for solutions. Accordingly, we suggest that in developing a strategy of research, students of effects would be well advised to broaden their conception to take into account the evolution of the transaction between media and audience. Certainly, effects do not flow only in one direction. The flow back to the media may be said to begin when someone recognizes a situation to be problematic. It comes full circle when there is an adjustment in the form of some organized regulation. We turn to a consideration of some conditions and mechanisms through which opinion is generated, expressed, and impressed in the media-audience relationship.

CONTROVERSY AND CONTROL

Paradoxically, controversy over mass communication emerges from a point of consensus bearing on the potential impact of the media: more and more people are spending more and more time in exposure to media content; this is incontrovertible. With the development and diffusion of ever more efficient technologies for the transmission of images, the world-wide opportunities for such exposure continue to accelerate. The United States continues to set the pace by creating and extending a communication system unparalleled in its magnitude.

This fact of ubiquity sows the seeds of controversy. Anything so massive that compels so much attention inevitably calls forth some critical reflection on grounds of sheer quantity alone. Such reflection is quickly nourished into specific complaint when considerations of quality are coupled to the assumed potency of size. It is not the machine alone (for who has not marveled at some aspect of this complex mechanical, electrical, and organizational mix?), it is the manner in which it is operated that calls forth the critical response. A persistent feature of that operation is the portrayal of violence. It must be acknowledged that this is but a single factor contributing to dissatisfaction with the state of the communication system. Dan Lacy (1965, p. 62) paints the broader picture by noting that

the banality and emptiness of most broadcasts and films, the "slickness" of magazines, the political bias of newspapers and news magazines, the cultural and political conformity of the mass media, sex and violence in books, films and broadcasts, illiteracy and superficiality in cultural life—all are the subject of thoughtful and continuous complaint.

In the American systems of mass communication, complaints, whether thoughtful or not, can be the beginning of a communicative process that may ultimately register an impact on the decision as to what content the media will offer their audience. Guided as they are by economic considerations intimately tied to audience size, the media can be acutely sensitive to audience feedback. If complaint generates controversy and if controversy generates consensus, then the probability of influence and the possibility of change is maximized. In some instances, complaint can also be effective apart from a real consensus because the media are prone to overgeneralize certain registered reactions. For these reasons it is important to attempt to identify the components and functioning of this interactive system in which complaint has such a significant potential.

Media-audience-critic. A first element to note is that complaint, as a forerunner to controversy, is a definition of a problem that may generate discontent, but does not uniformly arise from discontent. Since the media cater to a mass audience and attempt to satisfy the largest possible number of persons, it is not surprising that complaint does not generally emanate as a grass-roots response. It is, rather, the reaction of a select, articulate minority. Bernard Berelson's (1963, p. vii) characterization of the audience appraisal of television clearly represents what has been the case for each medium at the point where it begins to receive critical scrutiny.

For about fifteen years now, television has been at, or close to, the center of attention in America. The people have been watching television, and the critics, commentators, and educators have been watching the people watching television. On the whole, *the one has liked what it saw; the other, not* [italics mine].

At this point in the process, it might appear that the media, invoking their democratic calculus, would reveal little concern over the complaints of a critical minority in the face of support and approval from the vast majority of their audience. This, as we shall see, is too simple and too static a conception of the media-audience-critic relationship.

While the critics may not like what they see, they are not all of one cut, one mind, or one disposition to act. Some engage mainly in intellectual analysis of factors contributing to the decline of high culture, with resulting impressive symposia on mass media and mass society. Media managers are not insensitive to such efforts but have ready defenses for deflecting the argument at this level. The words of Dr. Frank Stanton (1961, pp. 90–91), president of the Columbia Broadcasting System, present a case in point.

Some sort of hostility on the part of the intellectuals toward the mass media is inevitable, because the intellectuals are a minority, one not really reconciled to some basic features of democratic life. They are an articulate and cantankerous minority, not readily given to examining evidence about the mass media and then arriving at conclusions, but more likely to come to conclusions and then select the evidence to support them. But they are an invaluable minority. . . . They probe around frontiers in their splendid sparsity, looking around occasionally to see where—how far behind—the rest of us are. We are never going to catch up, but at least we shall always have somewhere to go.

Another set of critics is disposed to translate abstract conviction into concrete action in the court of public opinion. Whether such initiators of complaint go on to become the molders of a controversy whose pressure the media cannot ignore or deflect is contingent upon a number of factors. It will depend, first, on the nature of the media content under question, its salience to a broader public, and the relevant traditions, values, and norms concerning public display of such content.

Value clusters. In American society, in sharp contrast to the situation in many other countries, a critic will not automatically muster support for his complaints about the portrayal of violence in the mass media. A number of value clusters are relevant here. One is the traditional aversion that Americans hold toward censorship and restriction of free expression. Another is a deep cultural commitment to violence extending back to frontier days. Throughout our history a great deal of violent behavior has been positively sanctioned. Many occupations allow for and even require the use of violence. Beyond that, the indicators of an abiding public fascination with violence are all around us, as witnessed in the popularity of certain athletic events, such as professional football (sometimes referred to as "Mayhem on a Sunday Afternoon"), the booming Christmas sales of toy weapons ranging from gun-shaped teething rings to simulated atom bombs, and the continued attraction of both real and fictional accounts of war and crime. While the mass media may whet the appetite for such materials, any would-be critic must ultimately come to recognize that such an appetite is rooted much deeper in American experience, if not in human nature. At the same time it may be acknowledged that the presence of other value clusters (for example, concern for the welfare of children) provides a counterbalancing context receptive to criticisms directed toward mass media violence.

Opinion leadership.   Thus, the cultural context in which the media content is received sets broad limits affecting the possibility of controversy and even the shape in which it may be formed and expressed. Equally important, however, is the interpenetration and operation of the persistent action-oriented critic whose power as an opinion leader becomes manifest in terms of (1) his professional status, (2) his access to platform or medium to amplify and spread his argument, (3) his linkage to sources of organized response from voluntary associations, and (4) the ability of such organizations to mobilize community concern, political investigation, the threat of new legal sanctions, and the possibility of some form of boycott of the media by a sizable portion of the audience.

In patterned sequence, these elements have, at one time or another, emerged to direct pressures against most forms of American mass communication to influence the manner in which they portray violence and other sensitive material. A feedback chain is forged as critics speak, opinions are amplified through various media, local groups pick up the argument, voluntary associations mount crusades, legions of decency appear, clean-up campaigns are organized, distributors of media content are challenged, petitions are circulated, politicians are alerted, hearings are held, authorities testify, resolutions are passed, and government intervention is threatened. The intricate elaboration of criticism into effective public opinion, through a maze of protest, publicity, community action, legislative investigation and, finally, media reaction has been analyzed in carying degree with respect to the motion pictures, the comic books, and the broadcast media. In each case, the feature that finally appears to compel the media to react in some visible and tangible way is the threat of restrictive laws or other intervention by governmental agencies.

Self-regulation.   In broad terms, the response of these media to the increase of public pressure has followed a similar form: after a defense of their performance in the name of a "free press," and after denouncing the evils of censorship, they take on the responsibilities of censors themselves as each develops an internal system of self-regulation. Self-regulation means that a communications industry taxes itself to establish an organization to police itself. A code of good conduct is formulated which prohibits the presentation of certain kinds of materials; media content is reviewed and edited in conformity to the code before it is released; some sort of "seal of approval" is appended to symbolize this conformity; and other efforts of a public relations sort are made to head off the kind of criticism that gave rise to self-regulation in the first place. As a result, for a time at least, controversy around a particular complaint, such as the excess use of violence, may tend to subside, and a wavering equilibrium emerges between the force of public opinion and the powers of media policy, as each side of the interaction adapts itself to the other.

The above is almost precisely what happened in the case of comic books, with marked consequences for those products with a heavy violence emphasis of the "crime" and "horror" variety. This medium developed in its present form in the 1930's and grew until the early 1950's when 600 titles of all varieties filled the newsstands and sales reached over 60 million copies per month. At the peak of the dynamic opinion process outlined above, industry self-regulation was instituted in 1954. The comics code forbids the use of the words "horror" or "terror" on the cover and also places restrictions on use of the word "crime." With reference to other materials bearing on the portrayal of violence, the code, consisting of 41 specific regulations and a "catch all" provision, includes the following restrictions:

No comics shall explicitly present the unique details and methods of a crime.

Scenes of excessive violence shall be prohibited. Scenes of brutal torture, excessive and unnecessary knife and gun play, physical agony, gory and gruesome crime shall be eliminated.

No unique or unusual methods of concealing weapons shall be shown.

Scenes dealing with, or instruments associated with walking dead, torture, vampires and vampirism, ghouls, cannibalism and werewolfism are prohibited.

Advertising for the sale of knives, or realistic gun facsimiles is prohibited.

Appraisal. After a decade of self-regulation, the Comic Magazine Association issued a booklet reviewing its efforts (Goldwater, 1964). While the booklet is not an unbiased appraisal, it argues:

Besides establishing and enforcing standards more stringent than any restrictive legislation legally enforceable under the constitutional guarantees of a free press, voluntary self-regulation is effective because it brings about willing cooperation rather than the reluctant, often inadequate or belated "compliance" given to coercive laws.

Then, of special relevance to the framework of the present analysis, it presents an impressive array of testimonials and commendations from church, civic, veteran, parent-teacher, business, and other organizations which leads to the conclusion that

their comments offer substantial proof that the comic magazine industry's program of self-regulation has well accomplished its purpose of providing an effective and practical means of eliminating undesirable material from comic magazines.

The battle over the content of the comic book has been a significant part of the war against violence in mass communication. It has brought to the arena of discourse, as the turmoil over the motion pictures did earlier and as current concern over television is doing, vital experience with a delicate mechanism of social control. While self-regulation appears to disarm many combatants, new issues around censorship call forth new disputes, and not all of the former critics are satisfied with self-regulation as a solution to old problems. Numbered among the latter is the single most influential critic in the long controversy over comics and an imposing figure in the continuing struggle to control violence wherever portrayed in the media—Dr. Fredric Wertham, the aforementioned New York psychiatrist.

Wertham has never relented in his long campaign against the comic books. His skepticism about self-regulation is indicated by a recent statement observing that "at present, with the threat of legislation receding, the number of crime comic books is again increasing by the millions (Wertham, 1965)." If for no other reason, Wertham continues to draw sympathetic attention because his basic concern is with children. As we have seen, he asserts that from the mass media they learn that violence is a constructive, socially approved form of settling difficulties. Accordingly children should be protected, and protected not by self-regulation but by law. He insists that social control for the protection of children has nothing to do with censorship for adults, although he recognizes that to make regulations applying only to children is not easy. He then reiterates his long-standing plea for a welfare law that would control crime comic books directly packaged, displayed, advertised and sold to children under fifteen years of age, noting that similar laws concerning the sale and consumption of liquor are never termed an infringement on civil liberties or a restraint of trade.

When Wertham turns to a consideration of violence on television, his enthusiasm for legal control is tempered by the fact that many adults look at television during children's viewing time, and many children watch it outside of this period. Furthermore, he observes that no control law could be limited to television alone but would have to include the movies which are so often shown on television. Despite these difficulties, Wertham (1965, p. 848) recommends two courses of action: (1) the formulation in legal terms of the permissible boundaries of the kind, quality, and quantity of sadism, violence, and brutality of television shows, along with strict licensing and powers of license revocation in terms of these standards, and (2) the improvement and translation of the relevant part of the industry's code into legal terms to stimulate the industry to strengthen facilities for content analysis and to grant them sufficient powers for enforcement. He concludes that "the best efforts of the best people in television would be aided by such a law, and children would reap a special benefit." And he closes with this observation: "Does the modern state need protection against the mass media? This is an issue with no easy answers. It will be debated for a long time."

Wertham, a man whose critical capacities have perhaps contributed most to the controversy feeding the forces that led to self-regulation, now (in 1965) takes a somewhat equivocal stance with respect to this mechanism. He clearly does not trust it in the hands of the comic-book publishers. For television, on the other hand, he would formalize its "best" elements and buttress them with the sanctions of law. As he notes, the debate over control will go on.

Charles Winick (1961), in a pioneering study of the activities of a program-screening department operating in television self-regulation, has sharply specified a prime requisite for the ventilation of the issue:

A close-up examination of how self-regulation of media actually takes place might help to cast light on those shibboleths or institutions of our society whose lengthened shadows are reflected in the censor's changes and could clarify the kind of use which is being made of the censor's power. Rather than debate censorship in the abstract, an examination of how it actually works might serve to make more real the concept of censorship.

Thus, concern over mass media violence moves from controversy to control and back again to controversy. Whether such cycles ultimately evolve into more satisfactory policy adjustments will depend on a better knowledge of effects, a clearer conception of alternative mechanisms of control, and a sharper understanding of how the two are linked.

MASS MEDIA AS SOCIAL SYSTEMS

Melvin L. De Fleur

... A PROMISING approach to understanding the relationship between mass media content and public taste, and for accounting in part for the remarkable continuity in the (low) cultural level of media content is provided by viewing the media as *social systems* which operate within a specific external system—the set of social and cultural conditions that is the American society itself (see Figure 1).

... The first major component of the social system of mass communication is the *audience*. ... The audience is stratified, differentiated, and interrelated in many ways ... that deter-

Excerpts and figure reprinted with the permission of the publisher from *Theories of Mass Communication*, copyright © 1966. David McKay Company, Inc., New York, 1966, pp. 145, 151–157.

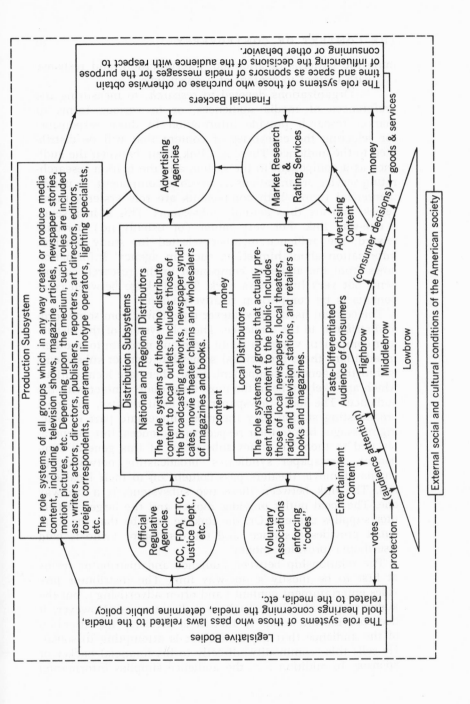

mine the patterns of attention, interpretation, and response
. . . with respect to content of a given type.

. . . Organizations devoted to *research*, to measuring the
preferences of media audiences, or to various forms of
market research provide information to those responsible
for selecting the categories of content that will be distributed to the audience. There is a link, then, between the audience as a component in the system and the market research-
rating service organizations as a second component. In purely
theoretical terms, both components are role systems themselves, and are thus actually subsystems. This is in a sense
a one-way link. For very minor (or usually no) personal
reward, the audience member selected for study provides
information about himself to such an agency. Information
flows from the audience component to the research component, but very little flows back. This linkage between components is by comparison relatively simple.

The content itself, of whatever type, flows from some form
of *distributor* to the audience. The role system of the distributor component varies in detail from one medium to another.
In addition, there are several somewhat distinct subsystems
within this general component. First, there are local outlets,
which are likely to be in the most immediate contact with the
audience. The local newspaper, the local theater, the local
broadcasting station play the most immediate part in placing messages before their respective audiences. But insepara-
bly tied to them are other subsystems of this general component. Newspaper syndicates, broadcasting networks, or
chains of movie theaters pass content on to their local outlets. The link between these two subsystems is a two-way
one. The local outlet provides money and the larger distributor supplies content. Or, the linkage may be that the local
outlet provides a service, and the distributor (who is paid
elsewhere) provides money.

The relationship between audience and distributor seems
at first to be mostly a one-way link. The distributor provides entertainment content (and often advertising), but the
audience provides little back in a direct sense. However, it
does provide *attention*. In fact, it is precisely the attention
of the audience that the distributor is attempting to solicit.
He sells this "commodity" directly to his financial backer or
sponsor. In addition . . . the audience supplies information

to the research component and this is indirectly supplied to the distributor in the form of feedback so that he may gauge the amount of attention he is eliciting. The linkages between components grow more complex as we seek the boundaries of the system.

To the audience, the research, and the distributing components, we may add the role system of the *producer* of the content. This component's primary link is with the *financial backer* (or *sponsor*) component and with the distributor, from whom money is obtained and for whom various forms of entertainment content are manufactured. There are a host of subsystems included in this producer component, depending upon the particular medium. Examples are actors, directors, television producers, cameramen, technicians, foreign correspondents, wire service editors, film producers, labor union leaders, publishers, copy editors, clerical staff and many, many more.

Linking the sponsor, distributor, producer, and research organization are the *advertising agencies*. Paid primarily by the sponsor, this component provides (in return) certain ideas and services. For the most part, it provides the distributor with advertising messages. It may have links with the research component as well.

Over this complex set of interrelated components, there are other subsystems that exert *control*. The legislative bodies, at both the state and national level, which enact regulative statutes concerning the media, constitute an important part of such a control component. Another important part of this role subsystem is the official regulative agencies, which implement the policies which have been legislated. The link between the legislative body (control component) and the audience is of course one of votes and public opinion, to which the component is presumably sensitive and dependent. Information lines between audience, legislative bodies, and regulatory agencies are more or less open.

To the regulatory components whose role definitions are found in legal statute can be added the private voluntary associations that develop "codes" and to some degree serve as a control over the distributors. Such distributors provide them with money, and they in turn provide surveillance and other services.

The regulatory subsystems draw definitions of permissible and nonpermissible content from the general set of *external conditions* within which this extremely complicated system operates. Surrounding the entire structure as an external condition are our society's general norms concerning morality, and the expressions that these find in formal law. Similar, although less likely to be incorporated into law, are our general cultural norms and beliefs regarding what will be likely to entertain or otherwise gratify Americans. Thus, we seldom see traditional Chinese opera, but frequently see western horse opera. . . .

• • •

. . . Within the system itself, the principal *internal condition* is, of course, a financial one. Most of the components in the system are occupational role structures, which motivate their incumbent personnel primarily through money. To obtain money, they are all ultimately dependent upon the most central component of all—the audience. Unless its decisions to give attention, to purchase, to vote, etc., are made in favorable ways, the system would undergo severe strain and would eventually collapse.

Almost any dramatic change in the behavior of the audience would cause the most severe disruption in the system for any given medium. . . . Such disruptions are infrequent, but they do occur. The key to heading off dramatic changes in audience behavior, of course, is to provide entertainment content of a type that will satisfy and motivate the largest possible number of audience members to carry out their roles in accord with the needs of the system. Such content will, in other words, *maintain the equilibrium of the system.* The ideal, from the standpoint of the system, is content that will capture the audience member's attention, persuade him to purchase goods, and at the same time be sufficiently within the bounds of moral norms and standards of taste so that unfavorable actions by the regulatory components are not provoked.

The type of entertainment content that seems most capable of eliciting the attention of the largest number of audience members is the more dramatic, low-taste content. Films, television plays, newspaper accounts, or magazine stories that stress physical violence, brutality, sexual gratification, earthy humor, slapstick, or simple melodrama appeal most to those whose educational backgrounds are limited. Their prior socialization has not provided them with sensitive standards for appreciation of the arts or for judging the cultural, educational, or moral merits of a given communication within complex frameworks. In the affluent American society, it is this type of audience member who is by far the most numerous. He has purchasing power in sufficient abundance so that his combined influence on the market can be overwhelming. He is in full possession of the media . . .

What we have called low-taste content is the key element in the social system of the media. It keeps the entire complex together. By continuously catering to the tastes of those who constitute the largest segment of the market, the financial stability of the system can be maintained. The critic who provokes public attention by denouncing media content and socially undesirable behavior may temporarily receive some recognition. He may also achieve some temporary disturbance in the system, or if he is persistent enough he may ultimately even displace some specific form of low-taste content from a given medium altogether. . . .

PART II
Inciting Social Sensitivity
to Media Violence

PART II

> The critics of mass media often seem intoxicated by their own rhetoric and sometimes seem misled by a nostalgia for a society which never existed; however, their potential contribution to averting and saving modern society from the fate they seem to fear is great, and I am all for it.
>
> ARTHUR SCHLESINGER, JR.

MOST PEOPLE are not particularly critical of mass media content. The ongoing routines of daily life do not ordinarily include concerted efforts to evaluate and criticize how the mass media bring the world of reality and fantasy to the household. In fact, exposure to the mass media gets to be a deeply ingrained habit, the selective features of which tend to reinforce satisfaction more than they stir complaint. The grip of this habit may first become visible through personal irritations that arise with a burned-out television set, a substituted program, a newspaper strike, or with the failure of a delivery boy to put the paper on the porch. In moments like these we become aware of our addiction.

Media addiction does not appear to offer a fertile base for the nourishment of social concern over some aspect of mass communication. Displeasure with media performance nonetheless does arise. When it does, individuals may cancel subscriptions, fail to show up at the box office, or write letters and make telephone calls to register complaints. Beyond personal irritation, and beyond individual expression of preferences, lies the perception of media content as a social problem and the development of collective action to cope with it. Critical publics emerge from previously unquestioning populations. Boycotts may be organized, legislation sought, censorship called for, and books banned or burned. The causes and consequences of this complex process will be examined throughout this book. For now, we focus on what must be present for sensitivity to be aroused and to crystallize into social attitudes and acts directed against media violence.

Widespread criticism and complaint about the mass media rarely emerges in an unguided, spontaneous fashion. Collective concern over alleged media ills can usually be traced to persons who know how to formulate indictments of the media in clear, sharp, normative terms that specify how media

33

content is a threat to cherished values. Where do we look for such persons?

Alarm bells regularly sound forth from institutionalized sources of criticism. The work of the mass communicator is routinely subject to the appraisal of fellow professionals and the often biting responses of intermedia critics such as book, television, and motion picture reviewers. While these reactions spark concern for artistic, professional, and technical matters, they do not automatically incite sensitivity about broader social issues. This requires that criticism be projected from a broader base of social values (e.g., concern for the welfare of children) where media performance is posed as a threat to the stability of such values. Such indictments appear most likely to emanate from sources external to the organizations of mass communication.

Once formulated, critical indictments must be transmitted in order to incite discontent and stir social unrest. Ironically, for criticism of the mass media to gain significant social force in modern society, the mass media must enter into the process. Whether or not media agencies provide exposure of media criticism of this sort depends in part on the characteristics of the critic. Access to the media, as well as the ultimate impact of a message, appears to be related to the personification of certain values (who one is), to competence (what one knows), and to strategic social location (whom one knows).

Though important, media diffusion of critical claims is not sufficient for the direct conversion of large numbers of persons from indifference to concern to militant action. Messages that mount social action do not move solely from the media to the masses. Intermediate steps of amplification and translation are involved. Media messages are amplified from local pulpits, platforms, and organizations. Here they are translated into local needs and adapted for local action. The manner in which this has taken place with respect to media violence will be examined in a later section (Part V).

For mass media violence to arise as a social problem, then, a complex communication network is forged for the multi-step flow of messages. It is difficult to locate the specific first step in what becomes a circular and cyclical interaction process. Clearly, an essential element is a critical reaction to media content. Messages must be formed that articulate alarm about media performance in such a way that they will spread, be amplified, and take root as *issues* in the action structures of society. These kinds of messages will now be illustrated.

The articles presented in this section articulate alarm about violence in the mass media. Each author has gained access to a significant national or international forum. A variety of critical claims is presented. At this point, the validity of the claims is not at issue. What is important is that their contentions about the scope and impact of media violence have disturbed established perceptions, induced concern, nourished protest, and for many persons have clearly defined media violence as the paramount problem of our time.

No one has been more persistent or effective as a critic of media violence than Dr. Fredric Wertham. Two of his many statements on this subject are included in this section. Whether one agrees with Wertham or not, it is a fact that his words have been used as rallying points for crusades by voluntary associations to inhibit the flow of media violence. He is the principal critic cited by preachers, teachers, lawyers, librarians, and others as they enter into the process of opinion instigation that mobilizes action either in attack or support of media performance. Violence in the mass media would not have become a public issue without the kind of effort that Wertham has extended.

SCHOOL FOR VIOLENCE

Fredric Wertham

THE British Government has recently set up a committee to study the effects of television on young people. The secretary of this Television Research Committee, sociologist J. D. Halloran of Leicester University, conferred with me last month about my material, methods and conclusions. He wanted to know particularly to what extent television, in relation to other influences, plays a part in shaping young peoples' attitudes and concepts. Inevitably the question of violence was in the center of interest.

The influence of televiolence is part of a much larger problem. Has the technological development of mass media, especially television, progressed so far that it transcends man and has outstripped its human controllers? I don't believe that we are pawns to advanced machines. Technology is everybody's servant. As spectators and viewers of TV, we are involved in the results and responsibilities, so we must inform ourselves what the real effects are.

Two sets of facts are indisputable. First, in real life certain kinds of violence have increased, and our attitudes about violence have changed. Secondly, there is an inordinate amount of violence on television. More than 15 years have passed since I pointed out that younger and younger children are committing more and more serious violent crimes. Today that is common knowledge. Murders by children under 14 used to be a rarity. They are not any longer. In addition, many of them show more brutality and cruelty now. As for young adults, it has become so prevalent for young parents to beat up and seriously injure their infants or very young children that the condition has been given a name, the "battered baby syndrome," and laws are being considered to cope with it. A new attitude on the public's part has been highlighted by recent cases where men and women were

---

attacked, beaten or killed on the street, in open buildings, on the subway or on ferryboats in front of bystanders who did not either help the victims or call the police.

MASS MURDER

The amount and matter-of-factness of violence on TV is easily documented. An innumerably repeated promotional blurb for *Cheyenne* (a Western series no worse and no better than others) illustrates its monotonous insistence. Within a few seconds two men are slugging it out and two men shooting it out, with one of them apparently killed.

One television station showed in one week, mostly in children's viewing time, 334 completed or attempted killings. Promotion spots showed over and over again 8 murders within 60-second periods (sometimes it was 30 seconds and 4 murders).

I have studied adolescents who in comic books, movies and TV have seen more than 10,000 homicides. Crime and violence are just that, whether shown in the setting of ordinary life, in pseudo-patriotic Westerns or pseudo-scientific settings in outer space. For the overall picture, quality is as important as quantity. A man brandishes a knife in a pretty girl's face on TV and threatens to cut her tongue out. A group of giggling attractive girls are shot down cold-bloodedly. A man is suspended by his feet with his head over a fire. Afternoon programs promise "hideous torture and terrifying horror"— and keep their promise. Typical are scenes of what I have called "sneering sadism," where the torturer or murderer expresses cynical contempt for his victim while hurting him. Children have learned to love that. For example, while one man lies on the ground with an arrow in his chest, a second man comments: "Don't worry, it won't hurt much longer" and pushes the arrow deeper into his chest and kills him.

QUESTIONNAIRE

The question is: Are there relationships between acts and attitudes in life and representations on TV?

This is not a matter for speculation and facile generalization. It needs sober and concrete scientific investigation. The much-used questionnaire method is not enough; even if they want to, children cannot tell you whether or how much they have been influenced. Artificially set-up experiments (similar to animal experiments) to measure aggression are not adequate either, because children are not rats. Moreover the immediate effects after seeing a show are relatively insignificant compared with the important long-range consequences.

We must study the whole child and not just one facet. The only method that can give valid results is the clinical method. That is to say, the child has to be examined and all the psychobiological and psychosocial factors with a bearing on his life have to be considered. The influence of TV has to be taken up and analyzed unobtrusively and incidentally. Follow-up study of development is necessary and what young adults say later about their childhood is most relevant.

I have been studying the effects of mass media (first comic books, then television) for many years. My definite opinion is that continuous exposure of children's minds to scenes of crime and brutality has had a deeper effect on them than is generally realized—just as the constructive effects of good shows (quite apart from strictly educational programs) are more far-reaching than is generally assumed. Television in the life of the young is either educational or miseducational —but never—in the long run—neutral. For children, the television screen has become a second reality.

When Lee Harvey Oswald was actually murdered on the screen, some adults for a moment did not believe their eyes. They did not understand what had happened. Children blended their realities and knew right off: "He shot him in the stomach." That is what always happens in the serials; they had seen it a thousand times. In one of my group therapy sessions, a boy brought up the point that Oswald was completely defenseless since he was handcuffed to two sheriffs when Ruby shot him point-blank. "Why not?" asked another boy.

Eliot Ness (the crime-fighter hero of *The Untouchables*) is a good guy and he gives a prisoner a terrific sock while two cops hold him. Many modern children fail to see the evil in horror and the wrong in violence and have lost their natural sympathy for the suffering of others. The trouble is not that they get frightened, but that they do not get frightened.

TV FACTOR

Of course the TV factor never works alone. The cult of violence lurks in many areas of our own social life. We speak glibly of the casualties of the next war in terms of minutes and millions. We kill each other recklessly on the highways. Human life has become more devaluated than the dollar. The fact that there are so many other influences working in the same direction does not make the television factor less potent, but more so. The witnesses who did not come to the aid of the girl who was being stabbed, the young people who shouted "Jump!" and "Chicken!" and "What's the matter—ya yellow?" to would-be suicides on the top of the building in Albany and the bridge in Brooklyn were conditioned in many ways. The mass media, and especially television, make up one part of this conditioning.

Whether crime and violence programs arouse a lust for violence, reinforce it when it is present, show a way to carry it out, teach the best method to get away with it or merely blunt the child's (and adult's) awareness of its wrongness, television has become a school for violence.

In this school young people are never, literally never, taught that violence is in itself reprehensible. The lesson they do get is that violence is the great adventure and the sure solution, and he who is best at it wins. We are training not only a peace corps but also a violence corps. I do not advocate that violence should be entirely eliminated from TV. But it should be presented as a fact of life, not as life itself. We want to show younger people how the other half lives; but that does not mean we have to overload their imagination with images of how the other half dies.

WE'RE TEACHING OUR CHILDREN
THAT VIOLENCE IS FUN

Eve Merriam

WHEN something becomes part of everyday life, we no longer notice it. By now, make-believe weapons for children are part of the daily scene, ranging all the way from bomber models to gun-shaped teething rings. On Christmas and birthdays, doting grandparents give toddlers the latest mock-up missile. This year, toy grenades are popular.

Also available in variety stores, dime stores and department stores are toy bazookas, rifles, machine guns and pistols. "Pull the trigger," say the ads, "loud bang is followed by whining noise of bullet. Wisp of smoke curls from the end of the barrel." Or "Load it with caps! Single shot or rapid fire—real live action—loads, fires and ejects shells!" All part of the everyday scene. . . .

Here, too, are newsstands proffering their accustomed children's wares: smoking guns and snarling faces peering from ever-new installments of Rawhide Kid, Two-Gun Kid, Space War, X-Men, Metal Men, Superman, Superboy, super violence. . . . Comic books have been in existence since 1937; it is estimated that 90 percent of all children between the ages of 7 and 14 read them. Part of the everyday scene.

And here, day in and day out, movie houses hawk the standard marquee messages: "Suspense shocker" . . . "sexy, sexy" . . . "brute of a man with the instincts of an animal" . . . "the bullet wasn't made that could stop him". . . "why did the thing want to devour women?" . . . "vividly depicts ax murders." A movie week like any other.

And, blaring endlessly, a television week like any other. Except for occasional pauses for national-conscience identification, business goes on as usual: the bullets whine in the Westerns, the police sirens shriek in the Easterns. To what dramatic purpose? Rarely is the brutality vital to the plot. The shooting scenes are thrown in for shock effect, to keep the viewer "entertained."

A report to the Federal Communications Commission states that between the ages of 5 and 14 the average American child witnesses the violent destruction of 13,000 human beings on television. If that figure seems exaggerated, consider that children spend more time watching television than on any other activity outside of sleep and school. Consider also what is available on "the children's hour," that period between four and nine p.m. when young people do most of their watching.

After a survey of one week's programming by four commercial channels in a major U. S. city, Stanford University published these findings: "The picture of the adult world presented on the children's hour is heavy in physical violence, light in intellectual interchange, and deeply concerned with crime."

In a five-day period, Monday through Friday, programs showed a stabbing in the back, four attempted suicides (three successful), four people falling or pushed over cliffs, two cars rolling over cliffs, two attempts to run cars over persons on the sidewalk, a raving psychotic loose in a flying airliner, two mob scenes (in one of which the mob hangs the wrong man), a horse grinding a man under its hooves, 12 murders, 16 major gunfights, 21 persons shot (apparently not fatally), 21 other violent incidents with guns (ranging from near-misses to shooting up a town), 37 hand-to-hand fights, an attempted murder with a pitchfork, two stranglings, a fight in the water, a woman being gagged and tied to a bed, and a great deal of miscellaneous violence, including a hired killer stalking his prey, two robberies, a pickpocket working, a woman killed by falling from a train, a tidal wave and a guillotining.

Scheduling for the 1964–65 season indicates that a high proportion of "action-adventure shows" is continuing, along with new private-eye and public mayhem features. And as television goes, so goes the rest of the entertainment scene. Movie battles are bigger and bloodier than ever, comic books and toys tie in with the goriest spectacles. It's all offered in the name of leisuretime "fun."

Combat, for instance, is a weekly hour-long show based

on World War II. Broadcast during an early-evening hour, it has millions of child viewers. In addition, 30 kinds of "play" items are licensed for sale by the show. A child can be in a state of total combat from morning until night. He can wear an official *Combat* uniform and helmet . . . wind a *Combat* watch . . . read a *Combat* comic book . . . play a *Combat* board game . . . carry a *Combat* field medical kit complete with bandages and stretcher . . . throw a rubber *Combat* grenade (10 points for knocking out infantry, 100 for a tank) . . . and he can sport several different kinds of official *Combat* guns.

In some societies children are taught the violence of hatred and prejudice, and the violence of war. But does any other society teach its children that violence is a form of entertainment? What will happen to a generation raised upon such an idea? We do not know, because today's children are the first guinea pigs.

Our nation's crime rate is high compared with most other countries' and has been rising steadily. The rate of juvenile crime has been rising even more sharply. What baffles authorities is the increasing number of youthful crimes committed for no obvious reason—not for revenge, not for greed, not for any cause that can be uncovered. These crimes are just for "kicks": slashing the tires of a car, beating up an old man on a dark street, and one of the newest teen-age "games"—the mock-up, where a couple of pals pretend to shoot or drag off a third, and what fun when the police come running!

Violence as a gimmick, as a toy, as a show. Why not? Isn't that the fashion? If you're too young or timid for active play, you can always tell a sick joke about a cripple or send some friend a "drop dead" greeting card. These acts of violence, big and little, are part of the everyday scene. And dominating the scene is the box in the living room in 91 percent of the total households in the continental United States, so that our nation's children can simply press a button and tune in.

We tend to think of children's television as a special category: cartoon programs, games, animal stories, folk songs. In fact, these programs take up little network time and little of the child's life. What they are watching, from babyhood up, are the adult programs. For every 100 sets tuned to *Gunsmoke* and *The Untouchables*, for instance, there are 40 child viewers.

We have not seemed to care much, at least not until now. The Bureau of Applied Social Research of Columbia University last year conducted an extensive study of family viewing habits. It was found that parents object most to violent programs; this element was mentioned overwhelmingly as the chief irritant. Yet only 5 percent of the families interviewed could recall trying to regulate their children's viewing. Parents who did exercise control merely limited the *amount* of television viewing per week, or the times it could be watched—after homework, for instance. The actual content of programs was ignored. Apparently, most of us are using television as a baby-sitter, and not bothering to ask for references. We do not reflect that this particular sitter may be a wicked influence.

Over a three year period a special U. S. Senate subcommittee has been investigating crime-sex-and-violence television programming for its possible role in juvenile delinquency. Senator Thomas Dodd of Connecticut, chairman of the committee, said:

Glued to the TV set from the time they can walk, our children are getting an intensive training in all phases of crime from the ever-increasing array of Westerns and crime-detective programs available to them. The past decade has seen TV come of age. However, the same decade has witnessed the violence content in programs skyrocket and delinquency in real life grow almost two hundred percent.

Further hearings were held last summer. Testimony already gathered provides insight into the attitudes of those who sell violence as entertainment. Here, for instance, is what the president of the Television Writers Guild of the West Coast told the committee: "Nobody ever sends you a memo saying 'Kill.' I feel that violence happens because . . . a producer feels he has an obligation to top the violence of the show opposite him."

Consider the paternalistic advice from a producer of *The Untouchables* to a member of his staff: "On page 31 of this script, I wish we could come up with a different device than running the man down with a car, as we have done this now in three different shows. I like the idea of the sadism, but I hope we can come up with another approach to it."

The vice president of the Television Writers Guild added a postscript out of his own experience: "I wrote one show recently that did not have a heavy gun in it or a weapon of any sort and it was well received by the studio. Regretfully, this show is now off the air."

But still on the air are syndicated installments of programs like *The Untouchables*. The Senate committee hearings revealed a script reader's comments to the studio producing the series: "This [installment] is loaded with action. Many exciting scenes. Opens right up on a lot of action —running gunfight between two cars of mobsters who crash, then continue the fight in the streets. Three killed, six injured—three killed are innocent bystanders."

We often hear the timeworn argument that the games children make up for themselves are far more frightening than anything that could pass the self-imposed codes of the comic books, publishers, movie makers, television authorities and toy manufacturers' council. Today's entertainment, the violence vendors say, is a pale reflection of children's naturally wild state.

Look at what parents and educators urge upon children (the argument continues), with no fear about their junior psyches being damaged. *Punch and Judy* is full of vicious beatings, and fairy tales are really horror stories.

Unfortunately, such parallels are not reassuring: for today's vicarious violence is both pervasive and *realistic*. Witches and dragons do not exist; getaway cars, bank robbers, and switchblades do.

Because the medium is relatively new, studies of the effects of indiscriminate and prolonged television viewing on today's children are still being evaluated. However, many studies have been completed describing the effects of radio, comic books and movies protraying violent scenes. The consensus is that reactions among children vary from mild anxiety to nightmares; from pulling the covers over their heads, to bed-wetting and to insisting on getting into bed with parents for protection. Yet radio offers no scary pictures, only sound effects: in comic books the pictures do not move;

and at the movies there is an adult alongside, or at least an extended period of "coming to" in the lobby and the street on the way home.

Reactions to a threatening scene on television are likely to be more intense; the child is already at home.

The violent entertainment forms affect children in other ways. If they are not becoming actively delinquent—our "good" middle-class children, yours and mine—they are becoming passively jaded. As a kind of self-protection, they develop thick skins to avoid being upset by the gougings, smashings and stompings they see on TV. As the voice of reason is shown to be a swift uppercut to the chin, child viewers cannot afford to get involved, for if they did, their emotions would be shredded. So they keep "cool," distantly unaffected. Boredom sets in, and the whole cycle starts over again. Bring on another show with even more bone-crushing and teeth-smashing so the viewers will react. The dramas reach new peaks of intensity; occasionally the continuity acceptance editor at the network has had to admonish: "On page 40, scene 85—delete the way Johnny kills Mrs. Zagano. As described it is not acceptable. . . . Delete the screams and gurgles. There's a commercial coming up." And further on, "Try to cut down on the killings please."

Please. Of another script, the network editor comments:

Violent death, pages 3, 19, 53, 61, 63, 64, 65. On page 4, scene 14, don't overdo the violence here—slapping woman, rabbit punch, etc. Page 53, scene 135—I don't see how we can do this scene acceptably. It's too gruesome a killing; a woman does it—the man is laughing—it's the end of an act before a commercial and we've got too much violent death in the show as it is. Please kill him another way. Even off camera it's too awful. This is a good show and I hope we can fix it for acceptance.

A good show. Sit back and watch the show as the world of entertainment crosses over to the real world. Newspapers tell how a youthful Midwest gang has modeled itself upon its favorite TV program. "We are untouchable," yells the 17-year-old leader when the gang is picked up after an attempted killing, "you can't do anything to us!"

And the real world crosses over to the entertainment world. A definition of true-life delinquency could just as easily apply to many of the amoral private-eye and Western heroes play-ing on movie and television screens.

Dr. Lewis Yablonsky, youth worker and sociologist, says that "one of the violent gang leader's vital functions for gang membership is to serve as a symbol of idealized violence."

The leader of a violent gang called The Bombers, for in-stance, demanded that new members, as part of their initia-tion, go out and beat up somebody, any somebody, some anybody. That behavior is recognized as socially delinquent. Yet here is socially acceptable behavior in the form of a character outlined for the hero of a projected "action-adven-ture" series on a leading network:

Curiosity is the keynote to Barton's character, curiosity to the point of danger and death. . . . He doesn't always find out, he may almost get killed, somebody always gets badly hurt, but the audi-ence gets a hell of a ride. Despite his many protests that he is only interested in research, it is obvious that he is fascinated with the amount of punishment and pressure the human body can sustain. The fact that it is quite often his own body that takes the punish-ment makes the razor's edge that much more fascinating.

Following a consultation with a high executive at the network, it was decided, in the interests of gaining a wider audience, to add a generous dose of sadism to the basic masochism.

As our protagonist is . . . in a hazardous occupation, the inclu-sion of sex and violence is not only desirable but can be accom-plished correctly and organically. . . . We look forward to a suc-cessful season.

A psychiatrist, Dr. Eugene David Glynn, raises some pointed questions about these sex-and-violence programs that children see. Doctor Glynn asks:

How high can excitement be raised? What will be the result of such constant stimulation? It is to soon to know what children so massively exposed to sex on television will consider exciting and sex-stimulating as adults. Will reality live up to the fantasies this generation has been nursed on?

The children are in a peculiar position; experience is exhausted in advance. There is little they have not seen or done or lived through, and yet this is secondhand experience. When the experience itself comes, it is watered-down, for it has already been half lived, but never truly felt.

· · ·

TV VIOLENCE—THE KIDS REACT

Mary Ann Guitar

TELEVISION, to no one's great surprise, has once again been judged guilty of contributing to juvenile delinquency. The 1964 hearings of the Senate Subcommittee on Juvenile Delinquency recently reaffirmed what 1954 and 1961 hearings had already established: Violence is a staple in the TV diet of millions of children. Senator Thomas J. Dodd of Connecticut and most of his committee agreed that this can have serious consequences. Their report states categorically: "The excessive amount of televised crime, violence and brutality can and does contribute to the development of attitudes in many young people that pave the way for delinquent behavior."

The day after the Dodd subcommittee report was made public, television received another blow. In a report to the American Academy of Pediatrics, two Air Force doctors asserted that too much TV can make a child actually sick. The so-called "tired child syndrome" was thus laid at the door of TV.

Everyone, it would seem, is talking about TV and its adverse effect on children, but no one has asked the victimized to testify in their own behalf. This midget survey, therefore, is to discover what children think about violence on TV.

Most youngsters queried agreed with the worldly 16-year-old who opined: "If you're a sadistic little monster, I suppose it could have an effect, but I don't think most of us are going to be affected."

If the young are frightened by what they see on television, they are reluctant to admit it. "No one takes it seriously," they protest. One wonders if they protest too much. Some of their examples are hair-raising. One boy recalled when "a guy's eyes popped out when he was run over by a car. We laughed ourselves sick."

Even if an episode produces shock rather than giggles, some older children believe it is a good thing. They think watching aggression provides a certain release. Asked if a TV scene might not provide an angry child with an unsavory model for behavior, the youngsters in this sample denied that they were susceptible. "I doubt if anyone would pluck his eyes out after seeing *Oedipus*," a high-school girl commented.

Perhaps so, but critics of TV violence point out that the child is a natural imitator. Even the experts, however, are not willing to state unequivocally that they know how children will react.

In an article written for *Scientific American*, Leonard Berkowitz contends (1964, p. 41):

The film might activate his aggressive habit so that he would be primed to act aggressively. Should he then encounter people with appropriate stimulus qualities, people he dislikes or connects psychologically with the film, this predisposition could lead to open aggression. [On the other hand, I would not] reject the argument that a frustrated person can enjoy fantasy aggression because he sees characters doing things he wishes he could do, although in most cases his inhibitions restrain him.

Youthful connoisseurs of TV agree with this diagnosis. One old hand of 15 says that the under-10 age group is the most susceptible to illusions of violence *cum* power. "They store away these ideas to get back at parents." But, he adds reassuringly, "You get mad at your father. You go to your room and work out how you would get back at him. But that's it." In other words, no one really follows through. No one, that is except the "dotards" (an ingenious condensation of dolt and retard used to identify the "Bruno's" or high ape groups).

Most young TV-watchers admit they are aware of TV fads

in violence, but insist that the various techniques are simply matters for conversational speculation. "Piano wire made it big for a long time," one observer noted. "They were always using it to strangle a guy or cut him up."

Children are said to hoard examples of refined sadism. As one boy explained, "They trade them like baseball cards." It is not uncommon to overhear a pair of 8-year-olds sharing sadism's shop talk. "Hey, did you see the cool thing they did last night? When they put flaming bamboo shoots under his fingernails?"

The young draw a fine distinction between what might be called the natural tools of childhood aggression and ones that have been displayed in action on TV. "Knives are just part of growing up," one boy asserted. "But the attraction of stilettos and switchblades is definitely stimulated by what you see." Then, while protesting that "only the peasantry is impressed with torture techniques," he contributed a chilling thought. "I'm sort of fascinated, too. I wonder what it would feel like to put your finger through someone. You can with karate."

It is precisely this sort of reaction that has led critics like Senator Dodd and Dr. Fredric Wertham, a longtime crusader against TV violence, to call for a clean-up of television programs. The latter argues: "Whether crime and violence programs arouse lust for violence, reinforce it when it is present, show a want to carry it out, teach the best method to get away with it or merely blunt the child's (and adult's) awareness of its wrongness, television has become a school for violence."

One astute 12-year-old said, "The scariest things are the things that are true." She points out that period drama is rarely terrifying, because "you know it's not of this time or place. The worst was when Oswald was shot." Dr. Wertham reports that many adults did not believe their eyes when Oswald was shot, but children knew instinctively what had happened—it was just like swift justice in the Westerns.

Clearly we cannot eliminate the violence of our own reality from the home screen. But, one wonders, must we compound the problem by presenting so much fictionalized violence? Senator Dodd has asked the networks to police themselves or face restrictive legislation. Meantime, parents can put limits on TV viewing. Many youngsters defend their addiction to the "idiot box" by saying, "If my folks thought it was bad for me, they wouldn't let me watch."

In point of fact, many parents rather relish some of the gunplay themselves. As Dr. Karl Menninger said recently: "We not only tolerate violence, we love it. We put it on the front pages of our newspapers. One-third or one-fourth of our television programs use it for the amusement of our children."

As long as this attitude prevails, the television industry may well conclude that, investigations and reports notwithstanding, it has a vote of confidence from the public.

IS TV HARDENING US
TO THE WAR IN VIETNAM?

Fredric Wertham

AT A RECENT panel discussion held by the International Writers Guild, James C. Hagerty, former press secretary to President Eisenhower and now an ABC executive, praised the television treatment of the war in Vietnam. The Vietnam war films, he said, show us war as it is and thereby help to advance the cause of peace. The daily exposure to the rigors of the battlefield, which for the first time in history everyone can experience in his home, will "convince people that war is the least sensible way of settling disputes." In other words, the mass coverage of the Vietnam war represents, in his view, a kind of electronic pacifism.

My observations are different. They are based on the reactions of teen-agers in individual and group sessions, when discussing war and its representation on the screen. I have also studied adult audiences. The conclusion became inescapable that if you want to condition people to accept war

Reprinted with the permission of the author and the publisher from *The New York Times,* December 4, 1966. Copyright © 1966 by The New York Times Company.

and violence, the present TV treatment is excellent. Our channels of communication are hardening us to war rather than educating us against it.

Bertolt Brecht has said that the truth can be concealed in many ways and can be told in many ways. That is certainly true. How can we get people used to the bombing of the countryside? The best way is evidently to show it to them all the time. In the Vietnam war this is supplemented by an occasional comment like that made by a high-ranking government official who said that our bombing is "miraculously accurate" and does not hurt civilians. One cumulative result of the war coverage has been that it has helped to transform us from Nervous Nellies into placid participants.

The effect of the war films cannot be evaluated in isolation. They hit a generation well prepared. No generation growing up in any epoch of history or in any place has had to face such a deluge of violence as modern American youth, now old enough to make history itself. The deluge begins in the nursery with the "kill toys"—as the children call them—guns and elaborate warfare weapons advertised as suitable for even the pre-school child. These toys teach that it is fun to play killing and that war is a good thing.

The education progresses to sadistic bubblegum cards, violent crime comic books, brutal movies and rough TV shows, crudely illustrated booklets like *Sin and Pain* sold under the counter to teen-agers, gorily presented murder news, etc. The audience so conditioned from childhood on finds the Vietnam fighting pictures really tame stuff and is easily manipulated with regard to violence by the huge public relations establishment that has been constructed at the top of the military set-up. And the well-accomplished task of these public relations experts is to teach us not revulsion against war and violence, but receptivity to it. Practically every TV newscast now has some war pictures. In effect, these really are war commercials.

The endless repetition of fragmented and fragmentary battle scenes, without indication of an over-all design, gives them a cliché-like character. What could be most moving scenes if presented in a sufficiently severe frame and with proper reverence for human life become a mere backdrop for violence and the expectation of violence. Our senses are being dulled. Big things become small.

What we are given is a hawk's-eye view of life and death. We have seen so many villages burn, so many soldiers going single file into the jungle, so many wounded being interviewed, so many helicopters taking off on desperate missions, that war is becoming routine and the corrosion of war commonplace. We claim to be concerned. But we view these scenes self-indulgently for their entertainment value and add them up subconsciously not to a yearning for peace but to a total belief in the morality of force.

The network news programs offer ever-increasing battle coverage. At the same time, more than a third of the new season's television series rely on physical violence as the climactic point of each story. In the minds of many, the war news films merge with the fictional action movies, especially Westerns. Teenagers have called Lyndon Johnson "the fastest gun in the West." Some have told me: "We have to kill the gooks—all the gooks!" Adults call that escalation.

Interspersed between fighting scenes are visual reports of benevolent efforts in Vietnam: "pacification in the countryside," programs for health, education and social rehabilitation, attempts to provide low-cost housing, efforts "to stimulate democratic institutions" among the peasants, construction of schools. Aline Saarinen reports our training of Vietnamese so that they can make "the thousands of artificial limbs needed." A small band of U. S. soldiers entertains Vietnam women and children with music.

In the midst of all the destruction, devastation and suffering, these minor politico-philanthropic endeavors seem incongruous. They remind one of the rich old lady who invited groups of wounded veterans for dinner. She asked the hospital to select as her guests those most severely wounded. Then she would tell friends: "Last night I had 12 veterans for dinner. And all together there were only 20 arms, 18 legs and 19 eyes!" French psychiatrists call that *philanthropie hysterique*.

The number of our troops in Vietnam has steadily increased. The Vietnam war reports on television do not as a rule announce these increases very forthrightly. Sometimes they are buried among other, much less important facts or they are given out as an aside "upon inquiry." Early in 1965 there were 30,000 U. S. troops in Vietnam. A little later

75,000 soldiers seemed a very large number. Now it is "more than 331,000" (only a few days ago it was 328,000). As feelers for the future, 600,000 and even three-quarters of a million are mentioned. It seems that when a "peace offensive" is loudly proclaimed it is accompanied or followed by a military expansion. We are being conditioned—like Pavlovian dogs—so that when the "peace offensive" bells ring we won't expect peace but accept an acceleration of bombing and an increase in the strength of the army.

Communication is the opposite of violence. Where communication ends, violence begins. When we do not communicate with one another, we cannot know one another; when we do not know one another, we can be stirred up to hate; when we hate, we are apt to resort to violence.

If we want to understand the effect of the Vietnam films, we must realize that over the years the mass media, of which television is the most potent, have helped to create the present international communication gap. There exists, in fact, what amounts to a vast machinery of hate. Any country that is regarded as a potential opponent, or any country that gets into the power orbit of a potential opponent, is vilified. No notice is taken of any good thing about it whatever and everything possibly bad is emphasized. Suspicion and denigration rule. Every utterance by its leaders is interpreted in the worst possible light. Special experts see to that. We have become so used to this that we are not even aware of it any more. In this way a warlike attitude is created. The peaceful messages get lost, the hostile one get priority.

Suppose, as an experiment, that I were to send a script of the Sermon on the Mount to a broadcasting station, suggesting that it be read on the air, with special attention to the passages about not killing and not being "angry with your brothers." The station would probably reply that it would have to give equal time to the opposite view.

But can't it be argued that the networks are just supplying the public with the kind of war coverage it wants? I do not think so. Nobody has expressed better what the audience expects than Truman Capote. "Watch," he writes. "You can see it on their faces. . . . It says: tell us truth, give us an answer, give us something which is not a smoke ring, but an emblem against our time." Surely we have had some very frank reporting. But frankness, as Katherine Mansfield said, is "truth's ugly and stupid half-sister." We need more. For Vietnam may be the prologue to a much bigger war which no television screen will be able to show at all.

PART III

The Content of Mass Media Violence

Bam! Powie! Zap!
BATMAN

IF THE mass media did nothing more but hold up a mirror to reflect reality, the content would be violent enough. But they do more; much more. They create a vast fantasy world peopled with violent characters. How much of mass media content has violence as a component? How is violence expressed? By whom, toward whom, and for what avowed purpose?

The articles presented below seek answers to such questions by examining violence in motion pictures, American literature, newspapers, paperback books, mass-circulation magazines, comic books, and television. In the case of films and literature, some effort is also directed to tracing the development of violence in these media and accounting for the forms it has taken. Throughout, both qualitative and quantitative approaches are employed to describe and analyze media violence. These procedures produce some results more open to verification than others. Nevertheless, the studies presented here probably provide as objective an estimate of the scope, form, and intensity of media violence as is currently available. Such research also suggests a need and displays some available means for a continuing audit of mass media content. Many consider it a lamentable fact that in this day of scientific measurement and social bookkeeping we keep better records of pig-iron production, annual rainfall, and flying-saucer sightings than we do of the content offered over the media of mass communication.

In considering this material, the reader must keep in mind the time-bound sample represented in these studies. Mass media content is subject to change (by forces to be outlined later). The illustrative studies presented here represent an appraisal at a given point or range of time. The content analysis of the comic-book material, for example, was undertaken at the peak of the controversy over comic books in America prior to the invocation of an industry code and self-regulation, which, as we shall see (in Part VII), greatly modified the permissible manner of presenting violence in that medium.

Another question should be kept in mind as we consider

the content of the mass media: What can be learned from a study of content? The research literature on mass communication clearly indicates that the effects of the mass media can only partly derive from the content being offered for audience attention. Audience predispositions, the social context of exposure, and other situational and motivational factors must also be considered. However, while the complex question of effects cannot be resolved by examining content alone, content analysis may yet be a highly instructive tool for exploring *potential* consequences and for deriving testable hypotheses about *possible* effects. Content analysis is also useful for identifying the manifest, and inferring the latent, intentions of communicators. Furthermore, systematic, objective, and repeated measurement of content, based on careful definition of concepts and close attention to the rules of sampling, can facilitate the more adequate application of critical standards to media content.

A content analysis typically involves the counting of symbols. But, for characterizing media violence and for understanding its effects, what shall be counted? In studies thus far, "violence" has for the most part been a loosely defined cencept. Some have merely engaged in noting the number of guns or the frequency of killings on television programs. Such information is undoubtedly more useful for spreading alarm about media violence than it is for understanding possible effects. A more sophisticated approach might attempt to discover underlying values repeatedly portrayed in a variety of mass media settings and situations. What, for example, do television programs such as animated cartoons, westerns, drama, and situational comedies portray in common with respect to violence? The last paper in this section postulates that effects are more likely to emerge over time, to the extent that such programs deal in *patterned ways* with basic goals and the mechanisms for their achievement, since a consistent portrayal of these affords the maximum opportunity for reinforcement of learning.

All the papers presented below indicate that violence is a prominent mechanism for goal achievement in the world of the mass media. For now, the reader may decide for himself if this model is real, or too real. How it is perceived and acted upon by media audiences calls for empirical studies beyond content analysis.

VIOLENCE IN THE CINEMA

Philip French

THE CINEMA is a peculiarly violent form of entertainment, developed in and catering for what we have come to think of as an age of violence. Undoubtedly one of the reasons that we think of our time *as* an age of violence is because of our vivid vicarious experience of destruction and brutality in newsreels and feature films. One can have lived the quietest of lives and yet feel that through the cinema one has looked upon the face of war and civil disruption, participated in bank robberies and murder, witnessed a hundred gun-fights and brutal assaults. Of all aspects of the cinema, the treatment of violence is perhaps the most complex, controversial, and in many ways central. It is only equalled as a controversial issue by the often closely related question of sex. The extreme views of its effects are on the one hand those of certain social observers who see it as one of the principal causes of crime and delinquency, and on the other of those psychologists who believe that it plays an almost essential cathartic role in diminishing aggression.

A not untypical reaction is that of an ex-secretary of the British Board of Film Censors who has been quoted as saying that "anyone who prolongs scenes of violence is only doing so to titillate a small unhealthy section of the audience". This generalization might find wide acceptance, but it does not stand up for a minute to close scrutiny. To begin with, a mass medium does not persistently set out to please small sections of its audience, so if an interest in violence is unhealthy, then it is one that is pretty widely shared. Furthermore the most obviously prolonged scene of violence ever made is the appalling carnage on the Odessa Steps in *Battleship Potemkin,* the most celebrated single sequence in the history of the movies. Although it is deliberately prolonged beyond the actual time which the real event would have taken, a rare thing in the cinema, no one could accuse Eisen-

---

Reprinted with the permission of the publisher from *The Twentieth Century,* Winter, 1964–1965, pp. 115–130.

stein of titillation. The view of the popular audience, which is too rarely heard in these matters (it votes with its feet at the box office), is no doubt expressed for them by Sammy Davis in *Robin and the Seven Hoods,* when he dances around a gambling den which he is wrecking with a sub-machine gun, celebrating the outrage with the mischievous song:

> I like the fun,
> Of reaching for a gun,
> And going, Bang! Bang!

This is the true spirit of the unselfconscious groundlings breaking through the rational carapaos of our nervous times.

Cinematic violence can be approached in terms of two closely linked questions: Why is there so much of it? How much of it is justified, and on what grounds? Naturally, some of the answers take one straight into the field of sociology and psychology, and where it seems better for them to be expanded by sociologists and psychologists I shall break off and leave it to them. There are already far too many film critics sitting in the stalls and treating the screen as if it were society on the couch. But these questions can only be posed against a historical background. There never has been a time when the movies have not been preoccupied with violence. (One of the earliest films of the Edison Company in 1893 was a one-and-a-half-minute film for Kinetescope viewing called *The Execution of Mary Queen of Scots*—the doomed lady walks to the block, an axe swings, a head rolls in the dust.) Before the end of the century it became apparent that the movies would take over the theatre's role of providing violence and spectacle, although the theatre's immediate response to the challenge was a vain indulgence in greater realism, more elaborate spectacle. But of one such attempt, the chariot race in a 1898 dramatization of *Ben Hur,* a contemporary critic observed: "The only way to secure the exact sense of action for this incident in a theatre is to represent it by Mr. Edison's invention."

If one is looking for the origin of the public opprobrium that is attached to movie violence, this too can be found in the 1890s. Terry Ramsaye, who lived through the period and was the American cinema's first serious historian, places it around 1897, two years after the invention of the movie projector. Faced with the limitless possibilities of the new

medium, the American pioneers could think of nothing
better to do than record prize fights round by round. Of the
consequences of this obsession with the ring, Ramsaye observed in his book *A Million and One Night* (1926):

> One marked effect of the Corbett-Fitzsimmons picture as the
> outstanding screen production of its day was to bring the odium
> of pugilism upon the screen all across Puritan America. Until that
> picture appeared the social status of the screen had been uncer-
> tain. It now became definitely low-brow, an entertainment of the
> great unwashed commonalty. This likewise made it a mark for
> uplifters, moralists, reformers and legislators in a degree which
> would never have been obtained if the screen had by specialization
> reached higher social strata.

The history of the cinema has since had running through
it a continuous battle between the "uplifters, moralists, re-
formers and legislators" and the practitioners in the medium,
its greatest artists as well as its most blatant commercial
exploiters, and the battleground has usually been the treatment of sex and violence.

The cinema was not exactly slow to realize its power,
though at first a trifle vague about its dramatic uses. When
Edwin S. Porter filmed the first important dramatic close-up,
it was of a menacing bandit firing his pistol directly into the
camera. But he stuck it on to the end of *The Great Train
Robbery* (1903) almost as an afterthought, and the Edison
Catalogue of the following year, while recognizing that "the
resultant excitement is great," suggested to exhibitors that
"this scene can be used to begin or end the picture".

Subsequent film-makers became more knowing in every
way as they came to understand the nature of the medium,
and as the society in which they lived grew increasingly
sophisticated in its appreciation of the nature of violence.
Since the turn of the century violence has been a constant
factor and I fancy that such evidence as there is for periodic
increases has been greatly exaggerated. It is the form and
intensity of violence that has changed rather than its quantity. This is a minority view, and a more generally accepted
one is that the German cinema was particularly violent in
the 1920s, the American cinema in the early 1930s and the
French cinema in the 1950s. Socio-political reasons—the
atmosphere of the Weimar Republic in Germany, the post-

Prohibition early-Depression era in America, the national confusion and colonial unrest in France—are usually given. What these backgrounds may have done is to give a unifying character to the bodies of films (i.e. all German expressionist pictures tend to look alike, all American gangster films share similar characteristics) and the violence may have had a more jarring effect through its repetitive, contemporary character. (Whereas paradoxically the repetitive, formalized violence in an established genre, the horror film say, or the Western, has the opposite result, making it almost cosy.) Yet if we look closely at the work of someone like Fritz Lang we see in the style and the treatment of violence a continuing personal development that links his German movies of the 1920s with his American ones in the following three decades.

As it happens there has never been a time when some critic hasn't been spotting a new upsurge of violence (and sex). There are at least four major instances in the case of the American cinema. First there was the outcry in the 1920s that brought into existence the infamous Production Code. (This followed an alleged cycle of violent movies that included De Mille's popular success of 1919, *The Cheat*, where Sessue Hayakawa branded his adulterous wife with a red hot iron, a sequence considered barbarous at the time but recently regarded as sufficiently innocuous to be presented during a sycophantic Tribute to De Mille on peak-hour TV.) A second outcry came in the 1930s with the gangster films, which contravened—directly or obliquely—almost every section of the Production Code, and yet a third in the mid-forties immediately after World War II. At this point an anonymous "Film Critic" contributed an article to *Penguin New Writing* (No. 30; 1947) called "Parade of Violence", which contained the following lament:

> Gone completely the sophisticated and adult attitude of American film-melodramas such as *Laura, The Maltese Falcon, Mask of Dimitrios*, etc.; instead we have the purposeless parade of violence for its own sake: physical violence unrelated to any known form of life and apparently catering for a supposed audience of sadistic schoolchildren.

Several of these pictures too are considered fairly innocent fare now that they have eventually reached the television

screen, and a handful of them are considered minor classics
—including two by Fritz Lang which "Film Critic" compares
unfavorably with those German pictures of the 1920s that
had been accepted as so dangerously prophetic by the ad-
herents of the heady thesis advanced in Siegfried Kracauer's
From Caligari to Hitler.

It is easy enough now to see these post-war pictures as
expressing the black mood of the time and reflecting Hollywood's belated discovery of abnormal psychology. The psy-
chopathic villain had arrived, to be joined soon by the psy-
chopathic hero, and both remain with us. Still, "Film Critic"
was in good company, and was talking about what G. Legman
described as "Hollywood's New Violence" (*Love and Death,*
1949), quoting "a working abridgment" of the production
code coined by an American Jesuit: "No tits—blood". Legman's well-known theory about the suppression of sex leading
to an increase of violence in all media, although taken much
too far, has a certain validity. Clearly the Catholic orientation of American censorship leads to a toleration of violence
and an intolerance of sexual frankness which, coupled with
the inescapable violence of American life, makes pictures
from the U. S. the most violent in the world. (They are
matched only, one is told, by a particular genre of sadistic
Japanese film which is anyway brewed for Oriental consumption.)

Still, within less than ten years of Legman's and "Film
Critic's" assumption that the situation could hardly get worse,
there was an article on censorship in *Sight and Sound* as-
serting as a fact, scarcely in need of support, that "The
ferocity of American films has undeniably increased". And
in the same issue (Spring, 1956) the magazine's associate
editor devoted a long essay to the "instinctive rebellion that
finds its expression in meaningless acts of violence" that
seemed to her to characterize the most significant of recent
U. S. social protest pictures. Again, one must observe that
there wasn't a real increase in violence but merely that it
was more disturbing on account of its confusion with in-
soluble social problems—*Rebel Without a Cause* (1955) is a
case in point. At its best it could even be the result of a
desperate honesty.

Now, eight years later, we seem to be involved in a similar
debate and it concerns movies from all over the world, in-

cluding—since the success of the James Bond pictures—our own film industry. From this we can draw some obvious conclusions. The most apparent is that yesterday's excess is today's restraint. When the searing brutality of *Barabbas* struck London there were those who looked back to the good taste of *Quo Vadis?*, forgetting that it was from this earlier film that many people, including a leading Labour M.P., had walked out in protest against its sadistic arena scenes. A 1955 reviewer of *Les Diaboliques,* the film which started a whole cycle of sick thrillers, recoiled with the observation that "rarely if ever has such a wallow in the sickeningly macabre been passed for distribution in this country"; five years later Hitchcock's *Psycho* made Clouzot's picture look almost like a production of the Children's Film Foundation. *Psycho* caused several critics disgustedly to quit the press-show. Though it is still going the rounds and scaring the pants off appreciative audiences, it is now regarded as a black comedy.

Another obvious conclusion is that just as screen violence needs to keep getting more intense to compete with preceding shocks in impact—especially where it is only the impact that matters—so there is a lag between national tastes. Where, say, Sweden is some years ahead of us in the tolerance of sexual frankness, so America is ahead in the tolerance of violence. Thus our censor cuts sex scenes from most Swedish pictures and can spot Eva Dahlbeck's nipples behind the screen better than Ingmar Bergman (who had to run this sequence for *Smiles of a Summer Night* through several times before glimpsing them). While he is rarely troubled in this way by imports from the United States, around two out of three American films leave on his floor a few hundred feet of violence of a kind that would scarcely disturb a sensitive youth in Dubuque, Iowa.

Violence on the screen tends, I have said, to take its character and form (if often obliquely) from the mood of the time and place in which it is made. This operates in two ways. On one level is the creative artist who is responsive to the undercurrent of the society in which he works, and reflects it in his personal vision. On another level is the skilful producer of films that are intended to meet what he divines to be contemporary tastes. Naturally there is a good deal of middle ground here. And one is aware that some directors, Hitchcock for instance, have ideas that usually and happily (in commercial terms) match the public mood, while others, such as Luis Bunuel, rarely do. Thus Joseph Losey, although he has worked in this country for over ten years, still has the personal approach to violence that was evidenced in his American pictures, though these at the time (the early 1950s) seemed very much of their period and place. The three James Bond films, however, are deliberately thought out in terms of exploiting current tastes, and as they get more certain in touch they become more decadent in treatment. If, then, someone wishes to see how violence is dealt with in a personal way, he might go to a Losey film, but if he wants to see the way in which the industry thinks the public want it serving up, *Goldfinger* is a better guide.

It might be interesting, therefore, to look at the opening sequences of a recent Losey picture, *The Damned*, and of the third Bond movie, *Goldfinger*. Both pictures contain a great deal of violence, but represent quite different approaches to it, and a comparison between the two will bring us on to the further consideration of the questions posed earlier about the amount of violence in the movies and its justification.

The Damned opens with the credit titles presented against the background of pieces of sculpture outside an artist's studio on a deserted cliff. The scene quickly shifts to the promenade of a quiet south-coast resort where a motorcycle gang are swinging on a statue of George III, and singing a rock song. An American visitor is then lured down a side street by the gang leader's sister to be beaten up and robbed. A few minutes later, battered and bleeding, he is carried into a nearby hotel and meets a civil servant (head of a secret atomic research establishment situated beneath the nearby cliffs). "I never expected something like this to happen to me in England," the American says, and receives the reply: "The age of senseless violence has caught up with us too."

The opening sequence in *Goldfinger* goes something like this. The setting is apparently a Caribbean republic—we see a seagull swimming on the water which turns out to be on the head of James Bond as he surfaces in a frogman outfit. With the aid of a rope fired from a dinky little gun he climbs a wall, kicks a Latin American guard in the teeth, and

plants a time bomb in a huge gas tank. He then peels off the
rubber suit to reveal a white tuxedo, in the button-hole of
which he places a carnation, and arrives at a night club just
in time to be relaxing at the bar when the bomb goes off.
(A semi-audible line is muttered which suggests that the
factory had been, I think, the HQ of drug traffickers.) Mis-
sion accomplished, Bond adjourns to the room of a dancing
girl. While kissing her he sees the reflection of an assassin
in her eye and uses her to receive the blow intended for him.
During the ensuing fight the would-be assassin falls into a
bath and while attempting to reach for Bond's gun, which is
hanging over the tub, is electrocuted by an electric fire
(equipped with a conveniently lengthy flex) that 007 hurls
across the room. After the obligatory wry crack from Bond we
at last get the credit titles—Some fancy designs of a gunman
firing through an eye-socket against the background of a
golden body.

The chief difference between these two sequences is that in
The Damned every shot is related to themes and incidents
that occur later in the picture, while the introductory episode
in *Goldfinger* is wholly gratuitous—it exists as a film in its
own right and its only function is to excite and amuse, to
establish a mood. Both pictures work in terms of what their
audience knows and understands, but the aim of *The Damned*
is to explore violence, that of *Goldfinger* to exploit it. (But
I don't wish to condemn violent entertainment *ipso facto*, and
Goldfinger is nothing if not entertaining.)

Take the characters in the two films. In *The Damned* the
American visitor is immediately recognisable as the two-
fisted adventurer (the part is played, incidentally, by an
actor associated with private-eye and Western roles), a suggestion of the perennial movie hero who usually carries a gun
or a sword and seems not merely prepared for violent encounters but positively to will them, though he is here deliberately thrown into a situation he cannot comprehend.
There is the teddy boy gang—traditional figures of group
menace, creations of social and psychological unrest, but
here set against the atomic scientist and *his* uniformed team,
men associated with a new destructive force too hideous to
contemplate. In *Goldfinger* Bond is played as a fantasy figure,
totally in control of his world, surrounded by stock figures
—the loyal American, the sinister Oriental, the treacherous

Latin American, the brilliant but deadly German—and when atomic science comes in, it does so as part of an action plot, a contemporary gimmick.

Then compare the treatment. In *The Damned* a sudden outburst of violence in a peaceful setting; the attack shown in brutal close-up, sadomasochistically presented from the point of view of both attackers and victim, disturbing and difficult to enjoy; and in the pick-up which precedes the assault is suggested an underlying erotic implication. From the very first frame of *Goldfinger,* on the other hand, we are disarmed—it is all a huge joke. The violence and sex is rapid and perfunctory (rarely lingered over as in the Fleming books), the association with sex is not implied but hammered home in knowing collusion with a pseudo-sophisticated audience, which is never genuinely involved in it. *The Damned* may be deliberately manipulating conventional material in its schematic way and operating at a symbolical level, but it is set in a real world where people get hurt, contaminated; *Goldfinger* is set in a fantasy world, with elaborately dazzling sets, and even the actual locations are made to seem unreal. The tradition in which it works is that of the violence of slapstick farce and of those sadistic cartoons where animals get squashed flat or have their fur blasted off only to reappear instantly, ready for further humorous punishment.

Finally, note the verbal exchange quoted above between the American and the scientist in *The Damned:* it's a trifle portentous, certainly, yet indicative of a serious awareness of the problem of violence on the part of the film-maker and assumed by him in his audience. *Goldfinger*, of course, is equally self-conscious and assumes in its audience a shallow knowledge of psychology, but this self-consciousness takes the form of deliberately sending itself up, of protecting itself against any serious charge by ensuring that no one likely to make such a charge could take the film seriously.

These films represent the two poles of contemporary screen violence. Superficially they have a great deal in common. They also share another quality that is not so superficial— that no other medium could have presented what is contained in these initial scenes so rapidly or with such impact —before, in fact, we had any knowledge in either case of the characters or the story other than that which we bring from other films.

I have dealt at such length with these two pictures because they highlight many of the ways in which violence is handled in the contemporary cinema, and because they help explain why there is and has been so much violence in the movies. The first reason is squarely faced by *Goldfinger*—there is a vast international public for such exercises in brutality, and the cinema is dependent upon the support of a mass audience. Indeed, the cinema (with the recent low-powered assistance of TV) now bears the main burden of satisfying this legitimate and enduring need. Secondly, as *The Damned* illustrates, serious artists are attracted by violent themes, perhaps today more than ever before, because of the urgent social issues involved, the extreme experiences they entail, and (it must be acknowledged) the "terrible beauty" violence has in itself.

There is a sense in which the cinema by its very nature is drawn towards violence. In writing on "Film Aesthetic" many years ago, Sir Herbert Read spoke of the camera as "a chisel of light, cutting into the reality of objects", and it can be maintained that the flickering passage of twenty-four frames per second through the projector, the vertiginous movement of the camera, the continuous shifting of viewpoint, the rapid change of image in both size and character, the very idea of montage, make films—irrespective of their subjects—a violent experience for the audience. Undoubtedly the technique of film is employed in this way. An obvious and conscious example is Alain Resnais's *Muriel*, where banal, undramatic material was deliberately presented in a violent and shocking manner primarily through its style of editing. In a far more obvious sense, however, the cinema—as the best description of it, "motion pictures", suggests—tends towards violence. It is concerned with movement, with the telling of stories, the conveying of sensations, the sharing of experiences, the expression of ideas, primarily in terms of the changing relationships of people and objects. True, sound effects, words and music have since come to play an important part in a medium that was developed without them, but their role is essentially ancillary; when the word dominates, as it too often does, the result is usually disastrous as either art or entertainment. The movies are predominantly about things happening, and the extreme form of things happening is violence. As everyone knows, the final word before shooting a scene is symbolically the director's call for "Action". Not surprisingly to the moviemaker and the moviegoer the words "action" and "violence" as relating to the content of a film are virtually synonymous.

This natural violent bent of the movies as art and entertainment has been compounded by the scenes of violence in the actual world that it has been the lot of the newsreel to record. And when one comes down to it, the task of distinguishing between the nature of newsreel material and that of the feature film is no easy one. We usually rely upon the context to do it for us, yet such is the basic similarity that the images of the two blend easily in our minds, and are frequently mixed in films. Occasionally there is an outcry when illegitimate use is thought to be made of documentary footage. For one thing it can be used to propagate falsehood—the Italian "documentary" *Mondo Cane* (where the individual scenes of violence and degradation were undeniably "real" and "true" in themselves) is an obvious and rather complicated example. And a few years back there were strong objections to actual combat shots of dying marines being inserted into an "entertainment" film, *Sands of Iwo Jima,* despite (or perhaps because of) the fact that few people could have told which were the real deaths and which the simulated ones.

The Oxford Dictionary defines the primary meaning of violence as "the exercise of physical force so as to inflict injury on or damage to persons or property", and this, the generally understood meaning in everyday life, is the sense in which I have been using it here. It shows how close the cinema is to violence in real life that one can discuss the widest possible range of films in these terms. . . .

• • •

For those in search of further descriptive and synoptic material I cannot do better than commend the special issue in February 1963 of the British film magazine *Motion,* a "Companion to Violence and Sadism in the Cinema". Like the recent programme at the Institute of Contemporary Arts, it raises the question of the intellectual's preoccupation with violence which is worth an essay in itself. Under "D" alone the Companion lists "Dark Side of the Light Fantastic, The"; "Dassin"; "Deaf Aid, Torture by"; "Dentures, Death by"; "Disease"; and "Doctor No"; and under "F" the editors choose their "Favourite Movie Scars". Even a cursory perusal of this document should save many a busy person the experience of sitting through a large number of tedious if not actually corrupting pictures. As the old saying goes: "The movies have ruined a lot more evenings than they have morals." I was struck the other day by the way in which the author of an advertisement for a recent horror picture touched in striking fashion on a fundamental aspect of screen violence. The film is called *Straight-Jacket;* it's described as "Entertainment Plus", and the poster depicts a screaming Joan Crawford, together with another photograph of that lady swinging an axe, above which is the slogan: "Keep saying to yourself—it's only a film—It's Only A Film—IT'S ONLY A FILM!"

VIOLENCE IN AMERICAN LITERATURE

David Brion Davis

FOR MORE than one hundred and sixty years American literature has shown a peculiar fascination with homicidal violence. Charles Brockden Brown, our first serious novelist presents us with one character who is driven by an irresistible impulse to kill, another who laughs ecstatically after murdering his wife and children, and a third who attempts to rape a heroine alongside the corpse of his latest victim. As one follows James Fenimore Cooper through innumerable pursuits, escapes, and battles, one soon loses count of the bodies of Indians and renegades strewn behind. The tales of Edgar Allan Poe are a gallery of dark and ghastly crime. George Lippard, a friend of Poe and the most popular American writer of the mid-nineteenth century, managed to include six rapes and a dozen murders in a single novel! The market Lippard helped to develop has been exploited even more cal-

Reprinted with the permission of the author and the publisher from *The Annals of the American Academy of Political and Social Science*, March, 1966, pp. 28–36.

lously in our own time by such writers as James M. Cain and Mickey Spillane. But on a loftier level, Melville's *Pierre* and *Billy Budd* both turn on acts of homicide. In Nathaniel Hawthorne's *The Marble Faun* we are told that when Donatello kills Miriam's persecutor, the lovers are bound together in an intimate union, closer than marriage, since they are now governed by a law created for them alone. Huck Finn is an eye-witness to two of the most unforgettable murders in American literature. *A Connecticut Yankee in King Arthur's Court* ends in a cataclysm of mass slaughter. A theme of raw, explosive violence runs through the works of Ambrose Bierce, Stephen Crane, and Jack London. It erupts with an almost predictable frequency in the novels of F. Scott Fitzgerald, Ernest Hemingway, William Faulkner, John Steinbeck, James T. Farrell, and Robert Penn Warren.

The significance of such literary motifs can easily be exaggerated. There has been considerable carnage, after all, in the world's great classics from *Oedipus Rex* and the *Song of Roland* to *King Lear* and *Crime and Punishment*. If the shootings, stabbings, lynchings, and fist-fights of American fiction present a different world from that portrayed by Jane Austen, Anthony Trollope, or C. P. Snow, there has been a strain of sadistic violence in English popular fiction from Matthew Gregory Lewis's *The Monk*, published in 1795, to Ian Fleming's recent *From Russia, with Love*. One might also compile a list of important American writers whose works contain little bloodshed—William Dean Howells, Henry James, Edith Wharton, Sinclair Lewis, J. P. Marquand, Saul Bellow, even Theodore Dreiser come to mind. Since literary fashions have almost a life of their own, and since much of the violence in American literature bears the imprint of Elizabethan drama, English Gothic romance, or Flaubertian realism, it would be naïve to conclude that the frequency of fighting and killing in American fiction is proof of an unusually violent society.

On the other hand, there can be no doubt that the treatment of violence in American literature reflects certain historical conditions and circumstances. Although we are handicapped by the absence of a fully developed sociology of the novel, we can make a number of tentative observations on the relations between fictional violence and American social patterns.

VIOLENCE AND THE MASS AUDIENCE

Perhaps the most obvious point is the sheer marketability of imagined violence. Literary historians have tended to ignore the prosaic fact that writers want to sell books and are usually sensitive to the tastes of their audience. This orientation may conflict with an artist's creative instincts or with the standards of his craft, but our greatest writers have usually established an equilibrium between the opposing forces. When we note that many of the themes and situations of the best twentieth-century fiction were anticipated in crude nineteenth-century pot-boilers which dealt with moral insanity, monomania, sex and sadism, the uninhibited violence of the South, and the dehumanizing effects of the Northern city, it is tempting to speculate on a "trickle up" process which refines literature from trash. Unfortunately, we know far too little about the influence of "subliterature" on serious writers. What does seem certain is the desire of the mass audience for a literature of violence. And this may be better explained by the limited attention span of the average reader than by theories of repressed aggression and vicarious release. As Alexis de Tocqueville suggested in the 1830's, at the very moment when American book production reflected a rapid increase in popular literacy, a mass market is not conducive to a literature of nuances, understatement, and delicate pleasures. Tocqueville misjudged America's capacity to produce a rich and diversified literature, but his theory that a democratic audience feeds on exaggeration, strong emotion, and striking effect helps to account for the violent sensationalism which today is so characteristic of mass media throughout the Western world. To hold the attention of the ordinary reader or even of the educated but fatigued mind in search of diversion, a story must be full of suspense, surprise, and startling contrasts. Violence is the cheapest means to a change of pace.

THE COMPACT OF REBELLIOUS BROTHERS

If the modern literature of violence has become as international as a James Bond movie, American writers have often been preoccupied with certain distinctive themes. Before the Civil War no genre was more popular than the historical romance of the American Revolution. To understand the significance of these highly standardized tales, one must recognize how much of our historical writing on the Revolution has been devoted to exorcising its radical spirit. Yet it has always been difficult to conceal the fact that the nation was conceived in violence, that its birth was accompanied by mobs and confiscations, and that a burden remained on the people collectively to validate their rebellion against lawful authority. For the first generations born after the event, there was a particular need to relate the violence of their nation's origin to their own experience and to affirm that a revolutionary heritage need not lead to a future of strife and anarchy. By the 1820's and 1830's young Americans professed unquestioning allegiance to the Founding Fathers, whom they saw as legendary demigods, and assumed that the cause of liberty lay not in further rebellion, but in fidelity to the true spirit of Washington and Jefferson. Anything that seemed to threaten the public welfare they pictured as a betrayal of tradition; change was justified as a removal of corruption and a restoration of former purity.

This mentality, which differed so markedly from that of European liberals who sought to throw off established privileges and powers, left a deep imprint on literary treatments of the Revolution. In the popular image, the War of Independence was not a challenge to sovereignty but rather a struggle between peers, usually symbolized by good and bad brothers, for the possession of land and women. The bad brother is the agent of an enemy power; the good brother often has the sanction of a Washington-type father, who gives legitimacy to the patriots' cause. But despite the effort to identify rebellion with a defense of tradition and lawful order, there is a tacit recognition that American society is characterized by a weakness of authority and an unregulated competition for power. And this literary view of the Revolution provided a model for later imaginary struggles for America's destiny, which usually involved conspiratorial brotherhoods linked, like the Tories, with the schemes of a foreign despot. The villains in early American fiction were seldom the bad father or wicked king figures so common in European literature. The hero's triumph was not a blow against evil authority but rather a defeat of the Tory, the renegade brother, the ruthless competitor who defied the sacred rules of the compact. These conventions, one suspects, gave expression to a widespread fear of factionalism and anarchy, and to a desire to identify one's own interests with a tradition of self-sacrificing unity.

THE WESTERN HERO

Yet the ideal of social unity might conflict with the ideal of the self-sufficient and omnipotent individual, who was celebrated in American popular culture from the Age of Jackson to the Age of the Robber Barons. One way of evading such a conflict was to project the image of the American hero into the vacant spaces of the West, where his aggressive self-reliance could be interpreted as a constructive and wholly natural force. "When the law of the land is weak," says Cooper's Ishmael Bush, "it is right the law of nature should be strong." And this meant, according to another of Cooper's characters, that when men lived beyond the law, they must be their own judges and executioners.

It was Cooper who inaugurated the great tradition of the American Western and who furnished the main ingredients for the American individualist hero. Leatherstocking and his countless descendents were isolated, solitary men. Far removed from the complexities of adult love, family relations, or vocation, they were the perfect wish-fulfillment of the preadolescent mind. Instead of shaping their lives to distant goals, they lived for the present moment and according to an understood code of natural justice and good-natured generosity. Their independent existence implied a repudiation of sexual and economic responsibilities; yet even their violence retained a certain innocence, since it was devoid of social consequence. There was also an element of primitivistic democracy in the physical heroism of the cowboy or forest scout, whose status was not enhanced by noble lineage or the loyalty of followers, but depended entirely on the exercise of natural abilities in a setting of unexpected dangers. If the European chivalric romance provided a model for testing character by the trial of combat, the American Western stripped the contestants of family ties or clan grudges and reduced their encounter to the most elemental struggle for survival.

As a young hunter who has not yet killed a man, Cooper's Deerslayer tells a hostile Indian that the world is large enough for both of them, but that if they meet fairly in battle, "the Lord will order the fate of each of us." In this archetype of Western combat, Cooper's hero is caught off guard when the treacherous Mingo suddenly raises his rifle to fire. Having caught only a glimpse of his peril, Deerslayer shoots with such lightning speed that the reports of the two rifles sound as one. The dying Mingo admires his killer's prowess, and gives him the new name of "Hawkeye," because "eye sartain—finger lightning—aim, death—great warrior soon." And though Deerslayer still believes it wrong to kill "a human mortal without an object," the West had provided an object, and in so doing had helped an undistinguished youth prove his manhood and win the esteem of his fellow frontiersmen. During the next sixty years the scene of combat moved from colonial New York to the deserts of Wyoming, but the formula changed very little. In Owen Wister's classic version, the Virginian faces an ultimatum from the bully, Trampas, and knows he must either flee and be thought a coward, or fight and risk the loss of his girl's love. As he confronts Trampas at sundown, "a wind seemed to blow his sleeve off his arm, and he replied to it, and saw Trampas pitch forward." The Virginian laconically informs the spectators that if anyone wants to see him about the shooting, he will be at the hotel. " 'Who'll want you?' asked Scipio. 'Three of us saw his gun out. . . . You were that cool! That quick!' " Unlike the ascetic Deerslayer, the Virginian can fulfill the boyish wish for triumph over all intimidating bullies, and also win the hand of Molly Wood. And yet in Wister's story the girl is really no more than a vehicle for adoring the hero and an instrument for revealing his conscience and manly tenderness. We know that in the next book or the next movie he will be married only to his faithful horse, and will be free to re-enact the drama of a quick draw and sudden death in the dusty streets.

INDIANS AND NEGROES

When one thinks of cowboys one also thinks of Indians, and as we have just seen, Leatherstocking's first victim was a Mingo brave. The convention of Indian-killing as a kind of rite of passage goes back in American fiction at least to 1799, when Charles Brockden Brown's Edgar Huntley overcomes religious scruples and tomahawks an Indian in order to rescue a captive maiden. By 1837 a father in Robert Montgomery Bird's immensely popular *Nick of the Woods* can boast that his son had killed his first "brute" at the age of fourteen, and had then "blubbered" all night after realizing he might have killed two. Such tales did not shock a reading public thoroughly familiar with the treachery and inhumanity of Indians, and convinced of the need for exterminating them as if they were poisonous reptiles. When we recall that for some two centuries Americans were engaged in a continuing racial war, it is not surprising that so much fictional violence should center on the red man. To kill an Indian was a ritual that sealed one's claim to the rights and privileges of the white man's civilization; it was a symbolic acknowledgement that American freedom and wealth depended on the sacrifice of the aborigine's blood. Of course, American writers often drew upon the European stereotypes of the noble savage, and portrayed "good" Indians who served the white man's cause. But even the most faithful brave could not be assimilated into white society. He was always the last Mohican, the dying warrior whose self-sacrifice contributed in some vague way to a greater America.

If American expansion required the forcible dispossession of the Indian, the American economy was long dependent on a system of coerced labor which began with the violent seizure of native Africans and which led to a militant society dedicated to the preservation of white supremacy and terrorized by the fear of racial war. From colonial times, the American mind associated the Negro with violence. This can be seen in the privately expressed fears of Southern slaveholders, in the debates of legislatures, in the Constitutional Convention, in countless court records, tracts, and sermons. Yet the Negro in American fiction, at least before the Civil War, was a peculiarly nonviolent being. Because pro-Southern writers were acutely sensitive to abolitionist attacks, they sought to prove that slaves were content and loyal and that masters lived a life of serene security, disrupted only by an occasional meddler from the North. When a Negro in such literature is involved in violence, it is almost always in the defense of his master or mistress. At the other

end of the spectrum, antislavery writers pictured the Negro
as the embodiment of Christian charity, dignified and for-
giving even in his suffering. He might flee his oppressors and
even fight in defense of his wife's honor, but except under
the most extreme provocation, he was incapable of revenge.
It is true that both Melville and Poe left haunting images of
Negroes in savage mutiny, of a black horror rising from
beneath the decks of society. But during the slavery era most
writers respected the convention of dissociating the Negro
from the violence of sadistic planters or Yankee fanatics.

By the beginning of the twentieth century, a tightening of
segregation and an increase in racial tension brought historic phobias to the surface of popular literature. The Negro
Gus in Thomas Dixon, Jr.'s *The Clansman,* from which the
movie, *The Birth of a Nation,* was made, is a far cry from
Uncle Remus or Uncle Tom. The brave sons of the Ku Klux
Klan know that Gus has raped a beautiful white girl. His
image was frozen in the eyes of the girl's dead mother, after
she had witnessed the event and had jumped with her
daughter off a cliff to shield their disgrace. But the men of
the "Invisible Empire" want to be sure of their justice, and
force Gus to re-enact the crime.

His thick lips were drawn upward in an ugly leer and his sinister bead eyes gleamed like a gorilla's. A single fierce leap and
the black claws clutched the air slowly as if sinking into the soft
white throat.

This is more than the calmest Southern man can take:

"Stop him! Stop him!" screamed a clansman, springing on the
negro and grinding his heels into his big thick neck. A dozen more
were on him in a moment, kicking, stamping, cursing, and crying
like madmen.

Needless to say, the battered monster is sentenced to death.

Curiously enough, the Negro is no less a creature of violence in Richard Wright's *Native Son.* Although Bigger
Thomas does not rape a white girl, he kisses and fondles the
drunken Mary Dalton as he takes her to her room and puts
her to bed. He does not sink his fingers into her soft white
throat, but he is panicked when her mother enters the
darkened room, and he smothers the girl to death with a
pillow. Fortunately, Mrs. Dalton is blind, so her eyes do not

record the image of Bigger Thomas. But the white power structure soon discovers that he has dismembered and incinerated the corpse and has proceeded to murder his colored mistress, Bessie. At the end of the novel, as Bigger is about to be executed, he tries to explain:

"What I killed for must've been good! . . . It must have been good! When a man kills, it's for something. . . . I didn't know I was really alive in this world until I felt things hard enough to kill for 'em."

Even earlier, Mr. Max, his heroic Communist lawyer, had tried to amplify the point:

"Every time he comes into contact with us, he kills! . . . Every thought he thinks is potential murder. Excluded from, and unassimilated in our society, yet longing to gratify impulses akin to our own but denied the objects and channels evolved through long centuries for their socialized expression, every sunrise and sunset make him guilty of subversive actions. . . . He was impelled toward murder as much through the thirst for excitement, exultation, and elation as he was through fear! It was his way of living!"

In *Light in August* William Faulkner refrained from such sermons when he came to the agonizing fate of Joe Christmas, who is beaten, flogged, and castrated after he has killed his white mistress and set her house on fire. But, like Bigger Thomas, Joe Christmas tries to strike off the depersonalized mask of his Negrohood and rebels against both the white man's hatred and paternalistic sympathy. As Alfred Kazin has said, Christmas is an abstraction seeking to become a human being, and it is for this that he is crucified. If abolitionist and proslavery writers once agreed that the Negro was a pacific being, in twentieth-century fiction he has become a focal point of violence and a symbol of man's infinite inhumanity to man.

VIOLENCE AND ANTIRATIONALISM

Thus far we have considered a number of themes which give a distinctive character to the treatment of violence in American literature and which reflect historic tensions in American values. But we should not forget that American literature is part of the literature of the Western world, and has echoed changes in intellectual climate that have usually originated in Europe. In the present century the role and meaning of violence in literature have been profoundly influenced by a complex shift in thought and values which, for want of a more precise term, may be called antirationalism.

When defending Bigger Thomas, Mr. Max refers to the murder of Mary Dalton as " 'an act of creation!' " This idea, if still incomprehensible to most people, has found wide expression in modern literature. Its antecedents go back to the romantic revolt against eighteenth-century rationalism, to the celebration of man's passions, fears, and irrationality as an antidote to the classic virtues of prudence, decorum, and moderation. When a mechanistic psychology threatened to deprive man of his moral autonomy, romantic writers increasingly turned to the spontaneous impulse as a source of truth, goodness, and beauty. In so doing, however, they tended to confuse virtue with desire, and freedom with revolt and struggle. Instead of thinking of violence as something to be suppressed, disciplined, or applied to rational ends, many of the early romantics became fascinated by Cain, Satan, and Dr. Faust, and showed undisguised sympathy for subline murderers and amoral supermen who were moved by demonic urges. In American literature such tendencies came to their highest artistic fulfillment with Melville and Poe.

Another source of the idea of creative violence can be found in the great revolutionary thinkers of the nineteenth century, who attacked the bourgeois synthesis of utility, Christianity, and private property. In spite of their obvious differences, such figures as Karl Marx, Mikail Bakunin, Friedrich Nietzsche, Jean Arthur Rimbaud, and Georges Sorel were united in their repudiation of the injustice and moral hypocrisy of bourgeois civilization, in their disgust with sentimentality and the cult of tender-hearted idealism, and in their view of violence as in some sense a regenerative, purifying force. As social radicalism merged with the more demonic strain of romanticism, one of the products was a literature designed to strip off pretensions and shock genteel sensibilities. The novel itself could be an instrument of aggression.

There were two sides to the new literature of violence. In an objective sense, it taught that all traditional ideals from

God to Christian charity were either illusions or instruments of class oppression; when one tore off the shams and myths, it was clear that society as it existed was ruled by brute force. In a subjective sense, man was found to be an irrational animal, moved by deep, destructive impulses which were either irresistible or were self-expressive, and, therefore, creative. According to Sigmund Freud, this Thanatos was part of man's basic nature; one might sublimate or displace one's darker desires, but the death-wish remained. And such pessimistic views were reinforced by a brand of Social Darwinism which found violent struggle to be the main theme of life; they seemed to be confirmed by the "lessons" taught by the First World War and the rise of totalitarian regimes which used terror as an instrument of policy.

It is unnecessary to trace the influence of such diverse intellectual movements on modern literature. Nor are we concerned here with aesthetic evaluation or the artistic uses to which violence has been put. What needs to be emphasized is that in twentieth-century literature violence has come to be identified with the very quintessence of reality, as opposed to abstract ideals, myths, and institutions. It is for this reason that Mr. Max could call Bigger Thomas's murder " 'an act of creation!' "

The theme of violence as reality has taken a variety of forms in modern American literature. It can stand for the true nature of class struggle: in Steinbeck's *In Dubious Battle,* Mac and Jim interrogate a high school boy who has been aiding the strikebreakers, and who has been caught with a rifle; in order to send him back as a warning to other youth, Mac beats his face to a pulp and breaks his nose; later, Jim's face is blown off by a shotgun blast as he falls into the strikebreakers' trap. It can be man's spontaneous outrage at oppression: Tom Joad, in *The Grapes of Wrath,* crushes the head of a policeman who has just killed Casy with a pickhandle. It can make sentimentality seem more hard-boiled: in *Of Mice and Men* George talks to Lennie, the giant half-wit, about their plans for settling on a little farm, but then shoots him in the back of the head, because poor Lennie had unintentionally broken the neck of Curley's wife. It can represent the puncturing of dreams and illusions: Fitzgerald's Jay Gatsby lies on a pneumatic mattress in his gorgeous swimming pool, surrounded by leaves and little

ripples from the gusts of wind. It can fulfill the design of
history: in *All the King's Men* Adam Stanton learns that his
revered father had been dishonest and that his sister has
become the mistress of Willie Stark, and he proceeds to
shoot the great boss and is cut down himself by Sugar Boy's
bullets. It can be the way life really is, no matter what the
priests and politicians say: in the orgiastic New Year's Eve
party which ends Farrell's *The Young Manhood of Studs
Lonigan,* Weary Reilley tackles the resisting and virginal
Irene, rips off her dress, beats her unconscious, and leaves
the bloody sheets in the bathtub. It can symbolize the brutality of a world to which one must be resigned: Hemingway's killers take over a lunch counter and prepare to am-
bush their victim.

But violence as reality can also stand for the supreme
moment of art and truth: in *The Sun Also Rises,* Romero
maintains a perfect purity of line in the bullring of Pam-
plona, only to be savagely beaten by a man who has no understanding of Hemingway's code of life. Or it can be a
nightmarish burst of horror, as in Marc Chagall's painting
of the falling angel or Pablo Picasso's "Guernica": in Faulkner's *Sanctuary* a lynch mob incinerates a man with gaso-
line, and the grotesque Popeye, who as a child cut up live
birds and kittens, rapes Temple Drake with a corncob. And
for some of our most recent writers, violence can be a
vehicle of unrelieved dehumanization: Herbert Selby, Jr's
amoral Tralala is raped by a mob in a vacant lot; her body
is then abused and covered with filth by children, while her
former companions roar with drunken laughter.

As we have suggested, there is nothing peculiarly American about such images of violence as reality. They arise from
an international disenchantment with the view that life is
essentially decent, rational, and peaceful. It would appear,
however, that American writers have wrought a synthesis
between such rebellious antirationalism and the older, native
tradition of the individualistic hero who seeks to prove himself by violent acts. It may not be wholly farfetched to see
an affinity between Cooper's Deerslayer and Hemingway's
Robert Jordan, between Melville's Ahab and Faulkner's Joe
Christmas, between Wister's Virginian and Spillane's Mike
Hammer. Moreover, the theme of patriotic violence against
conspiratorial Tories, which was first developed in the his-

torical romances of the Revolution, seems to have been end-lessly reworked in comic strips and popular fiction, the Tories, of course, having become Communist subversives. Critics who interpret violence in contemporary literature as a symptom of a sick society may be reassured to know that American writers have always been preoccupied with murder, rape, and deadly combat. Yet, in so far as the older themes have been assimilated to an antirationalist philosophy, and as the individualistic hero has been moved from the open seas or prairies to a dense society in which only the most brutal survive, the treatment of violence in our literature has grown increasingly ominous for a people who profess to believe in peace and human brotherhood.

SEX AND VIOLENCE ON THE
AMERICAN NEWSSTAND

Herbert A. Otto

OVER THE past five years especially, and to some extent prior to that time, considerable attention has been focused on the prevalence of two themes—"Sex" and "Violence"—in our mass media of communication. However, with few exceptions (notably the comic book industry study and re-form movement), the spotlight of public attention has been turned primarily on the television and motion picture media. Lately and to a lesser degree, literature (i.e., hard cover pub-lications) has been in the public eye, mainly due to certain judicial and administrative rulings, culminating in unex-purgated publication of Henry Miller's early works by Amer-ican publishers.

It is surprising that in view of the interest paid to the themes of sex and violence as they appear in television, motion pictures and hard cover books, a significant segment

Excerpts reprinted with the permission of the editor from *Journalism Quarterly*, Winter, 1963, pp. 19–26 (graphs and footnotes omitted).

of our mass media of communication—magazines, newspapers and pocketbooks—has been almost totally neglected. It is the purpose of this article to summarize three research projects undertaken to study the scope and range of incidents of sex and violence as found in the magazines and newspapers generally available on U. S. newsstands.

• • •

METHODOLOGY

Magazine Study

On April 17, 1961, all magazines available for sale at a representative newsstand in Salt Lake City, Utah, were purchased, with the exclusion of certain special types. Magazines dealing with such special areas as astrology, science, news and sports were excluded from the survey. A total of 55 magazines was thus obtained. It was then found that the magazines could be placed into five groupings:

(1) Police and detective magazines, (2) romance magazines, (3) family magazines, (4) men's magazines, (5) intellectual magazines.

There were 17 men's magazines with such representative titles as *Male, Playboy, Stag.* Romance magazines numbered 14 with such titles as *My Confession, Real Confessions, True Love.* Next were the police and detective magazines with 11 titles such as *Master Detective, True Detective, True Police.* Family magazines included 10 titles such as *The Ladies' Home Journal, Redbook, Reader's Digest.* Finally, the intellectual magazines numbered three—*Atlantic Monthly, Harper's* and the *New Yorker.*

A preliminary survey was conducted to define the types of incidents involving sex and violence found in magazines. Fifteen categories ranging from "killing" to "torture" to "verbal attack" were found to cover the scope of violence. Similarly, 17 sex categories, such as "adultery," "kissing and hugging" and "rape," defined the incidents dealing with sexual themes. Each of these categories was defined separately, uniform counting procedures were developed, and two grids were designed to facilitate analysis of the material. To insure accuracy, the definitions, counting instructions and other materials were mimeographed and a number of training sessions held with the 10 researchers to insure thorough comprehension of counting procedures and uniformity in analysis.

The contents of all 55 magazines were then analyzed and a count made of the number of incidents of violence and sex found in each magazine. The number of words devoted to the description of incidents of violence and sex were also counted and the column inches of pictures devoted to these subjects measured. Advertisements were excluded from this survey.

The Newspaper Study

A list of leading United States newspapers was obtained and those newspapers selected which had the largest circulation and which at the same time would be geographically representative. A total of 10 newspapers was thus selected. They were the *New York Daily News, Chicago Tribune, Los Angeles Times, Philadelphia Bulletin, Detroit News and Times, Baltimore Sun, Cleveland Plain Dealer, Washington Post, St. Louis Post-Dispatch* and the *Houston Post*. The date chosen for analysis was Wednesday, April 11, 1962, and a copy of each paper for that date was obtained. This date was chosen after a survey of literature revealed that Wednesday was the day a maximum of actual news stories could be expected.

The criteria used for analysis were similar to those established by the group which analyzed magazines in the 1961 study. Seventeen sex categories and 18 violence categories were defined. A set of grids was prepared and standard counting procedures developed. Column inches was the measurement used to record all data. Advertising, comic strips and radio and television guides were excluded from the survey. Analysis was by the number of column inches devoted to each sex or violence category. Percentages of the total were then computed for each sex and violence category.

Paperback Books Cover Analysis

This study was concerned with an analysis of the cover of paperback books. The newsstand which represented the largest single source of paperback books found in Salt Lake City was selected as the locale for this study. A preliminary study of the contents of the pocketbook section of the newsstand was undertaken. It was found that all paperbook books could be classified in eight groups. These groups were fiction, historical fiction, detective, science fiction, war-military, western, educational-informative and humor.

The percentage of books found in each area was then determined. A random sample method was used to select an equivalent percentage of books from each category. A total of 296 book titles was thus selected from all areas as the sample for this study. Analysis of the covers of paperback books was conducted, both on the basis of cover illustrations as well as classification of titles. A set of 10 classifications of cover illustrations was developed. These were: (1) female seductive, (2) female non-seductive, (3) sadistic, (4) violent, (5) male seductive, (6) male non-seductive, (7) military or weapons without violence, (8) natural scene, (9) humor, (10) non-illustrative.

The cover illustration category "female seductive," for example, was defined as follows:

This would include any illustration designed to connote any impression of lewdness, sensualism or provocation in which a female is the central illustrative figure. It would include any females in stages of undress or attempting to undress, nude or semi-nude, dressed or in any provocative costume, or in sensuous juxtaposition with a male.

Classification of titles was under five categories: (1) seductive title, (2) violent title, (3) title with sadism, (4) neutral or normal titles, (5) questionable and not definite title. The following is the definition for the category "violent title": "This would include any title in which the reader is given a definite impression of death, violence, crime, war, or aggression."

To minimize elements of subjectivity and bias, each of the three researchers conducted an independent evaluation of the sample using the definitions and tally sheets. The three separate sets of results were then compared, found largely similar, and averaged.

MAJOR FINDINGS

Magazine Study

Fifty-five magazines, representative of the reading matter generally bought by the public, were analyzed. These magazines had in their reading matter the astounding total of 2,524 incidents of violence, and 1,261 incidents dealing with sexual themes. A total of 282,710 words was devoted to these subjects.

As might be expected, there were marked contrasts in the amount of sex and violence included in the content of the different groups of magazines. For example, the amount of violence in Police and Detective magazines was 542% higher than found in Family magazines. Comparing incidents dealing with sexual themes in Family and Romance magazines, it was discovered that Romance magazines had 1150% more sexual incidents than the Family type magazines.

If a reader bought a Police and Detective type magazine he could expect to find an average number of 6,199 words devoted to incidents of violence. A man's magazine would have about 4,157 words. In contrast, Family magazines would devote 926 words to this topic. The buyer of a Romance type magazine would find an average of 3,222 words on incidents dealing with sex. (Men's magazines have 1039% more picture space devoted to sex themes than Family magazines.) Romance magazines have less than half the amount of picture space devoted to violence and sex than Men's magazines. In contrast, 79% of the pictures found in Police and Detective magazines deal with themes of violence and 21% depict sex themes.

Detailed content analysis revealed a number of interesting facts:

(1) Men's magazines (having such titles as *Male, Rogue, Stag*) have the largest number of pictures depicting themes of sex and violence of all magazines surveyed.

(2) Although a Police and Detective magazine (with an average of about 30 killings and 7 robberies per issue) had over 10 times as many killings as a Family magazine, both groups of magazines had nearly the same number of incidents of "verbal attack." Verbal attack is defined as "to quarrel with, be abusive, use violent language." However, the Family magazines used almost double the number of words to describe an equal number of verbal attacks.

(3) Whereas physical torture received detailed treatment in Men's magazines as well as Police and Detective and Romance magazines (in that order), other magazines generally avoided this topic.

(4) Police and Detective magazines lead the field in the description of incidents of rape. This group of magazines had twice as many descriptions of rape as the Romance magazines, which ranked second. Men's magazines closely followed the Romance group in the number of rapes described. The Police and Detective magazines had almost 1000% more incidents of rape than the Family magazines.

• • •

Newspaper Study

The 10 newspapers devoted a total of 29,841 column inches to news. Of this total, 1,518 inches, or 5% of the total, dealt with descriptions of incidents of violence. *This surprisingly low total is one of the significant findings of the study.* Of the separate categories, War Violence was highest with an average of less than one percent (.8%) of all news being devoted to this topic by the papers surveyed. This was followed by news of Accidental Violence (.5%) and news devoted to Killings (.4%).

The figures cited represent an average of all papers surveyed with the exception of the *New York Daily News.* Inclusion of the averages of this tabloid in the summary would have resulted in a marked distortion of the results. For example, the *New York Daily News* devoted 3.3% of its total news to subjects dealing with sex. Of the papers surveyed, the *Philadelphia Evening Bulletin* was next highest with only .42% of the total news content dealing with this topic. The *New York Daily News* therefore devoted seven times the amount of news space to this subject. A total of 33.5% of news in the *Daily News* covers topics of violence. Of the other papers surveyed, the *Detroit News* comes closest with 8.8% of news content devoted to violence. The *St. Louis Post-Dispatch* had the lowest percentage of column inches on this topic, 2.1%.

Correlating the Deutschmann categories with the sex-violence categories, our findings are generally in agreement with Stempel's recent analysis of content patterns of small and metropolitan dailies. Stempel's figures indicate that in most small metropolitan dailies studied, War and Defense News receives roughly twice as much space as the two categories Crime and Accident and Disaster combined.

Cover Analysis of Paperback Books

Of the sample of 296 paperback books whose covers were analyzed, a total of 44% had covers or illustrations falling in the seductive-sadistic-violence categories. (Thirty-three percent of this total had "female seductive" cover illustrations.) Another 6% of the cover illustrations were of the "weapons or military without violence" type which had considerable sensational, eye-attracting value. Therefore, 50% of the pocketbooks were found to have covers with illustrations of a seductive, sadistic, violent (weapons or military) nature. Non-seductive and natural scene material accounted for 38% of the covers and the remainder (12%) had no illustration.

It will be recalled that it was found that paperbook books could be divided into a number of groups: (1) fiction, (2) historical fiction, (3) detective, (4) science fiction, (5) war and military, (6) western, (7) education-informative, (8) humor. Certain major trends were discovered in the use of cover illustrations by the different groups of paperback books. For example, the fiction type of pocketbook had 40% female seductive covers. By contrast, the detective-type pocketbook utilized 61% female seductive covers, while 22% of this type pocketbook had covers depicting themes of violence and sadism. In the western type pocketbook, 39% of the cover illustrations were found to show scenes of violence. On the other hand, in the educational-informative type pocketbook, 51% of the cover illustrations were of a non-seductive or natural scene type.

Analysis of pocketbook titles disclosed generally similar findings. Fifty-seven percent of the titles were judged to be "neutral or normal" and 14% were classified as "questionable and not definite" as no judgment could be formed about this group. A total of 29% of the pocketbooks had titles which were classified as being in the seductive-violent category (10% violent, 19% seductive titles).

DISCUSSION

The three studies which have been undertaken indicate that television and motion pictures are not the only segment of our mass media of communication heavily saturated with themes of sex and violence. With the exception of certain special categories, namely the family and intellectual type magazines, *most magazines available on the corner newsstand are riddled with a metastasis of sex and violence themes.*

A spot check was made of magazine content published 10 years ago. The number of magazines specializing in violence and sex (such as Men's magazines and the Police and Detective group) has increased markedly since that time. Based largely on this heavy increase in the group of magazines specializing in violence and sex, there are definite indications of a *significant increase in the quantity of violence and sex themes found on the newsstands over the last 10 years.* The amount of space devoted to these magazines as well as the number of incidents portrayed has been rising. This upward trend shows every sign of continuing. The cover analysis of paperback books seems to bear out this trend. The writer, in his travels over the country, has noted that in many of the major cities the larger newsstands are increasingly reserving a number of racks (usually located well to the rear of the newsstand) for pocketbooks having cover illustrations which can be classified as ranging from "mildly seductive" to "extremely seductive." Sample titles of such publications are *Mass Orgy, Lust Market, Hungry Thighs* and *Orgy Club.* A spot check of these specialized sections reveals that these pocketbooks deal almost entirely with highly erotic and sadistic themes.

The newspaper study presents markedly different results indicating that a representative segment of the American press is not as preoccupied with themes of sex and violence as are some of our other mass media of communication. However, a study of tabloids can be expected to yield significantly different results. A comparative study needs to be made of the amount of news space devoted to sex and violence by tabloids as differentiated from other metropolitan dailies. It would also be of value if a base V/S Index (violence/sex) for newspapers was developed.

On November 16, 1962, the writer was asked to testify before a subcommittee of the Utah Committee on Children and Youth concerned with the effect of the mass media of communication on youth. In the course of a spirited debate with the regional wholesale news distributor, the distributor pointed out that he was exercising a voluntary form of censorship by keeping 95 magazines, deemed objectionable by him, from Utah newsstands. On the basis of previous records, he estimated that the gross sales volume of these magazines would exceed $90,000 annually. It should, therefore, be noted that this study is markedly biased on the conservative side. Similar studies conducted in other parts of the nation can be expected to yield a significantly higher concentration of incidents of sex and violence to be found in the contents of the newsstands.

The question whether the preoccupation with themes of sex and violence in our mass media of communication has an effect on the personality and character formation of our growing generation is currently the subject of widespread debate by behavioral and social scientists. Implicit in this debate is the issue whether the publisher or those in control of our media of mass communication have a responsibility to the public in a similar way the comic book industry, some years ago, was discovered to have a responsibility to the young people of America.

There is a pressing need to conduct a comprehensive comparative study of the sex and violence content as well as the nature of publications found in the newsstand 10 years ago and today. An imperative need exists to "pull together" the different studies of violence and sex in television, radio, motion pictures and the other media. More research in this area must be initiated and a *comparative analysis of this vast mass of information should be undertaken*. This, coupled with a review of related research and literature may give us specific clues to two very pressing questions: (1) Does the American public need this continuous consumption of violence and sex? If so, why? (2) Can our understanding of this phenomena be used positively in terms of strengthening the nation's health and well-being?

The three modest studies which have been reported here can only be considered in the nature of pilot projects. It is hoped that interest will be stimulated so that broader and more extensive research projects can be undertaken which will examine the phenomena of the themes of sex and violence in our mass media of communication.

VIOLENCE IN COMIC BOOKS
(Before Self-Regulation by the Comics Industry)

Marilyn Graalfs

HOW MUCH physical violence and horror is there in comic books? In what stories is the greatest amount of physical violence and horror found? How are they portrayed? What is the role of language, plot, or story sequence in portraying violence and horror?

To provide some answers to such questions, a content analysis of 351 comic books, all those available on the newsstand during the first three months of 1954, was undertaken. In the 351 books there were 1,325 stories. On the average, each story included 6.8 pages and 42.2 frames. The frame, defined as a picture enclosed by a border with or without dialogue, was the basic unit for the quantitative analysis but the descriptive results were much the same whether the unit was the frame, the page, or the story. A group of trained investigators classified the frames and acts according to definitions worked out after repeated pre-testing. Ten general categories of story types were developed. However, three types were dominant: *Humor,* 35.4 per cent; *Crime,* 27.5 per cent; and, *Romance,* 20.6 per cent.

SUMMARY OF QUANTITATIVE FINDINGS

1. A violent physical act appeared once in seven frames in comic books (14 per cent of 44,653 frames).

2. While some physical violence is portrayed in all major types of stories, it is more prevalent in some settings than others. The per cent of the total frames with violence by story types is as follows: Western Crime, 25.8; War, 22.4; Conventional Crime, 19.5; Fantasy Crime, 18.2; Fantasy Non-Crime, 12.5; and Humor, 6.1.

Excerpts from *A Survey of Comic Books in the State of Washington,* A Report to the Washington State Council for Children and Youth, June, 1954, pp. 19–29.

3. In none of the War stories were American soldiers shown dead or injured.

4. The most frequently portrayed type of physical violence was striking with a weapon (one out of four frames of violence).

5. One in four of the violent frames showed a person dead, dying, or injured.

6. One in twenty of the violent frames showed people being attacked or mangled by animals.

7. Death is shown in comic books mainly in Fantasy stories. The highest proportion of violent frames showing persons dead or dying was found in Fantasy Non-Crime stories, 29.5 per cent, followed by Fantasy Crime stories, 24.7 per cent. The lowest proportions were found in Humor, .5 per cent, Western Crime, 4.8 per cent, and War, 7.9 per cent.

QUALITATIVE FINDINGS

Physical acts are not the only means for portraying violence in comic books stories. Three additional means will now be described and illustrated.

1. *Character, plot, setting.* The majority of fantasy stories, which exhibited relatively few physical acts of violence, dealt with supernatural people and events. Most frequently the supernatural phenomena involved werewolves, vampires, zombies, witches, people returning from the dead, and animal monsters. Physical violence occurred in only one or two frames. However, the total amount of violence cannot be measured by counting isolated frames taken out of context. *Each* frame in these stories contributed to the horror and suspense.

One method of portraying horror identifies supernatural phenomena with real people and things.

CASE 1: A monster being, ape-like in form, stalks a city. The police, particularly one sergeant, repeatedly attempt to destroy him. While the story shows little physical violence, tension mounts with each frame until near the end. In the last few frames *the police sergeant* is shown changing from his human form into the monster. He remains undiscovered and is shown in natural human form in the last frame which has the caption: "How many more lives will be snuffed out by the evil Grakku [name given the monster] safe in his human disguise as Sgt. Grunsky?"

CASE 2: A story uses for its plot a Pied Piper theme. The Piper tells the animals to revolt against their slave conditions. When they attack, the hero refuses to listen to objections from the villagers when he kills the animals by destroying a bridge. "Don't you understand all those animals have learned to hunt humans and they will pass that hatred on to their descendants if we let them?" The story ends with the caption: "Where are the descendants of those animals today? Ever catch your cat staring steadily at you in the firelight or watch a horse look back at you as you cross behind him?"

CASE 3: A man dreams that zombies have taken over the earth and set up an oppressive dictatorship. The story is obviously a dream. However in the last frame, after seeing the world ruled by zombies in a dream, the man awakens and says, "People don't realize I'm really a zombie!"

In each of the above cases horror was portrayed not only by making use of fantastic supernatural powers but by identifying these powers with people and animals that really exist. That is, by association it is suggested that real policemen may be ghouls who prey on the denizens of a city. The next-door neighbor may be a zombie who is secretly plotting with other zombies, also neighbors, to take over the world. Ordinary house pets are actually man's enemies awaiting the opportunity to destroy him.

Another device for portraying horror not only uses supernatural beings (werewolves and vampires) but places these characters in a highly realistic setting. Therefore, horror is identified not only with real people but also with real situations.

CASE 4: The central character in this story is an orphan whom the matrons of the home are eager to have adopted for some secret reason which is never clear to the reader. The boy is portrayed sympathetically as wishing with all his heart that his real parents will someday return. A young attractive couple finally adopt him. The remaining frames rotate between showing them feeding him lots of milk, eggs, and cake, and his restriction to a barred and locked room. In each frame he asks about his confinement and each time the lovely couple reply that they will tell him the secret someday. The action progresses to the climax in the last three frames.

Frame 1: The picture shows the inside of the door to the boy's room. Through the door comes the following dialogue: "I was hoping you'd tell him tonight. I couldn't have waited another day."

Frame 2: They enter (boy not shown), fangs exposed, saying; "You're just right . . . fat and full of rich blood. . . . We're Vampires!"

Frame 3: Boy's body exposed to the reader. He leaps to the attack—as a werewolf!

These cases illustrate that violence and horror in comic books is not restricted to the isolated action shown in each frame. Though there are no frames with physical violence, a whole story may create "horror" by its selection of characters, sequence of events and situations.

2. *Language.* Words alone or in conjunction with pictures may describe violence and horror more vividly than the graphic techniques. In comic books, language contributes to horror in the following ways.

a. *Anticipation.* The following are introductions to stories.

This first tale of Death and SUSPENSE will keep you CHILLED to the BONE right up to the TERROR-FILLED conclusion! The BLOOD spills FAST and OFTEN as Hazel [main character who murders husband] reaps the REWARD of a successful MURDER.

This tingling tale of MURDER with its SHOCKER ENDING should satisfy the most demanding of CRIME LOVERS.

Hee, hee, hee [we've] served the main course and now you should be ready for the DESSERT. Your hungry bellies have become BLOATED, consuming the HORROR and GORE in the preceding Tales . . . but yet there is room for MORE. Just ONE *more* tantalizing scrumptious tidbit . . . the FROSTING ON THE CAKE, so to speak.

b. *Reinforced beliefs.*

"Who can doubt the age-old horror of cosmic ghouls that roam the earth in search of prey . . . of countless things that walk by night," is the preface to a story about werewolves.

c. *Describe desires.*

As a man gropes toward the figure of a woman outlined behind a lighted dressing screen, the caption above says, "Now you know why you were so interested in her white alabaster skin . . . the beautiful red lips, the creamy neck . . . now you know. He says, "Can't wait any longer . . . must go to her . . . must kill, kill, kill!" The last frames show he is a werewolf.

d. *Language used to describe killings.* One of the most important functions of language in crime comics is to replace graphic portrayals of brutal killings. In these types of stories pictures did not show weapons in contact with victims, nor was the victim's mangled body exposed to the reader. However, the act of killing and its effects on the victim were imaginatively described by the texts. The following will serve to illustrate the technique.

CASE I: A man is shown lifting an axe preparatory to striking his wife on the floor. In the next frame he lowers the axe; the wife is not shown but the caption reads: "Bertha squealed as Norman brought the axe down. The swinging of steel and the thud of the razor-sharp metal against flesh cut the squeal short." In the next frame he holds the axe poised again, the body still is not exposed and the caption reads: "He brought the axe down again and again, hacking, severing, dismembering."

CASE 2: CAPTION: "His [victim's] shrieks died to a bubbling moan . . . then a final death rattle. . . . You did not stop swinging the chair until the thing on the floor was nothing but a mass of oozing scarlet pulp." No body is shown but the entire frame is *colored red.*

CASE 3: A woman kills her husband with a kitchen knife. Picture shows blood on the knife but no injury on the husband's body. "The rapier sharp blade SLICED him directly between the shoulder blades. . . ." Then the woman dragged him to the pen where a crazed bull was kept. *Caption:* "Even a STOMACH as STRONG as Hazel's couldn't stand the sight of the Bull's attack on Ezra's corpse. GAGGING she turned and FLED back to the house."

CASE 4: The husband drags his wife out to the forest to kill her. The frame shows him frantically beating while only an outstretched hand of the woman is exposed. CAPTION: "He snatched up the lead pipe and in a desperate fury pounded and beat her."

CASE 5: The train operator says of a woman who was pushed in front of the onrushing subway, "I've never seen anyone so mangled to pieces in my life. She ain't a woman anymore, she's a mess." (The woman is not shown with injuries.)

CASE 6: "I didn't want to kill you. You were good to me," says the perverted murderer whom she had befriended. The frames show him drawing forth the knife and the contorted face of the woman as he grabs her. The next two frames show the actual killing. In neither is the woman shown but the captions read: "The scalpel edge of the butcher knife was hot on Lola's neck. She tried to scream but no sound came—only a choking gurgle. There was a fluid red haze and then blackness. . . ." In the first frame the man is with the knife in swinging motion and the background is colored red. In the second his face is contorted, one hand clutches the woman's hair, only her forehead is exposed, but the man is holding the knife in a horizontal position ready to sever her head.

3. *Sequence.* Another way in which horror or violence may be shown is by the sequence of events. Stories may be constructed so that each frame stimulates the imagination of the reader up to a shocking climax in the last frame. The sequence may be carried out through the use of words and pictures which in themselves are unrelated to horror. Consider, for example, the following two cases.

CASE 1: In the first few frames several characters are apparently repulsed by some weird creature. The frame does not show the thing but one character points in its direction and says, "Ugh! What is it?" The tension is built about the strange creatures who are only described verbally until the last frame where they are shown as huge grotesque frogs.

CASE 2: The story is about a man who gets entangled in a swamp. One frame shows him in the swamp and a huge vulture circling above in a downward direction. The next frame shows the man being carried out on a stretcher with *bandages over his eyes.*

Violence can be portrayed both pictorially and verbally in comic books. Among fantasy stories, particularly, violence is underestimated if only actions shown in the frames are counted. The types of characters, plots, and settings contribute to violence by identifying them with realistic people and events. Language may be used to heighten the degree of horror by (1) encouraging the reader to anticipate it; (2) reinforcing superstitious notions about supernatural beings; (3) describing the feelings and attitudes of characters which cannot be revealed to the reader through pictures; and (4) replacing pictures of brutality. Finally, the sequence of events may in the absence of either words or pictures of any action create horror.

ACHIEVING GOALS THROUGH VIOLENCE ON TELEVISION

Otto N. Larsen, Louis N. Gray, and *J. Gerald Fortis*

THE PRESENT paper uses content analysis to explore and illuminate certain dimensions of program presentation that could serve as models for viewers' behavior. Goals, methods, and combinations of goals and methods presented on programs viewed by various segments of the television audience will be analyzed. The degree to which approved goals are portrayed as being successfully achieved by either approved or disapproved methods will also be studied. Are viewers exposed to essentially similar models of behavior in these respects regardless of the type of program involved? Since many critics appear to worry less about the content of children's programs and are more concerned about the adult programs which children are known to watch, it becomes of interest to attempt to determine the exent to which content differs over program types relative to the amount of difference within program types.

RESEARCH PROCEDURE

Units for analysis of goals. In this study a goal was defined by any verbal act or behavior by any character indicating a desire or wish for an identifiable situation. By situation is meant a state of affairs, an identifiable system of relationships (social or otherwise). The desired identifiable situation need not require a change in existing situations or relationships, i.e., the preservation of the status quo may be a goal. Once this general definition was agreed upon, seven mutually exclusive and totally inclusive classes of goals were defined:

Excerpts reprinted with the permission of the authors and the editor from "Goals and Goal-Achievement Methods in Television Content: Models for Anomie?" *Sociological Inquiry,* Spring, 1963, pp. 180–196 (footnotes and one table omitted).

1. *Property.* A character has expressed desire for a property goal when he makes a verbal statement indicating a wish for any situation of objects (physical or social) which would have material or economic value, i.e., give comfort, accumulate wealth, or generally wish for situations of material success. An expressed desire for leadership situations, dominance situations, particular social positions, etc., do *not* fall into this category.

2. *Self-preservation.* A verbal act by a character indicating a desire for attainment or maintenance of safety and protection or of freedom from fear, care, danger, or doubt for oneself or intimate associates; desire for preservation of the status quo, desire for escape from situations of explicit physical danger, desire to satisfy minimal bodily needs, desire to be rid of affliction, etc.

3. *Affection.* A verbal act by a character indicating a desire for gratification of a passionate affection, devotion, friendship, dislike, or hate or other affective relationship between the speaking character and one or more other characters whether explicitly specified or not; desire to be liked, loved, befriended; desire for the preservation of the status quo in affective relationships *only;* desire for others to be considerate of oneself in social relationships; desire to be idolized or worshipped by others, etc.

4. *Sentiment.* A verbal act by a character indicating a desire for justice, revenge; desire for change in a nation's, city's, county's, culture's, political system or social system because of one's beliefs or values rather than for power; desire for the preservation of the status quo of a social or political system in a city, county, nation, culture, because of one's beliefs or values rather than for power, prestige; desire for a state of fairness, impartiality, and reward or penalty as deserved because of one's beliefs or values rather than for power; desire for retaliation, balance in nature; desire to forward religious movement, etc.

5. *Power and prestige.* A verbal act by a character indicating a desire for a position of dominance, leadership, the ability to control or influence the behavior or attitudes of others; desire for a particular or generalized position in a system of social relationships which are not primarily affective; desire for membership in groups of certain social positions; desire to exercise authority in formal or in-

formal social situations; desire to be respected, consulted, etc., though not necessarily liked.

6. *Psychological.* A verbal act by a character indicating a desire for a satisfaction of a psychological drive, escape from "reality," engaging in an encounter with danger; desire for unusual or daring experience; desire to be artistically creative; desire for education; desire to engage in violence for violence's sake; desire for unnatural satisfactions; any desire due to psychological abnormality, etc.

7. *Other.* A verbal act by a character indicating a desire for anything not listed thus far.

Units for analysis of methods. A method of goal achievement was defined as a verbal or non-verbal act by a character which is identifiably connected with a specific goal and is presumably being employed by the character in question, directly or indirectly, to increase the probability of goal achievement insofar as the character is able to interpret the situation. Eight classes of methods of goal achievement were defined:

1. *Legal.* A verbal or non-verbal act by a character directed toward the attainment of a specifiable goal which is authorized by law or is in conformity with rules that can be enforced in a court of law, i.e., lawsuits, appeal to police or armed forces, appeal to established government, self-enforcement of acknowledged legal principles, etc., but non-violent.

2. *Non-legal.* A verbal or non-verbal act by a character directed toward the attainment of a specifiable goal which is made without regard for moral or legal standards but which is not performed with intent to injure, damage, or make other use of physical force. This may involve acts of embezzlement, slander, libel, rumor formation, theft, confidence games, non-violent white-collar crime, cheating, lying, etc.

3. *Economic.* A verbal or non-verbal act by a character directed toward the attainment of a specifiable goal which involves buying, selling, trading, or bartering of goods or money, use of commercial channels, etc.

4. *Violence.* A verbal or non-verbal act by a character directed toward the attainment of a specifiable goal which involves the use or threat of use of forceful means regard-

less of the actor's legal or non-legal attachments; use of power, roughness, or physical force to injure, damage, maim, render helpless, etc.; threat of the use of such power, etc.

5. *Organization, negotiation, and compromise.* A verbal or non-verbal act by a character directed toward the attainment of a specifiable goal which involves combining forces with other individuals or groups, discussing methods, compromising all or part of original goals, scientific investigation of problem, and conferring or bargaining *non-economically.*

6. *Escape.* A verbal or non-verbal act by a character directed toward the attainment of a specifiable goal which, to the viewers' perception, appears to be an attempt to avoid facts inherent in accomplishing the goal, shunning or shirking of the problematic situation, avoidance of channels of action so as to escape decision making, forgetting goal, relinquishing *all* of goal, escaping from situation in which goal arose, withdrawing from situation, etc.

7. *Chance.* Verbal or non-verbal acts directed toward the attainment of a particular character's goal which arise through accidental circumstances, fortuitous events, or outside intervention without apparent cause or design. Not acts by character's (or characters') intimates designed for the attainment of specifiable goals; luck, good fortune, etc.

8. *Other.* A verbal or non-verbal act by a character directed toward the attainment of a specifiable goal which does not fall in the above categories.

Classification and selection of television programs. While several systems of program classification based on form, substance, and source have been employed in television content studies, it was decided preferable, for the present purposes, to devise a classification system on the basis of the following criteria: (1) Audience composition stratified by broad age-categories as determined by national rating-service and audience studies; (2) for programs that were designed mainly for entertainment purposes; and (3) that were national network releases during the evening hours after 6 p.m. Analysis of data from Nielsen and ARB rating-services indicated the feasibility of classifying entertainment programs into the following three types.

1. *Adult.* Programs where the child or teen-age audience was no greater than 15 per cent of the total audience.
2. *"Kidult."* Programs where the child or teen-age audience maintained at least a 30 per cent share of the total audience but no more than 38 per cent of the total audience.
3. *Children.* Programs where the child or teen-age audience exceeded 38 per cent of the total audience.

Lists were compiled of programs falling in the three categories which appeared on network stations in Seattle. From these lists the following eighteen programs were selected for observation, six in each of the three program categories:

1. *Adult programs:*
   a. *Alcoa Presents* (NBC, 10 p.m. Tuesday).
   b. *Dick Powell Show* (NBC, 9 p.m. Tuesday).
   c. *Bus Stop* (ABC, 9 p.m. Sunday).
   d. *77 Sunset Strip* (ABC, 9 p.m. Friday).
   e. *Twilight Zone* (CBS, 10 p.m. Friday).
   f. *Adventures in Paradise* (ABC, 10 p.m. Sunday).
2. *Kidult programs:*
   a. *Bachelor Father* (ABC, 8 p.m. Tuesday).
   b. *Cheyenne* (ABC, 7:30 p.m. Monday).
   c. *Rifleman* (ABC, 8:30 p.m. Monday).
   d. *Donna Reed Show* (ABC, 8 p.m. Thursday).
   e. *My Three Sons* (NBC, 9 p.m. Thursday).
   f. *Car 54 Where Are You?* (NBC, 8:30 p.m. Sunday).
3. *Children's programs:*
   a. *Bugs Bunny* (ABC, 7:30 p.m. Tuesday).
   b. *Deputy Dawg* (NBC, 6 p.m. Tuesday).
   c. *Huckleberry Hound* (NBC, 6 p.m. Thursday).
   d. *Bullwinkle* (NBC, 7 p.m. Sunday).
   e. *Flintstones* (ABC, 8:30 p.m. Friday).
   f. *Walt Disney Presents* (NBC, 7:30 p.m. Sunday).

• • •

FINDINGS: VARIATION OF GOALS
BY PROGRAM TYPE

Adult programs presented an average of 24.6 goals per show; kidult programs presented an average of 22.2 goals per show; and children's programs presented an average of 17.7 goals per show. Thus it appears that the number of goals appearing in a television show will increase as the relative proportion of children and teenagers watching the show decreases. An analysis of variance test for a significance of difference among the means of the three categories is, however, not significant (F for the analysis of variance table is .31, indicating greater variation within categories than between categories).

In order to examine the variation of particular types of goals by program types, seven analyses of variance were computed, one for each of the seven goal categories. The interval scale for these analyses was the frequency of presentation of the goal in question. The absolute frequency, rather than relative frequency, was used since the primary interest here is in absolute exposure to models of behavior rather than relative exposure.

TABLE 1. *Average Presentation of Specific Goals by Program Type*

	PROGRAM TYPE				F RATIO		
Goal	*Adult*	*Kidult*	*Chil-dren*	*Total F*	*Adult and Kidult*	*Adult and Child*	*Kidult and Child*
1. Property	1.8	4.5	4.5	1.52	2.44	2.50	—
2. Self-preservation	8.3	2.3	2.2	3.43[a]	—	—	—
3. Affection	8.2	3.0	3.8	1.41	2.54	1.23	—
4. Sentiment	5.2	8.8	3.5	.66	.49	—	1.24
5. Power and prestige	1.5	2.2	3.2	2.50	.33	1.00	—
6. Psychological	2.2	1.0	.5	1.96	1.29	5.00[b]	—
7. Other	1.5	.3	0.0	.75	—	—	—

[a] At 2 and 15 degrees of freedom $F_{.10} = 2.70$.
[b] At 1 and 10 degrees of freedom $F_{.05} = 4.96$.

Table 1 indicates the mean frequency of each of the seven goals for each of the three program types. The fourth column of the table indicates the F ratio for the analysis of variance over the three sets. The final three columns show the F ratios computed for pairs of program types in cases where it was felt that significant differences might be found.

Only two significant differences are found in terms of the

three program types: *self-preservation* goals differ significantly over all three program types, and *psychological* goals differ significantly between adult and children's programs.

In order to further examine these differences additional analyses of variance were computed for two of the goals. These second analyses were computed on the basis of time-corrected data. The data were time-corrected by dividing the frequency of presentation of each goal by two for the sixty-minute programs to make them more comparable with thirty-minute programs. This method assumes an even distribution of goal presentation within each program.

The time-corrected analyses were made for two of the goals: *self-preservation* and *power and prestige*. The first of these was significantly different over the entire set; the second approached, though it did not reach, significance. . . .

From this, then, it may be concluded that the differences in the three program types for *self-preservation* goals is due to the slightly higher average length of programs in the adult category. The nearly significant difference found in *power* and *prestige* goals appears to arise from the effect of a single hour show in the children's category, which tends to disappear when time is controlled.

Generally, in terms of desired goals presented, the three types of programs differ only slightly. The single remaining significant difference occurs between adult and children's shows on *psychological goals*. The nature of plot structure of the two types of programs seems to explain this difference. It will be noticed that in several cases the F ratio is lower than 1.00, which tends to indicate, not only that the categories do not differ significantly, but that the differences within categories are actually greater than the differences between them.

Table 2 shows the percentage distribution of the seven types of goals in the three categories and the combined percentage over all three program categories.

Table 2 allows somewhat different assessment of the differences in goals over the three program types. It will be noted that the most frequent goal presented on adult programs is that of *self-preservation*—almost 30 percent. On the kidult programs the most frequent goal portrayed is *sentiment*—almost 40 percent. On the children's programs the most frequent goal presented is *property*—about 25 percent.

TABLE 2. *Percentage Presentation of Specific Goals by Program Type*

Goal	Adult (N = 172)	PROGRAM TYPE Kidult (N = 133)	Children (N = 106)	Combined percentage (N = 411)
	%	%	%	%
1. Property	6.4	20.3	25.4	15.8
2. Self-preservation	29.1	10.5	12.3	18.8
3. Affection	28.5	13.5	20.8	21.7
4. Sentiment	18.0	39.8	19.8	25.6
5. Power and prestige	5.2	9.8	18.9	10.2
6. Psychological	7.6	4.5	2.8	5.4
7. Other	5.2	1.6	0.0	2.5
Total percent	100.0	100.0	100.0	100.0

Thus while the only significant difference for a specific goal occurred between the adult and children's programs for *psychological goals*, it is reasonable to conclude that the pattern of goal presentation differs over the three types of programs. The relationship is, however, low enough to prevent specific predictions as to the nature of the differences in presentation which will occur.

FINDINGS: VARIATION OF METHODS BY PROGRAM TYPE

The same procedures were used to analyze the variations in methods. The average frequency of presentation of methods per program was 39.5 for adult programs, 32.9 for kidult programs, and 30.2 for children's programs. These differences are not significant when analyzed by analysis of variance techniques (F ratio in this analysis was .33).

• • •

It will be noted in Table 3 that the only significant differences arise for *organizational methods* and *escape methods*. Organizational methods appear significantly more frequently in kidult programs, next most frequently in adult programs, and least frequently in children's programs. Escape methods appear most frequently in adult programs with kidult and children's programs about equal.

In order to investigate these differences further, separate

TABLE 3.   *Average Presentation of Specific Methods by Program Type*

| | PROGRAM TYPE | | | | F RATIO | | |
Methods	Adult	Kidult	Chil-dren	Total F	Adult and Kidult	Adult and Child	Kidult and Child
1. Legal	3.2	4.8	2.0	.80	—	—	—
2. Non-legal	2.8	1.7	2.8	.14	—	—	—
3. Economic	1.8	3.7	1.8	.23	—	—	—
4. Violent	12.5	6.7	14.2	.70	.47	—	1.23
5. Organizational	3.3	6.5	2.5	6.29^a	—	—	—
6. Escape	6.8	1.2	1.8	5.05^a	—	—	—
7. Chance	2.8	3.3	2.7	.08	—	—	—
8. Other	6.0	5.2	2.3	1.05	—	2.37	3.24

^{a} At 2 and 15 degrees of freedom F.05 = 3.68.

time-corrected analyses were computed on both organizational methods and escape methods. The F ratio for the time-corrected organizational methods was 2.19, which is not significant at either the .10 or .05 level. The F ratio for escape methods was 3.56, which is significant at the .10 level. Thus it appears that the difference noted on organizational methods was due to hour shows in the kidult categories, while the difference noted on escape methods was due to factors other than program length since the relationship does not cancel out when time is controlled.

It would appear, then, that the three program types do not differ greatly in terms of the presentation of specific methods of goal achievement. The extremely low value of some of the F ratios in Table 3 indicates that for methods, even more than for goals themselves, there is frequently a greater amount of variation within categories than between categories.

Table 4 shows the percentage presentation of specific methods of goal achievement by program type.

A factor of immediate importance in this table concerns the relative frequency of *violence* as a method for the three program types. It will be noted that each of the program categories makes use of violence as the most frequent method. Thus knowing the program type is of no particular value in predicting the methods used to achieve goals.

TABLE 4. *Percentage Presentation of Specific Methods by Program Type*

Method	Adult (N = 236)	Kidult (N = 198)	Children (N = 181)	Combined percentage (N = 615)
	PROGRAM TYPE			
	%	%	%	%
1. Legal	8.1	14.6	6.6	9.7
2. Non-legal	7.2	5.1	9.4	7.2
3. Economic	4.7	11.1	6.1	7.2
4. Violent	31.8	20.2	47.0	32.6
5. Organizational	8.5	19.7	8.3	12.0
6. Escape	17.4	3.5	6.1	9.6
7. Chance	7.2	10.1	8.8	8.7
8. Other	15.1	15.7	7.7	13.0
Total percent	100.0	100.0	100.0	100.0

FINDINGS: VARIATION OF GOAL-METHOD COMBINATIONS BY PROGRAM TYPE

Since we have defined eight methods of goal achievement and seven goals, there are fifty-six possible combinations of goals and methods. Before attempting to examine significant differences for specific combinations, one interesting side-light should be discussed. This sidelight concerns a loose measure of *plot complexity,* defined here in terms of the number of different combinations of goals and methods presented on a particular type of program. Adult programs presented an average of 11.5 different combinations of goals and methods, kidult programs an average of 9.3 different combinations, and children's programs an average of 8.3 combinations per program. An analysis of variance test indicates that these differences are not significant (the F ratio in this test was .56). From this we may conclude that, insofar as we have defined plot complexity, in terms of the number of different goal and method combinations appearing, there appear to be no differences between the three categories. . . .

In order to examine the variation of specific goal and method combinations, analyses of variance were computed for each of the fifty-six possible combinations. . . .

. . . Only two of the combinations are significantly different over the set of programs: *self-preservation—other* and *sentiment—other*. In the first of these cases adult programs carry most of the share; in the second kidult programs have most of the cases. . . .

FINDINGS: DEGREE OF SUCCESS IN GOAL ACHIEVEMENT BY APPROVED AND DISAPPROVED METHODS

How successful were the television characters in pursuing the seven goals defined for observation in this study? Were there any differences in degree of success by program types? Some answers to these questions can be gained since the observers also noted which of the combinations of goals and methods used in any program were portrayed as being successful and how often. The answer to these questions becomes more interesting if one assumption is made concerning the goals and a reclassification of the methods of goal achievement is made for the analysis. Concerning the goals, let us assume that the seven goals designated for observation in this study represent aspirations that are socially approved, not only in the world of television content, but for the most part in the world of the television viewer. Concerning the methods, let us take the eight original categories and re-classify them into three categories as follows:

1. *Socially approved*—Legal.
2. *Socially disapproved*—Non-legal, Violence, and Escape.
3. *Either*—Economic, Organizational, Chance, and Other.

With this re-ordering the question then becomes, are there any differences between program types in the degree of success in goal achievement by approved and disapproved methods? For the students of *anomie*, this question may be of particular importance. When approved goals are achieved on television, are they most apt to be portrayed as being reached through approved or disapproved means? To the extent that there is a prevalence of the view that socially disapproved behavior is necessary to achieve socially approved goals, television could be said to be presenting models for anomie.

The analysis of the data was made with seven two-way

analysis of variance tests, one for each of the seven desired goals. This test allowed assessment of the data in three ways: (1) a significance test for differences among three types of methods of goal achievement for each of the seven goals; (2) a significance test for differences among the three program types for each of the seven goals; and (3) a significance test for interaction which would indicate whether the relationship between success in goal achievement and type of method used to achieve the desired goal differed over program types. The data were converted to percentages to control for the slight though insignificant tendencies for some types of programs to present a larger absolute number of goals. Table 5 shows the average percentage representations of each of the combinations of goals and types of methods in each of the three kinds of programs.

The final three columns of Table 5 indicate the F ratios calculated for each of the seven goal categories. The F ratios were above the .10 level of significance in eight cases. The following point stands out: with a single exception, regardless of the goal, the method which seems to have the greatest likelihood of achieving the goal is in the *disapproved* or in the *either* category. The exception lies in the *Power and Prestige* goal category for Kidult programs where the *approved* methods seem to have the greatest likelihood of success. For the most part, this general relationship appears to hold for each program type. When interaction is found to be significant it appears to arise from cells in the *disapproved* or *either* category rather than from the *approved* methods of goal achievement.

The data in Table 5 also suggest some interesting points concerning the probability of the successful achievement of various goals. When *property goals* are portrayed on children's programs, they have a relatively high chance of being achieved. In adult programs, *self-preservation, affection,* and *psychological* goals have a high degree of achievement. The probability of success in goal achievement seems to be related to the relative frequency of goal appearance (Table 2), but it appears to be even more strongly related to the type of program on which it appears (compare Tables 1 and 5). Thus a *property goal* appearing on a children's program is more likely to be achieved than when the same class of goal is portrayed on either of the two other program types,

TABLE 5. *Percentage of Successful Goal Achievement by Program Type and by Approved or Disapproved Methods*

GOAL-METHOD	PROGRAM TYPE			F RATIOS		
	Adult	Kidult	Chil-dren	Pro-gram type	Method	interaction
Property						
approved	0.0	31.7	16.7	3.53[b]	2.68[a]	2.48[a]
either	20.8	5.5	72.8			
disapproved	30.5	70.3	49.8			
Self-Preservation						
approved	33.3	0.0	0.0	2.70[a]	1.90	.87
either	44.5	29.5	27.7			
disapproved	40.8	16.7	55.5			
Affection						
approved	50.0	16.7	16.7	1.33	2.85[a]	1.66
either	43.5	58.3	47.5			
disapproved	94.3	16.7	33.3			
Sentiments						
approved	33.3	33.3	33.3	.86	.39	1.35
either	66.7	72.1	16.7			
disapproved	38.3	17.8	47.0			
Power and Prestige						
approved	0.0	33.3	0.0	1.10	2.05	2.51
either	16.7	16.7	50.0			
disapproved	16.7	0.0	50.0			
Psychological						
approved	0.0	0.0	0.0	4.74[b]	5.51[b]	2.56[a]
either	41.8	50.0	0.0			
disapproved	66.7	16.7	0.0			
Other						
approved	0.0	0.0	0.0	.50	.50	1.25
either	0.0	16.7	0.0			
disapproved	16.7	0.0	0.0			

[a] $F_{.10}$ at 2 and 45 degrees of freedom (or 4 and 45 for interaction term) = 2.44 (or 2.09 for interaction term).
[b] $F_{.05}$ at 2 and 45 degrees of freedom = 3.21.
NOTE: in some cases (where interaction was not significant) the interaction sum of squares was thrown into the total sum of squares in these cases $F_{.10}$ = 2.42 at 2 and 49 degrees of freedom.

particularly if the method of achievement is not of the approved variety.

The major finding here lies in the suggestion that methods that are *not* socially approved seem to be portrayed in television content as having a better chance of achieving the desired goal than those methods which are socially approved. This finding appears to be quite general and for the most part unrelated to either the particular goal which is sought or the type of program on which it is portrayed.

CONCLUSION

In studying seven goals and eight methods and their fifty-six combinations as portrayed in television programming, only five significant differences were found in their relative frequency of presentation over the three program types. There seems to be a real, though weak, relationship between desired goals and the methods of goal achievement used. Thus it would appear that, if one is willing to disregard conditions of context or surroundings, i.e., animated cartoon presentation, age and occupation of characters, etc., all types of programs present similar models of behavior. Whether one is a member of an audience containing a relatively high proportion of children and teenagers or whether one is a member of an audience containing mostly adults makes little difference in terms of the models of goals-methods behavior available for viewing.

These findings tend to question the assertions of many critics of television content, who have frequently stated that certain types of programs may have more undesirable effects on children's behavior than other types of programs. Our data suggest that children would be exposed to essentially similar material regardless of which type of program they watched most frequently.

Some researchers have asserted that there is a strong tendency for the mass media to support the common values or to reassert the existing mores of the culture in which they operate. The present data suggest a definite tendency for television programs to project content in which socially approved goals are most frequently achieved by methods that are not socially approved. This finding appears either to cast some doubt upon current assessments of the state of societal

values, or television's interpretation of them, or upon the findings of earlier research. That is, it would appear that a state
of anomie is consistently being portrayed on television dramatic programming. Whether or not the television audience
perceives it in this form or is influenced by this pattern is a
matter for further study. Such studies might be carried out
with school populations where length of exposure to television might be more subject to measurement and control than
with other populations. If, in such studies, belief in the necessity for using socially disapproved methods of goal achievement proves to vary directly with the length of exposure
time to television then this would have obvious implications
as to the effects of this medium.

PART IV

Effects of Mass Media Violence: Empirical Studies

But simply agreeing that violence is bad resolves nothing.
                                    BRUNO BETTELHEIM

TWO FACTS are now before us: (1) Mass media content is heavily saturated with violence, and (2) more and more people are spending more and more time in exposure to such content.

Isn't it reasonable, then, to assume that some kinds of effects must follow from these facts? Many observers believe it is. Furthermore, it is difficult for them to imagine that these effects could be anything but harmful either for the person or for the society.

However, it is one thing to make this judgment and quite another to demonstrate by objective procedures the actuality of such effects. The latter involves the kind of demanding labors illustrated by the selections presented below. These readings show various ways in which researchers make observations to ascertain an order of occurrence between exposure to media violence and specified effects. They also indicate that research is a continuing, cumulative, and highly self-critical enterprise. Otherwise stated, a scientist must ask, "How do you know, and how can I come to know this too?" Thus research on the effects of media violence involves not only the conduct of particular studies, but a continuing dialogue between researchers on the shortcomings of studies, the feasibility of alternative strategies, and the necessity for the fresh pursuit of new leads.

What kinds of effects could media violence have? Most public concern with this question is directed toward the potential that the media have for directly inducing aggressive, deviant behavior in individuals through the repeated portrayal of violence. But there is a wider range of possibilities. Effects may be direct or indirect, and immediate or long range. It is also conceivable that exposure to media violence could reduce aggressive action tendencies rather than create or reinforce them.

A distinction can also be made between effects for individuals and effects on the social level, although the social effects of media violence have largely been ignored in the literature thus far. Even if empirical studies demonstrate that media violence induces aggression in individuals, and allowing that this is evaluated as a negative or undesirable effect, what may be negatively evaluated for individuals, could, under some circumstances, be positively valued in a collective form. For example, violence can serve as a catalyst for social change as when alienated sectors of the population take recourse to violence and aggression to overcome blocks to social-economic achievement. An important and largely unexplored question here is the role of the media in stimulating or schooling persons for such action either through the portrayal of fantasy violence or through the reports of actual collective violence.

The first selection, by Eleanor E. Maccoby, provides an instructive general guideline for considering the rang of possible effects: "When we ask about the effects of the mass media, we must not phrase the question in terms of *whether* the media have an effect, but rather *how much* effect on *what kind* of [people], and under *what circumstances* will the effects be exhibited." Under any circumstance, it is extremely difficult to sort out the impact of the media from other variables operating in the social and psychological setting of audience experiences. One approach to this problem is emphasized in the article by Bandura which reports findings of studies based on controlled laboratory experiments. The controlled experiment is generally acknowledged as a sophisticated research design because it goes beyond descriptions of association to sequences of causation. However, the controls imposed in the laboratory leave serious problems associated with understanding the perception of media violence in a natural setting. Criticisms of laboratory studies are brought to light in Klapper's summary of Ruth Hartley's critique of laboratory research.

A number of the investigators cited in the articles below are engaged in continuing programs of basic research on the impact of violence—works reported in many professional journals and books. Their work is also reported in nontechnical sources (e.g., Bandura's report in *Look*), which facilitates comprehension and relates to the general interests of this book in another way. Mass communicators, critics, government officials, and other laymen interested in the effects of media violence are most apt to learn about scientific studies from popular sources. Accordingly, such accounts, usually stripped of technical details, are often cited when "decision-makers" want to report scientific findings relevant to their views. It is perhaps not too cynical to suggest that the use of such materials stimulates controversy as much as it clarifies issues.

As the reader will observe, controlled experiments lend considerable support to the contention that mass media violence has both direct and indirect effects on individuals which pose problems of short- and long-range consequences for us all. Thus laboratory studies clearly suggest that the portrayal of violence can, under specified conditions, reduce inhibitions against violent behavior, teach forms of violent expression, and provide cues that aggression is socially acceptable.

These studies also explore basic issues implied in such longstanding formulations as the frustration-aggression hypothesis and the catharsis principle. The laboratory evidence on the latter formulation, supported by data from the field and clinic, tends largely to suggest that exposure to media violence does *not* drain off aggressive tendencies.

But the pursuit of evidence goes beyond psychological issues and proceeds in places beyond the laboratory. The need for a broad-based attack on the impact of violence is emphasized in the last two articles of this section.

James Halloran, an English sociologist, includes in his extensive review of research an acknowledgment of Wertham's influence as a critic of media violence, but goes on to challenge the "highly subjective and selective framework" from which Wertham proceeds. Halloran's article also provides a general assessment of research on the effects of television violence—the medium currently at the center of the controversy. He concludes with this penetrating challenge: "No state of mind, no perceptual patterns, no needs, no reactions, no effects, no criticisms and no condemnations can be fully understood unless these factors are related to those forces in society which both produce and require the violence." Halloran adds, "In a manner of speaking, society gets the violence it deserves or, perhaps more accurately, it produces the violence it needs." In the final article of this section, an American sociologist, Walter Gerson, explores some ways to pursue an inquiry into such basic societal "needs."

EFFECTS OF THE MASS MEDIA

Eleanor E. Maccoby

• • •

THE NATURE OF POSSIBLE EFFECTS

THERE are several ways in which exposure to the mass media could influence children. The first is indirect. The media can exert an influence by taking children away from other activities. If the other activities would be harmful to the child (including, for example, activities of a delinquent gang), then the effect of the media would be wholesome. If, however, extensive TV-watching or comic book reading were taking the child away from needed physical exercise, or from cultural activities such as practicing on a musical instrument, then we would be more likely to judge the effects to be harmful. In any case, if we wish to appraise the effects of the media, it is clear that we must be concerned with the child's total pattern of activity, so as to discover if possible what is being given up in favor of the hours spent with the media.

The more direct effects of repeated exposures to the media may be either immediate or long range. Under immediate effects we would include the emotional reactions of the child while he is viewing, listening, or reading, and the immediately ensuing repercussions of these in defensive reactions, fatigue, excitement, dreams, and so on. The long-range effects concern the *learning* that is produced: both the learning of content (vocabulary, items of information, beliefs) and the strengthening or weakening of certain personality traits of the child, such as aggressiveness, passivity, and the like.

The connotation of the word *learn* is such as to make one think of the classroom, or at least of the documentary film, whose intent is to impart information . . . by far the largest portion of children's exposure to the mass media is not of

Excerpts reprinted with the permission of the author and the publisher from Eleanor E. Maccoby, "Effects of the Mass Media," in Martin L. Hoffman and Lois Wladis Hoffman, eds., *Review of Child Development Research*, Russell Sage Foundation, 1964, pp. 325–329.

this instructional sort, yet it is clear that he learns from the mass media nonetheless. The child's interest lies primarily in being entertained, and he achieves entertainment primarily, we believe, through putting himself in the place of one or more of the characters depicted in the film or book and experiencing vicariously the events that involve this character. Although the viewer may be sitting quite still while the hero shoots it out with the villain, the fact that he is sharing the hero's experiences to some extent is suggested by the nature of his emotional reactions while viewing. Many years ago, Dysinger and Ruckmik (1933) took physiological measures of children's emotional responses (galvanic skin response, breathing, heart rate) and noted that the viewers showed changes in emotion that reflected the action on the screen. Furthermore, which screen characters and which action most fully engaged the viewer were found to be a function of certain characteristics of the viewer. For example, boys became most aroused during fight scenes and other adventurous episodes; girls were most emotionally responsive during romantic scenes.

We must assume from this that the kind and degree of vicarious experiencing depends upon the individual viewer's preexisting interests and motives to some degree, and upon the match between these characteristics of the viewer and the events on the screen. It is possible, by watching the eyes of movie viewers as they watch a movie, to determine which screen character they are looking at most of the time. In one study (Maccoby, Wilson, and Burton, 1958) it was found that male viewers spent more time watching the hero, and female viewers more time watching the heroine, during romantic scenes involving just the male and female leading characters. We assume that in stories which present more than one leading character, a viewer makes a choice of a character who will be his primary "identificand," and experiences the actions vicariously through this character. It follows that he learns more about this character's actions (and those elements of the stimulus situation that are most relevant for triggering this character's actions) than about other elements in a story. We also assume that the depth of the viewer's involvement with the character will vary, depending on the nature of the action and the extent to which the action meshes with the viewer's own motivational system. A demonstration of these phenomena may be found in a study of seventh-graders and their learning (memory) of the content of a class-B entertainment movie (Maccoby and Wilson, 1957). Boys remembered aggressive content better, girls remembered romantic content; *but* this preferential memory was found only for the aggressive or romantic content for which the same-sexed leading character was the actor. Thus boys remembered best the aggressive actions performed by the boy hero, but were not especially good at recalling aggressive actions of the heroine. We see then that similarity between the viewer and the actor, both in role (for example, sex) and in preferred action systems, influences which elements of movie content will be absorbed.

It should be noted here that the differences among viewers in what is seen and remembered from films is small, though reliable. Many films offer little choice of an identificand, having essentially a single hero, and the efforts of the writer and the director are to draw the viewer into empathic engagement with that character. The question of just what characteristics of a screen character will produce fullest identification among viewers is a fascinating and still largely unexplored issue. The ability to lead viewers into identification with the characters is a major part of the screen writer's skill, and so far belongs more to the sphere of art than science. We merely wish to indicate here that we believe that the nature and degree of this identification is important in determining what the viewer will take away from the viewing experience.

For this and other reasons, then, it would be a mistake to assume that the impact of the mass media would be constant, or even similar, from one child to the next. The child is not a passive entity, simply absorbing like a sponge whatever is offered to him. He is an active selector of what mass media materials he will expose himself to in the first place; and even during exposure, as noted above, he deploys attention selectively, and what he remembers varies accordingly. Furthermore, what a child does take in has a different effect, depending on his preexisting level of information, the nature of his needs, and the quality of his adjustment to his life situation. So when we ask about the effects of the mass media, we must not phrase the question in terms of *whether* the media have an effect, but rather *how much* effect on

what kind of children, and under *what circumstances* will
the effects be exhibited. The mass media may teach children
skills they will never perform (for example, how to take the
oath as President of the United States), or attitudes that will
never be elicited (for example, toward men from Mars). So
the effects depend in some degree on the probability that
situations relevant for the application of the content acquired from the mass media will occur in the real life of
the child.

METHODS OF STUDYING MASS MEDIA EFFECTS

. . . If present-day children are different in some ways from
the children of previous generations, it is tempting to attribute the changes to television and the other mass media.
But it is obvious that modern children are growing up in
surroundings which differ in many ways from earlier patterns of life. In recent years, society has been recovering
from the effects of a major war and living in the shadow of
another one; population has grown rapidly, with crowding
of houses and schools, and population has shifted from rural
to urban to suburban areas, with accompanying changes in
the demands that are placed upon children; more mothers
are working; and income and living standards have been
rapidly rising. To sort out the effects of the mass media in
the complex of changes that are occasioned by all these
other shifts in our pattern of life is difficult indeed.

The advent of television has created a few "experiments
of nature"—situations in which certain areas share in most
of the social changes of modern times but for some reason
are late in acquiring television. Such areas may be contrasted
with other similar areas which do have television, and the
characteristics of children in these pairs of areas may be
compared. There are certain risks in these comparisons. For
example, if a particular town is late in getting television, the
reason is likely to be that it is geographically isolated to
some degree, and the residents may be exposed to fewer cultural influences of many sorts in addition to being unexposed
to television. Still the findings of several such studies have
proved instructive.

Another related technique for studying the effects of television has been to contrast the behavior and attitudes of

children who live in homes with television with those of children whose homes are without television. Here the problem is that in most American communities the saturation of television sets is extremely high, with more than 90 per cent of all homes having a set. In such a situation, the homes which do not have TV are an unusual population in many respects. The group without TV includes intellectuals who believe that the quality of programs offered is too poor to justify their buying a television set, and it also includes a small group of very poor or very disorganized families who cannot obtain credit for the purchase of a set. Obviously, children growing up in these homes are subject to many other special influences from their environment—they are likely to be different from the children in the TV-owning households in many ways other than those produced by the influence of television. Valid comparisons between set-owners and nonowners may be made only during the early days of the introduction of TV into a community, when it is possible to find groups of owners and nonowners who are reasonably well matched with respect to characteristics other than set ownership; and even here, as will be noted later, it is necessary to be cautious about inferring effects of television. For when one compares a family who bought televesion as soon as it was introduced with another family having the same income, same number of children, same age parents who did not buy it, the two families must have different philosophies concerning the allocation of their economic resources —differences which undoubtedly have implications for the values taught to children.

Perhaps the most powerful technique for the study of the effects of television has been the before-after study. In a few notable instances, it has been possible to study a community *in advance* of the introduction of television, and then to restudy the same population (including the same children) after television has been established and individuals have had a year or two of exposure to it. The most notable example of a study of this kind is the one made by Himmelweit, Oppenheim, and Vince (1958) in Great Britain. A later, highly valuable before-after study, patterned upon the British one, was made by Furu (1962) in Japan. . . .

Even with a carefully executed before-after study, however, there are limitations in how much can be learned with this method. Our knowledge of the effects of exposure to the mass media has been much advanced through the use of smaller experimental studies in which one group of children are shown a movie, comic book, or television program, and another prematched group are *not* exposed to this material. The two groups of children can then be tested to see whether there are any differences in beliefs or behavior that might be related to the content of the material. Experimental procedures of this sort cannot tell us much concerning the long-term, cumulative effects of continued exposure to the media. But they can serve to pinpoint specific effects of individual exposures with a high degree of precision. And they can provide better tests of theoretical issues concerning effects, since they permit control of irrelevant variables to a degree not possible in studies which are conducted in preexisting natural settings. . . .

WHAT TV VIOLENCE CAN DO TO YOUR CHILD

Albert Bandura

IF PARENTS could buy packaged psychological influences to administer in regular doses to their children, I doubt that many would deliberately select Western gunslingers, hopped-up psychopaths, deranged sadists, slapstick buffoons and the like, unless they entertained rather peculiar ambitions for their growing offspring. Yet such examples of behavior are delivered in quantity, with no direct charge, to millions of households daily. Harried parents can easily turn off demanding children by turning on a television set; as a result, today's youth is being raised on a heavy dosage of televised aggression and violence.

Reprinted with the permission of the publisher from *Look*, October 22, 1963, pp. 46–52. Copyright © 1963 by Cowles Communications, Inc.

Testimony in recent U. S. Senate hearings revealed that the amount of violence in television programs has increased substantially over the years. One network executive claimed that this rise in violent action-adventure programs reflects nothing more than technological advances in photography; new films and camera techniques, he said, make it possible to catch action that previously went unrecorded. Other investigators, however, charged that some television shows deliberately used brutality to attract and hold a larger audience.

What happens to a child who watches aggressive personalities on television slug, stomp, shoot and stab one another? Spokesmen for the broadcasting industry generally claim that television has no demonstrable ill effect on viewers. Many mental-health workers and a large segment of the general public assume that exposure to violence can be cathartic —i.e., as children identify with the aggressor, their pent-up hostile feelings are drained away—and that television thus serves as a harmless cultural pacifier. A minority considers television a demonic influence that must be stamped out completly.

Several widely circulated survey studies contend that televised violence has neither harmful nor beneficial effects, except perhaps on highly insecure and emotionally disturbed children. It is surprising how this view has won uncritical acceptance, particularly because it is based on little more than findings from public-opinion polls and survey questionnaires that seldom, if ever, directly examine the *children's* attitudes and social behavior.

If you wished to assess the full effect of a particular medicine on children's physical health, you would hardly do it by soliciting opinions from parents, teachers and self-defined "experts."

Precise information can come only through carefully controlled laboratory tests in which the children themselves participate. For this reason, we recently conducted a series of experiments at the Stanford psychological laboratories to provide some real basis for evaluating the impact of televised aggression on preschool children.

We designed a series of experiments to test the extent to which children will copy aggressive patterns of behavior, when these patterns are shown by adult models in three different situations: in real life, on film and as cartoon characters on film.

The first group observed real-life adults. An experimenter brought the children, one by one, into a test room. In one corner, the child found a set of play materials; in another corner, he saw an adult sitting quietly with a set of tinker toys, a large, inflated plastic Bobo doll and a mallet. Soon after the child started to play with his toys, the adult model began attacking the Bobo doll in ways that children rarely would. For example, the adult sat on the doll and punched it repeatedly in the nose, pummeled its head with the mallet, tossed it up in the air aggressively and kicked it around the room while saying things like "Sock him in the nose!" "Hit him down!" "Throw him in the air!" "Kick him!"

The second group of children saw a movie of the adult model beating up the Bobo doll. The third group watched a movie—projected through a television console—in which the adult attacking the doll was costumed as a cartoon cat. Children in the fourth group did not see any aggressive models; they served as a control group. This gave us a basis of standard behavior to compare with the actions of the groups who were exposed to the aggressive models.

At the end of 10 minutes, the experimenter took each child to an observation room, where we recorded his behavior. For reasons that I will explain later, we mildly annoyed each child before he came in.

The observation room contained a variety of toys. Some could obviously be used to express aggression, while others served more peaceful purposes. The "aggressive" toys included a mallet, dart guns and the three-foot Bobo doll. The "nonaggressive" toys included a tea set, crayons and coloring paper, dolls, cars and trucks and plastic farm animals. Each child spent 20 minutes in the room, and his behavior was rated by psychologists observing through a one-way mirror.

The results leave little doubt that exposure to violence heightens aggressive tendencies in children. Those who had seen the adult model attacking the Bobo doll showed approximately twice as much aggressiveness in the observation room as did those in the control group.

We reached two important conclusions about the effect of aggressive models on a child.

1. The experience tends to reduce the child's inhibitions against acting in a violent, aggressive manner.

2. The experience helps to shape the *form* of the child's aggressive behavior. Most of the children from the first three groups sat on the Bobo doll and punched its nose, beat it on the head with a mallet, tossed it into the air and kicked it around the room. And they used the familiar hostile remarks, "Hit him down!" "Kick him!" and so forth. This kind of conduct was rare among the children in the control group.

Our observations led us to a third, and highly significant, conclusion. We noticed that a person displaying violence on film is as influential as one displaying it in real life. The children were not too inclined to give precise imitations of the cartoon character, but many of them behaved like carbon copies of both real-life *and* film models. From these findings, we must conclude that televised models are important sources of social behavior and can no longer be ignored as influences on personality development. As audio-visual technology develops, television will become even more influential.

I would like to make one point clear: A child who watches violence on a screen is not necessarily going to attack the first person he sees. But if he is provoked enough on some future occasion, he may very well copy aggressive patterns of behavior that he has learned from a pictorial medium like television. This is clearly illustrated by an episode in which a boy was seriously wounded during the reenactment, with a friend, of a switchblade knife fight seen in a television rerun of the movie *Rebel Without a Cause*. The impact of the scene upon the boys did not become apparent until the day after the program, when one of them adopted the James Dean role and challenged his friend to a fight. Only after the fight had begun did the *Rebel*-style knife play emerge.

That is why we deliberately irritated each child in our experiment before he entered the observation room. We wanted to see if the children who had viewed aggressive models would display more aggression than those in the control group after all were exposed to the same degree of annoyance. They did.

In assessing the influence of televised violence on viewers' behavior, however, we must distinguish between *learning* and *doing*. Though children readily learn patterns of social behavior from television programs, they do not copy indiscriminately the behavior of television characters, even those they like best. There are at least two reasons for this:

1. Children rarely have access to the weapons necessary for showing off what they have learned. If they had switchblades, blackjacks and six-shooters, it is safe to predict that the incidence of tragic imitative aggression connected with television viewing would rise sharply.

2. Most parents quickly suppress any learning that conflicts with what they consider desirable conduct. This is particularly true of verbal affectations that arise frequently, are irritating to parents and can be readily identified as television-produced.

Therefore, the impact of television can be isolated and measured precisely only when partental influences are removed and the children are given the instruments they need to reproduce behavior they see on television. These are the conditions we achieved in the laboratory. No one should forget, however, that television is but one of several important influences on children's attitudes and social behavior, and other factors undoubtedly heighten or suppress its effects.

PUNISHING THE BAD GUY

Most people believe an ethical ending to a program, in which the bad guy is punished, will erase or counteract what a child learns from exposure to aggressively antisocial models. To test this assumption, I conducted another experiment.

One group of nursery-school children watched a movie, again projected through a television console, in which Rocky, the villain, seizes all of Johnny's favorite toys. He kicks him and hits him with a baton and finally takes the toys in a big sack. In this version, aggression pays off handsomely.

A second group of children saw the same program with a punishment ending added to show that aggression does not pay. As Rocky tries to seize the toys, Johnny overpowers him and thoroughly thrashes him.

We tested the two groups of children to see how much they behaved like Rocky. Children in the first group—who saw Rocky's aggressive behavior rewarded—readily imitated his physical violence and his hostile remarks. Children in the other group—who saw him punished by Johnny—showed very little imitative aggression. We then asked each child to evaluate the behavior of Rocky and Johnny, and to decide which of the two characters he would prefer to copy. The replies were both interesting and surprising.

As might be expected, children who had seen Rocky punished for his aggressive behavior rejected his as a person to emulate. Also, as expected, most of those who had seen Rocky's aggression pay off said they would copy him.

What did surprise us, however, was the discovery that all the children were highly critical of the way in which he behaved ("Rocky is harsh," "Mean," "He whack people"). Their comments indicate that they imitated Rocky, not because his aggression was intrinsically desirable, but because it paid off ("Rocky beat Johnny and chase him and get all the good toys." "He was a good fighter. He got all the good toys"). One little girl provided a striking example of how a child will adopt objectionable patterns of conduct if they prove successful. She denounced Rocky for the way in which he grabbed Johnny's toys. Nevertheless, at the end of the experimental test session—during which she exhibited much of Rocky's aggressive behavior—she turned to the experimenter and asked, "Do you have a sack here?"

This experiment involved only a single episode of aggression that was rewarded or punished. In most television shows, the bad guy typically wins power over important resources and amasses considerable material rewards through a whole *series* of aggressive exploits. For example, he may gain control over grazing land, water supplies, gold mines, steers, nightclubs, blondes, the constabulary and perhaps the whole town. Generally, he is not punished until just before the last commercial—and punished only once—whereas he has probably succeeded several times during the program. Such punishment of the villain at the end may have only a weak inhibitory effect on the child viewer. In the learning process, immediate rewards have much more influence on a child than delayed punishment.

Although seeing the televised villain punished may discourage children from copying his antisocial behavior immediately, it does not erase from their minds the methods of aggression that they have learned.

In a related experiment, three seperate groups of children

observed a model's aggression rewarded, punished or left without consequences. When tested, children who saw the model punished displayed less imitative aggression than the other two groups. Then we offered all the children attractive rewards if they would reproduce the model's behavior. The introduction of rewards completely wiped out the differences between the three groups of children. They *all* reproduced with considerable accuracy the model's physical and verbal aggression.

From these findings, we can conclude that if children see the bad guy punished, they are not likely to imitate his behavior spontaneously. But they do acquire—and retain—concrete information about *how* to behave aggressively, and punishment of the bad guy does not make them forget what they have learned. They may put his knowledge into practice on future occasions, if they are given enough provocation, access to the necessary weapons and the prospect of sufficiently attractive rewards.

EFFECTS ON ADULTS

Are the effects of televised violence revealed in these experiments confined to children? The answer is no, according to a recent study by Dr. Richard H. Walters at the University of Toronto. Grown-ups can be just as deeply influenced by exposure to aggression.

Dr. Walters asked a group of adult males and adolescent boys to help in a study of the effects of punishment on learning. The participants could give an electric shock to a "learner" every time he made a mistake on a test. They could vary the length and intensity of the shock. Before the test began, each sampled a few shocks to become familiar with the different pain levels.

The learner then proceeded to make intentional mistakes, and Dr. Walters measured the length and strength of the shocks he duly got. (Unknown to the participants, the electrodes were disconnected, and the learner felt no pain.)

In the second step of the study, half the participants watched the switchblade scene from *Rebel Without a Cause,* while the other half saw a short film about picture making. Then they all repeated the shock-administration test.

Those who had seen the picture-making film administered

relatively weak shocks. But the *Rebel* group gave longer, more powerful shocks. Indeed, if the electrodes had been connected, they would have caused considerable pain. Moreover, this group showed a pronounced increase in aggressiveness and hostility on an objective personality test.

All the laboratory studies that I have reported deal with the immediate impact of a single exposure to aggression on the viewer's attitudes and conduct. While the questions about immediate effects have been clarified to some extent, we need much more research on the cumulative impact of television, and the way in which the medium combines with other beneficial or adverse influences in the shaping of people's thoughts and acts.

But what about those immediate effects? We now see clearly that violence on a television or movie screen affects viewers by:

1. Reducing their inhibitions against violent, aggressive behavior.

2. Teaching them *forms* of aggression—that is, giving them information about how to attack someone else when the occasion arises.

And, third, let us keep in mind that the ethical ending, in which the villian is punished, may keep viewers from reproducing villainy right away, but does not make them forget how to do it. The ethical ending is just a suppressor of violence; it does not erase.

Since the amount of time that children are exposed to television makes it one of the most important influences in their lives, these laboratory findings do not present a pretty picture—unless our society is interested in increasing the aggressive tendencies of a growing generation.

THE IMPACT OF VIEWING "AGGRESSION": STUDIES AND PROBLEMS OF EXTRAPOLATION

(Summary of a Paper by Dr. Ruth E. Hartley)

Joseph T. Klapper

INTRODUCTION

A NUMBER of studies conducted in the last several years have dealt with the effect of depictions of "aggression" on the subsequent behavior of viewers, in particular child viewers. Though many of these were laboratory studies, a number of their authors have asserted that the findings indicated what results could be expected from the viewing of such material in real life situations. The statements of these researchers differ markedly from the findings and statements of other equally qualified researchers. The social importance of the entire topic accordingly demands an objective evaluation of the studies in question.

In reference to any study, such an evaluation should involve two steps: (1) evaluation of the study itself, i.e., assessment of the validity of its methodology and its findings, and (2) evaluation of the validity of "extrapolation" or "generalization" of the findings to real life situations—i.e., assessment of the validity of statements or beliefs regarding the degree to which the findings of the laboratory study are indicative of what does or would occur in real life as a result of real life viewing situations.

Office of Social Research, Columbia Broadcasting System, Inc., June 24, 1964. Copyright 1964 by Joseph T. Klapper. In a foreword to this summary, Klapper writes: "Dr. Hartley's paper is a professional discussion of a series of technical studies. Specialized language is often employed and the paper cannot be put into ordinary everyday language without omitting many important technical points. It is possible, however, to produce a summary, confessedly superficial, indicating the scope and some of the major points of Dr. Hartley's paper. This document is in fact such a summary. It has been cleared by Dr. Hartley as a fair and just statement of her views, insofar as these are reflected in this necessarily superficial abstract of a long professional work."

For such extrapolation to be valid, certain minimal prerequisites must be met. (1) The group of people studied (the "subjects") must be representative of any larger group to whom the results are extrapolated. (2) The viewing conditions must be reasonably like those which occur in real life. (3) The "stimulus material" (i.e., the films or exhibitions used in the experiment) must be similar to the material viewed in real life on television or the movie screen. (4) The "criterion behavior" measured (i.e., the post-viewing behavior of the subjects and the manner in which it is interpreted) must be similar to the real life behavior whose likelihood of occurrence is being predicted. (5) The social context of the criterion behavior must be similar to the social context of real life, in which the behavior whose likelihood of occurrence is being predicted would occur.

DEFINITION OF AGGRESSION

Authors of scientific works often and quite legitimately redefine a common word, stating the specialized meaning it is to be understood to carry in the work at hand. If such definitions are not presented, considerable misunderstandings may occur. These are the more likely to occur if the word in question is relatively common, and if the scientist, without providing definitions, uses the word to refer to something different from its "consensual" meaning—i.e., unlike the meaning the word ordinarily carries for the general public.

All of the studies here discussed deal with what they call "aggression" (or, in some cases, related words such as "hostility"). The dictionary definition and consensual meaning of "aggression" involves three elements: intent, damage or hurt, and interpersonality—i.e., interpersonal aggression, as commonly understood by persons concerned therewith, involves the intent and attempt to hurt or damage another person. In discussing the studies at hand it will always be necessary to note whether the behavior regarded as "aggression" conforms to this consensual meaning.

Age Range and Procedures

The discussion of studies is arranged in terms of the age groups of the people ("subjects") involved, as follows: (1) children of pre-school age; (2) elementary school children;

(3) young adolescents and adults. As there is only one study in the recent group of experimental studies bearing on elementary school children (in this case six to seven years old), it will be discussed along with those bearing on preschool children. Studies bearing on the two broad age groups should be discussed separately, since "methodology must be adapted to the developmental level of the subjects."

STUDIES INVOLVING YOUNG CHILDREN

The studies involving young children ordinarily use the term "aggression" (or some very similar word) to describe the behavior observed by the children (the "stimulus material") and occurrence of the same or related behavior on the part of the children being observed ("criterion behavior").

In most instances, the studies followed some variation of the following scheme. Some children ("experimental subjects") viewed a film or exhibition of so-called "aggression," while others ("control subjects") did not. The degree of "aggression" evident in limited play behavior of the two groups was thereafter compared. In some instances the comparison bears on behavior before and after viewing the stimulus material.

"Aggressive" stimulus material included exhibitions by live adults and films. Typical content included rough handling of toys, "adults dressed as children . . . hitting each other, cartoon characters in a wrestling match, a cartoon of Woody Woodpecker having an aggressive contretemps with another character, and an animation of a weed choking a flower."

Aspects of criterion behavior which were rated as "aggression" were for the most part restricted to rough handling of toys, the choice of playing with "aggressive" or non-aggressive toys, and verbal "aggression" directed, for the most part, toward toys. Various specific experiments rated as "aggression" hitting a Bobo doll (a two-to-four foot plastic clown with a round bottom, designed to recover position after being hit); playing with a toy in which one toy prize fighter hits another; saying "yes" when asked by an adult whether he (the adult) should "pop" a balloon; and the like. In only *one* experiment were the children provided with an opportunity to exhibit "aggression" toward other children (by attacking them with rubber daggers, hitting them, or the like). In fact, this was the only experiment in which the child was in contact with any other child (or anyone else, except in some cases the adult observer) during the measurement of "criterion behavior" [Siegel, 1956].

Experimental Controls

All experiments must include "controls"—i.e., situations which permit the comparison of the occurrence of criterion behavior on the part of the experimental group with the occurrence of such behavior when there has been no exposure to the stimulus material. Three methods of control are employed in the various studies. To produce valid results, each must be employed in characteristic ways.

1. When experimental and control groups are used, the two groups should be "matched," or large groups should be used in order that differences between them are randomized (i.e., cancelled out by chance individual variations). The studies of young children which employed this type of control used small groups, and in most instances attempts to match the two groups in reference to characteristics which could be crucial to the study results were imperfect or incomplete.

2. When the behavior of the same child before and after exposure to the stimulus material is compared, it is nevertheless necessary to use a control group. Otherwise the experimenter cannot tell whether differences are due to the influence of the stimulus material, or simply the result of being in a similar behavioral situation twice within a brief period of time. Again, group matching is necessary, but was not always achieved in the studies of young children here under review.

3. The behavior of the same child can be observed before and after exposure to various different types of stimulus and/ or neutral material. In such a procedure, it is desirable to have knowledge of the *range* of the pertinent behavior which is normal to each child. Otherwise normal variations may be fallaciously ascribed to the influence of stimulus material.

Individual Studies with Young Children

Studies by Bandura and his colleagues (1961, 1963) are discussed in detail, and certain methodological questions are raised which are insusceptible of brief summary.

Bandura and his colleagues extrapolated their findings to real life situations, ignoring the major ways in which the laboratory experiments differed from real life, as, for example,

—that the "aggression" consisted of hitting, kicking, and otherwise attacking a Bobo doll, which is a toy rather than a person. It is also to be noted that the toy was designed for this purpose, and virtually invites attack.

—that the stimulus material for the experimental group consisted *entirely*, or *very nearly entirely*, of exhibitions of such attack by adults, outside of any context at all, and untempered by exhibitions of other activities, or by the presence of other adults in the exhibition.

—that the early Bandura experiments included no "sanctions," i.e., no adult (or child) at any time during the experiment indicated that the "aggressive" behavior was in any way disapproved or might entail any unpleasant consequences.

—that the children were placed for the criterion behavior period in a physical situation identical in every respect with the situation of the adult in the film.

—that the so-called heightened aggression was observed very soon (a few minutes) after exposure to the stimulus material, and no attempt was made to determine the duration of effect.

—that "play behavior cannot serve as an accurate predictor of non-play behavior" since because of its permissiveness children act in ways in which they would not act in non-play behavior. Bandura himself in fact states that [quoted words are Hartley's] "ratings of 'aggressiveness' made of the subjects in their nursery school groups showed no significant correlation with the criterion behavior shown after viewing the films."

In a later study Bandura introduced "sanctions." Some children saw a film in which an aggressive child was punished for his aggressive acts and some saw a film in which he was rewarded. Compared with the others, the children who saw the aggressive child punished imitated his activities significantly less during the criterion behavior period. They were able, when explicitly asked, to imitate him, which Bandura regards as evidence that they "learned" how to be aggressive. The question arises, however, as to why they should *not* remember something they had recently seen, and on what basis this can be regarded as "learning" how to be aggressive.

Studies by Løvaas (1961) and by Munsen and Rutherford (1961), both cited in support of the hypothesis that depicted "aggression" evokes aggression, are discussed at length. Both the methodology and the validity of extrapolation from the Løvaas study are severely questioned. Munsen and Rutherford themselves denied any basis for extrapolation, stating, "There is no evidence in the data to suggest that in an unselected group of subjects, those who increase in the measure of aggression used here become more hostile toward the other children . . ."

A study by Siegel (1956), mentioned above, in which children were actually given the opportunity to be aggressive toward other children, revealed no significant heightening of such aggression occurring after exposure to stimulus material. A study by Walters, Leat, and Mezei (1963) found, as did Bandura, that children are greatly influenced by the depicted *consequences* of "aggression."

In reference to the various studies of young children, Dr. Hartley concludes that the stimulus material often did not depict "aggression" in the socially accepted sense of the term, and that the criterion behavior involved "aggression" only in the case of Siegel (1956), where the results were negative. She finds no basis for the alarmist statements made by some of the laboratory experimenters.

STUDIES OF YOUNG ADOLESCENTS AND YOUNG ADULTS

A detailed description is provided of a study by Feshbach (1961) which suggested that exposure to fantasy aggression (a film) *reduced* aggression among previously insulted persons. A series of more elaborate studies on the same subject by Berkowitz (1963), which allegedly suggested the opposite, are criticized both in reference to methodology and to statements extrapolating the findings to real life. A somewhat sounder study to the same effect by Walters, Thomas, and Acker (1962) is described, and questions and objections are raised regarding the significance of the reported statistics and, again, extrapolation to real life situations.

A series of studies which do not support the increased-aggression hypothesis are described and discussed. In one such study, Albert (1957) found no increase in aggression resulting from any of three versions of an entire Western film: a version in which the hero won, a version in which the villain won, and a version in which the conflict was not resolved. In another study, Emery (1959), also using a complete film, again found no increase in "hostile aggressiveness," although he did find "a shift in . . . feelings of being threatened by a powerful and hostile environment and a shift in the direction of greater activity in changing the environment and in defending one's situation" [quoted words are Hartley's]. Maccoby and Wilson (1957), using complete motion pictures, found that

. . . subjects identified with the figure most like themselves or like what they aspired to be; that they remembered significantly more of the events and behaviors involving the figure with whom they identified; and that they did *not* remember aggressive material more than nonaggressive material if it did not involve their identification figure. On a reconstruction measure, on which subjects had to indicate what went before and after a cue, aggressive material remembered made up so small a proportion of the responses that it could not be statistically considered in comparisons. [Quoted passage from Hartley.]

It is noted that Bandura's subjects, who remembered but did not spontaneously imitate the actions of a punished aggressive film character, saw no competing material and could exercise no selective memory.

The final described study was pursued by Bailyn (1959), who dealt primarily with comic books, but found that young people who read many comic books also tended to be heavy consumers of movies and television programs. Her elaborate study led her to conclude that persons with certain existing combinations of problems and behavioral difficulties may react to certain media material in undesirable ways, but that only 3 per cent of her subjects fell into the extreme group in this category. Since the susceptible combination of personality and environment included a variety of chronic conditions not dependent on the media, the latter did not seem to be the prime movers.

Dr. Hartley's summary and recommendations follow verbatim.

Summary

It is impossible to predict accurately or even usefully from the results of the laboratory studies reviewed here to everyday viewing situations, partly because individual differences in response to the stimuli used were ignored in the reports. Additionally, the stimuli used were often vastly different from the materials of ordinary exposure in relation to several crucial elements and the behaviors and contexts of behavior used in indices of effect were so contrived as to resemble ordinary life only tenuously. The investigators who have linked the laboratory results with real-life events have done so by the device of using the same generalized label— e.g., "aggression," "violence," "punitiveness"—to bracket quite different behavioral referrents. Thus far, the connection between the kinds of behavior thus bracketed remains theoretical and hypothetical.

Recommendations

The collection of data which could shed light on the effects of viewing specific types of material, under ordinary conditions of living, would have to combine the qualities of Siegel's (1956) excellent study with Bailyn's (1959) awareness of complexity. It would be necessary to conduct separate investigations with subjects of different developmental levels—i.e., preschool, early-middle school ages, preadolescence, early and later adolescence. The stimulus materials used to represent the independent variable should by choice include those actually used in television programs known to be watched by large numbers of children of the developmental levels used as subjects. Post-viewing criterion behavior, used for testing the effect of the stimulus material, should be of two kinds, spontaneous and unprovoked, and provoked, but by the sorts of stimuli that are likely to occur in ordinary living. If aggressive behavior is the focus of interest, its definition should include the elements of intention, damage or hurt, interpersonal contact and feedback from other persons—e.g., the victim, authority figures, onlookers. Numbers of subjects in each experimental sample should be substantial, and samples should be representative of the viewing population in terms of relevant elements, as far as they are known. Levels of pre-exposure behavior in relevant categories should be equalized for experimental and control groups. Results should be examined in terms of proportion and constitution of subjects showing significant effects. Subjects should be re-examined after a substantial interval of time, measured in weeks, not minutes, for the occurrence or re-occurrence of the criterion behavior, preferably outside of the experimental situation. Follow-up records of behavior from persons in a position to observe the subjects closely, in a natural milieu, should be particularly useful in indicating what segment of the subject's total behavioral repertoire has been affected. A comprehensive program of research along the lines outlined here may appear formidable, but it is needed.

TELEVISION AND VIOLENCE

James D. Halloran

IF ONE is to judge from the results of inquiries, the evidence recorded by committees such as the Pilkington, letters to the press, and the formation of "protection" societies and organizations, many people are deeply concerned about what they imagine to be the effects of the mass media in general, and of television in particular. Most of the charges that are made have been heard before in relation to comics, radio and cinema, and usually take the form of unsubstantiated generalizations and condemnations which accuse television of encouraging anti-social attitudes by offering undesirable models for imitation, stimulating aggressive tendencies and in general of being a major contributory factor in the development of delinquent and criminal behavior. Although the debate does not go on at a very high level it would be wrong to dismiss this concern as coming entirely from cranks and over-eager moralizers. Although a recent survey carried out in June 1964 by Research Services Limited on behalf of the Independent Television Authority found little spontaneous criticism about violence in television programmes, in answer to more specific questions 34 per cent of those

Reprinted with the permission of the publisher from *The Twentieth Century*, Winter, 1964–1965, pp. 61–72.

interviewed thought that the statement that there was too much violence on television was "very true" and another 22 per cent thought that it was "partly true."

The Pilkington Committee found that disquiet at the portrayal of violence was expressed on three main grounds: namely, that small children were disturbed and frightened by scenes of violence, that such scenes could lead children to dangerous and even disastrous experiments, and that the showing of violence encouraged anti-social, callous and vicious attitudes and behaviour. Many of those giving evidence to the Committee felt that there was too much violence on television, that constant repetition of violence was bound to be damaging, that violence was unnecessarily emphasized and lingered over and that, quite often, it was used gratuitously—thrown in for kicks—without adding materially to plot or characterization. Moreover, the concern and disquiet are not confined to this country; the Hearings before the United States Senate Sub-Committee to Investigate Juvenile Delinquency, and reports from several European countries, record the same story.

But what does all this amount to? Neither the Pilkington Committee nor the Senate Sub-Committee used any sort of population-sampling techniques and even if they had been more refined in their methods they would still only have provided evidence of what a more representative sample of the population *thought* or *felt* about the effects of violence on television. Obviously, this is not the same thing as the actual, established effects. It should be remembered that even a complete consensus on this or any other problem need not mean that public opinion represents an accurate picture of what really takes place.

We need to ask then, whether or not there is any justification for this disquiet and concern, and for an answer to this question we might look to the experts, to those who have studied the problem within their own particular discipline. But this is where the trouble begins, for the poor layman will quickly find that the experts are not agreed, and that the available evidence, such as it is, points in both directions. As I hope to show later the situation, although confusing, is not quite so hopeless and unhelpful as it might appear to be at first glance. Still, it is not surprising that a bewildered public does not readily turn for help to experts who seem to be providing evidence in partial support of every view, who at times appear to be generating more heat than light in their own incomprehensible disputes, and who certainly do not provide definitive answers to what the public may consider to be urgent social questions.

Who are the experts and what do they have to say? It is not quite accurate to split them into two camps, with the cautious sociologists and social psychologists in one and the rather more critical psychiatrists in the other, for there are important exceptions on both sides. By and large, however, the evidence provided over the years by those in the former group suggests that it is wrong to blame television for outbreaks of violence and the alleged increase in crime and delinquency rates. Generally, social scientists refer to television as a reinforcing agent, rather than as a direct causal or creative factor in the formation of attitudes and behavior patterns. To take this line, however, is not to absolve television producers from their responsibility; for in any society there will be some tendencies which it will not be considered desirable to reinforce. To these social scientists television, like the other media, is seen as working in and through a variety of other social factors, such as relationships and experiences with parents, brothers, sisters, teachers, companions, etc. Consequently, even if a link could be established between certain viewing patterns and some form of "social damage" these social scientists would suggest that the roots of this damage would probably be found in home, school, neighbourhood or other social setting. Only in certain circumstances, as for example when attitudes in a certain area have not been formed or developed, is television seen as being a direct cause of some particular attitude or form of behaviour in that area.

However, not all sociologists would adopt this line. In this country Bryan Wilson, like many non-sociological critics, has suggested that the mass media over-dramatize and pay too much attention to violence, provide those with anti-social tendencies with vivid fantasies, stimulate and satisfy criminal, violent, sensational and salacious appetites, provide technical knowledge and the glamour of publicity, and help to produce an atmosphere of greater tolerance for many forms of deviant behaviour. Supporting evidence is not produced by Wilson and indeed this type of indictment is more characteristic of those psychiatrists, most of them American, who have been so outspoken in their condemnation of the heavy dosage of violence on the American small screen. Again, it can be unfair and misleading to generalize, and by no means all psychiatrists in the United States would wish to associate themselves with the formidable Dr. Fredric Wertham and his supporters in their frequent and vociferous condemnations. Yet, as far as the experts are concerned, the main attack on the television companies for their portrayal of violence has been mounted by the psychiatrists. What is more, it would appear that their attacks have been pressed home with some success, for judging from the preliminary reports received in this country the United States Senate Sub-Committee on Juvenile Delinquency, which received several submissions from Dr. Wertham, has stated that it has found that a relationship has been conclusively established between televised crime and violence on the one hand, and anti-social attitudes and behaviour among juvenile viewers on the other. At first glance (the full report is not available at the time of writing) it would appear that the Committee has been more impressed by the unequivocal evidence of such as Dr. Wertham than by the more cautious statements of the social scientists. Wertham himself has little sympathy with the methods and works of the social scientists and he considers that their "statistical-question-naire-control group method" is quite unsuitable for the intricate problems involved in measuring the effects of violence on young people. In one of his submissions to the Senate Sub-Committee he gives considerable space to a destructive criticism of the work of such well-known authorities as Hilde Himmelweit, Wilbur Schramm and Joseph Klapper. According to Wertham the clinical method is the only one capable of dealing with the effects of mass media in a scientific way. The clinical method includes a study of the whole child, a diagnostic evaluation of his personality and emotional life, his thinking, his background, his real satisfactions and dissatisfactions, the application of psycho-diagnostic tests and—most important—a follow-up of his further development and response to guidance and therapy.

Wertham bases his statements of the effects of television violence on his clinical studies of over 200 unselected cases. He finds that the surfeit of brutality, violence and sadism has made a profound impression on young people who are becoming more and more "teledirected," more hostile, more callous, more insensitive. He claims that inhibitions are lowered, resistances removed and sadism perpetuated or aroused. The media have helped to create and foster the belief that brutality is an expedient regulator in all social relationships, says Wertham, and slowly but surely we are raising a generation of violence worshippers.

As a sociologist I do not feel that Wertham supports his case with valid or objectively measurable evidence. Needless to say, controls are not used and little attempt is made to assess the part played by other social factors. He works within his own highly subjective and selective framework and, to mention but one point, appears to take at face value many statements made by his subjects although it is surely possible that such statements as "I saw it on television" can often be the delinquent's own rationalization of his behaviour. In many ways it is unfortunate that Wertham and others go too far and over-state their position, for a more sober, more objective and better argued case against the excessive use of certain types of violence on the screen is gradually being built up by some of the social scientists whom Wertham apparently despises.

The cathartic or abreaction hypothesis has long been used by authors, producers and critics as a justification for the presentation of violence. It is frequently argued that the viewing of aggressive scenes brings about a reduction in the aggressive drives of the viewer, that children get rid of hostility feelings in an innocuous way by watching violent television programmes, and that such programmes provide a necessary social function by presenting young people with a harmless outlet for latent hostility and by enabling them to relieve their pent-up aggression. Aristotle, and to a lesser degree Freud, are used as authoritative backing for these claims and although it might be mentioned here that this demonstrates a fundamental misunderstanding of both the philosophy of Aristotle and the psychology of Freud this is hardly the point, for in this context a correct understanding of the work of these great men is not so important as the views which the defenders of violence attribute to them. The labels of authority and respectability are given to phoney arguments and help to get these arguments accepted.

I use the word phoney, for gradually it is becoming clear that the bulk of the social scientific evidence available does not lend support to the cathartic argument but indicates that television violence can instigate aggressive behaviour immediately following the viewing experience. Although an early experiment by Seymour Feshbach, an American psychologist, had given some support to the cathartic argument, the results of an experiment carried out in the mid-1950s by Eleanor Maccoby suggested that aggressive content could be learned and levels of aggression influenced by the viewing of violent scenes on television. Eleanor Maccoby questioned the validity of the discharge of aggression theory, as also did Leonard Berkowitz from the University of Wisconsin in his criticism of the interpretation of the results of the Feshbach experiment. In this experiment a group of students, previously angered, were divided into two sections; one section was shown a film of a boxing match and the other a more neutral film. After seeing the films all the students were tested and those who had seen the boxing match showed less hostility than the others. It could be that the anger of these students had been discharged vicariously as Feshbach suggested. But there are other possible explanations, and Berkowitz has suggested that the students could have inhibited their hostile reactions, because as a result of viewing the boxing film they had become uneasy about their own aggressive tendencies and had begun to think that their aggressive behavior might be wrong.

Another experiment demonstrated that young children who had been exposed to a cartoon film with an aggressive theme played more aggressively with their toys than did other children who had seen a less aggressive film. Moreover, these findings on aggressive behavior are not confined to children, for in another experiment some adult males who had seen a film which included a knife-fight displayed more severe punitive attitudes to their colleagues, soon after the viewing, than did some comparable adults who had seen a less violent film.

Within the last few years some most ingenious experiments have been carried out by Berkowitz and his colleagues, and by Albert Bandura and his colleagues at the University of Stanford. Bandura holds that film models are as effective as real life models in transmitting deviant patterns of behavior and that some forms of deviant behavior are "released" by children who have been exposed to film models who have displayed the deviant behaviour freely on the screen. In one experiment he established that children subjected to mild frustration tended to imitate the aggressive behaviour of an adult they had seen on the screen. Of course, most of these experiments are carried out in relatively artificial conditions and in some cases the experiment proves only that the aggressive children learned to take out their aggressions on the same target as used in the experiment. Whether they would generalize this tendency and act aggressively toward other persons or objects in real life would obviously depend on other external social factors which were not controlled in the experiments. Much more research is required before clear-cut general statements can be made, but it should be noted that television does provide a continually available source of experience which children may readily imitate.

Despite the experimental limitations, however, it now seems quite clear that the viewing of filmed and televised violence does not necessarily lead to a discharge of anger or aggression to the extent and degree that many of those on the production side would like us to believe. Fortified by these findings and by the general confirmatory results of his own ingeniously contrived experiments, Leonard Berkowitz argues that there is no such thing as free-floating aggressive energy which can be released by viewing violence or aggression, or, for that matter, by any other activity. A person may derive pleasure or satisfaction from the viewing experience, as he views actors doing things he would like to do but is normally prevented from doing, but this need not be accompanied by a discharge of hostility. The hostility which will still persist to the extent that the frustrations and aggressive habits persist. In fact, even when the angered person carries out an act of overt aggression himself, it seems likely that unless he thinks that he is attacking the known source of the frustration, the hostility will not be reduced. According to this view effective catharsis occurs only when the angered person perceives that the source of his anger or frustration has been attacked and damaged.

But the lessons that can be drawn from these experiments may be taken a little further. Cinema and television productions depicting crime and violence are often defended on the grounds that there is a "good" ending and that it is made perfectly clear that "crime does not pay." In many of these productions justice is not only done, it is seen to be done, and the method invariably used in punishing the evil character, the villain, is to repay violence with violence! This may give the audience a degree of satisfaction, probably because people approve of hurting those who hurt others, but it could also have harmful consequences for, according to Berkowitz, when a villain is defeated aggressively the restraints of audience members may be weakened, a sort of permission or warrant is given, and angered members of the audience, primed for aggressive action, are more likely to attack those whom they perceive as "villains" in their own lives immediately following their viewing experience.

Of course, it must be emphasized that these points stem from laboratory experiments and they are not put forward here in an attempt to establish a general law on the direct causal link between televised violence and crime, and anti-social attitudes and behaviour. Although it will be seen that these give little comfort to those who regard fantasy-aggression as having socially beneficial results, it is still necessary for us to make a distinction between potential or readiness for aggression and actual overt aggressive behaviour in social situations. In real life, as distinct from experimental situations, other factors operate and many of these will serve as constraints. In all probability the aggressive reaction will not be an enduring one and will gradually disappear as the person moves into new situations and has new experiences. Moreover, people react differently to different people. An angered man will strike some people more readily than others and this selection of target is not just a function of size or apprehension about the ability to hit back, for it seems probable that we are more likely to be aggressive toward those whom we can associate either with the source of the provocation of our anger or frustration, with the aggressive film we have just seen or, not surprisingly, towards someone we just dislike.

This draws attention to the significance of the link-up between what people see on the screen and their own real worlds, for in addition to the importance of the association already mentioned it would appear that viewers' emotions

are most affected by what they see on the screen when they
are able to link the filmed events with their own lives and
experiences. Where the programme is associated with the
types of conflicts which a person is experiencing or where
the identification has some connections with his social life,
the person is more likely to carry the stimulation over into
real life with an increase in the amount of directly expressed
aggression.

Again it is necessary to draw attention to the very real
limitations in the research from which these points are
taken. Admittedly, much more research will be required
from psychologists and sociologists before the gap between
the experimental and the real-life situation is adequately
bridged. But these experiments are important starting-points
and maybe in years to come they will be regarded as the
beginning of a vital breakthrough in mass-media research.
We may not feel justified at this stage in accepting the
direct link findings of the Senate Sub-Committee, still less
may we feel able to join with Dr. Wertham and his associates, but I think we may accept with Berkowitz, Bandura
and others that the heavy dosage of violence in the mass
media, although not a major determinant of crime and delinquency, heightens the probabality that someone in the
audience will behave aggressively in a later situation. The
catharsis fallacy is by no means the only one in this field
of discussion. Statements from all sides, from producers,
professional critics and over-enthusiastic moralizers, show
that the whole debate on the effects of filmed and televised
violence is riddled with misconceptions.

Professional critics, whatever their sect, with their pen-
chant for loose, pretentious judgments write of the artistic
handling of violence, the responsible treatment of violence
controlled by first-hand observation, violent incidents made
acceptable by being presented in context, by being deeply
embedded in the master plan, by delicate treatment, by being
digested into the body, and it would appear that in a "really
good work" even gratuitous violence can be explained away
as being in character. These critics may be right, these may
be accurate accounts of their own reactions and of the reactions of the authors and producers. But can we leave it
at that? Are there not numerous implied assumptions about
how other people will react? The whole field of film and

television criticism abounds with élitist evaluations and superimpositions. It is implied that if they (the critics) see it in a certain way then others will also see it in that way; that if the violence is cushioned and made acceptable to them and if this is what the producers intend then it will also be made acceptable to others. That individuals bring different needs and predispositions to the screen and that they perceive content selectively and subjectively is either not appreciated or ignored. One frequently gets the impression that many of the critics work on the assumption that basically we are all the same under the skin, and that we all see the world in the same way.

Producers, too, are not free from these misconceptions. Several studies in the United States have shown that what the producer intends to convey to his audience and what is actually conveyed or perceived can be two very different things. The possibility of the existence of a "hidden message" which obviously relates to perceptions, needs and dispositions of the viewers and may be much more important than the overt message, is often not taken into account. A recent investigation in this country into the response of children to television, conducted pointly by the University of Cambridge and A.B.C. Television, drew further attention to the gap which exists between intention and perception and provided the makers of the programme with "a humiliating, funny, illuminating and humble-making experience."

The world does not appear to children as it does to adults, consequently adults do not see the same thing in a television programme as children do. The adult watching fairy stories will not take the fictional characters seriously, the young child probably will, because he believes he is seeing real people. Children do not respond uniformly, some children may be frightened, others amused and others totally unimpressed by the same stimulus. Moreover, what frightens and disturbs an adult may not produce the same reaction from a child. For example, death on the screen will elicit quite different reactions from the adult and the child and, similarly, aggressive action is likely to evoke different responses.

In general, we would expect response differences between adults and children to be greater and more varied than those between different adults, but the differences between adults are quite marked and can be linked to social, political, re-

ligious, economic and educational factors as well as to general personality. Violence in the content of a Bible story or
even in a Shakespearian play will draw less adverse criticism
than in the content of a western or a detective thriller, yet
the response could be the same. When people complain about
violence on television they rarely illustrate their complaints
with references to news reels, rocket trials, the explosion of
hydrogen bombs, historical documentaries or war films. Yet
it is possible that for some people these may, in the long run,
produce more injurious reactions than Westerns and detective thrillers. Several years ago Professor Grunhut, then
Professor of Criminology at Oxford University, suggested
that we ought not to be surprised if young people solve their
problems in a violent way, for the nation has been solving
its problems in this way for some considerable time. Television reminds us of this problem-solving ability and the
methods employed, quite frequently.

An important point to make here is that the field of research must be widened so that the attitudes, reactions,
needs, states of mind, perceptual patterns can be fully understood in relation to the many sociological factors (family
experiences, education, social-economic position, religious
and political affiliation, social class, etc.) that produce and
require them.

It would be unfortunate if in making these remarks about
different people seeing things in different ways and if in
drawing the attention of readers to the gap that exists between the intention of producers and the perceptions of
viewers I gave the impression that those who make the decisions at various stages and levels in the production process
were irresponsible and cared nothing about the possible injurious effects of their work. Such is not the case. The
B.B.C.'s programme policy governing violence produced in
1960 by the Controller of Television Programmes, Kenneth
Adam, is indicative of the concern and care which is shown
in these quarters, and although the independent companies
were criticized on this score in the Pilkington Report it
would be quite misleading to present the officials and producers of the companies as irresponsible people. In any case
the I.T.A. now promises to play a more active role in this
respect than it has done in the past.

But although concern and responsibility are important

matters, they are not the main issue here. Even when these qualities are not in question, as in the case referred to above, it is still possible that the stereotyped misconceptions and fallacies which I have instanced and which abound in this field will persist and continue to play their part in determining what is presented on the screen, what is repeated, what is banned, what is praised and what is condemned.

Is there too much violence on television? Is it increasing? The U. S. Senate Sub-Committee says "yes" to both these questions as far as the U. S. is concerned. The position in the United States is, of course, quite different from our own and although my own impression is, that in so far as any satisfactory definition of violence can be agreed on, there is far more violence on the American screen than on the British screen, there are many people in this country, as we have seen, who feel that there is too much violence on our television also.

But can these questions really be answered? First of all we have to answer the question, What is violence? and this as I have tried to point out is no easy matter. I am not denying that a common denominator of acceptance could fairly easily be established and used as a basis for decision making, but it must be emphasized that the traditional methods of content analysis are inadequate. The established, conventional procedures are crude and limiting and a much more refined and sophisticated approach to content analysis will be necessary before any real progress is made. Analysis in terms of deaths, blood, weapons, number of incidents, or even in the more sophisticated categories of the professional critics will not do. If we wish to examine the content of television programmes which contain violence and aggression, in an attempt to assess the effects of these programmes, then the most relevant categories of analysis should stem from the perceptions of the viewer. This is not to say that there is no place for the professional, evaluative critics; they have their own disciplines and skills, and bring valuable insight to the problem. But it cannot be stressed too often, that if we wish to ascertain the effect of violence, then it is more important to know how people really react, than to know how a small group of people *think* they will react.

But why all this concern and apparent preoccupation with violence? There are many other aspects of life which do not seem to attract the same attention. Could it be, as Gerson Legman speculated in his book *Love and Death,* that this concern and preoccupation and this "fixation on violence and death in all our mass-produced fantasies is a substitution for a censored sexuality, or is, to a greater degree, intended to siphon off—into avenues of perversion opened up by the censorship of sex—the aggression felt by children and adults against the social and economic structure."

This may or may not be true, but the statement does contain an important pointer and that is, that violence on television cannot be studied in isolation. We need to look at the whole social and economic structure of society and examine the portrayal of violence and the concern and disquiet which this brings about in this wider setting. No state of mind, no perceptual patterns, no needs, no reactions, no effects, no criticisms and no condemnations can be fully understood unless these factors are related to those forces in society which both produce and require the violence. In a manner of speaking, society gets the violence it deserves or, perhaps more accurately, it produces the violence it needs.

VIOLENCE AS AN AMERICAN
VALUE THEME

Walter M. Gerson

THIS ESSAY contends that more studies should treat violence in media content as a dependent variable and emphasize the social and cultural structure of American society as the independent variable. From this perspective, two important foci of empirical analysis would be: (1) the complexity of the value structure of American society, and (2) the reciprocal relationship between the mass media and public opinion.

In the recurrent discussions of mass culture by sociolo-

This article was prepared for this book. The footnotes appear in the Notes and References section at the end of the book.

gists, social commentators, humanists, and other observers of the American scene (e.g., Olson, 1963; Rose, 1962; Gerson, 1965), the "democratization" of culture is a prominent theme. Democratization implies that the masses of people come to control the content of the mass media, and that the media, on the other hand, comes to control the masses. In other words, control of cultural content has been transferred from highbrow cultural elites to the masses and the media.

Wilensky (1964) furnishes some support for this line of reasoning. He documents how cultural uniformity grows in America, even though social differentiation persists. Wilensky points out various forces at work that tend to produce cultural standardization: the mass education system resulting in widespread literacy, high rates of vertical and residential mobility, and the emergence of national markets which make use of nationwide media of mass advertising and entertainment. So, modern society tends toward the widespread sharing of tastes, beliefs, and values which cuts across group lines. If this is the case, it may be hypothesized that the majority of people get whatever content they want in the mass media.

Further, if the rational pursuit of money is a commanding force for the American mass media—and this has been relatively well documented (Wright, 1959)—then supposedly the media institutions give the people what they want, i.e., the present content which is popular with the masses. Again, the emphasis on violence suggests that there is a relatively substantial public demand for violence. At the very minimum, a large minority of American people evidently continue to read or view the violent materials in the media.

A key question is: *Why* is there public demand for violence? To a large extent, the answer to this question lies in the social and cultural structure of American society. I would suggest that violence constitutes a significant and recurring theme in the American value structure. Accordingly, analytical emphasis should be on violence itself and its place in American culture.

DIMENSIONS OF VIOLENCE

Violence has usually been defined in terms of physical force resulting in physical injury. For research purposes, a broader and more comprehensive definition might yield more significant findings. Violence need not be limited solely to physical behavior. Violence can also be conceptualized to include non-physical behavior resulting in social or mental injury, such as damage to one's self-concept or to one's reputation.[1] This is not a new approach; Simmel espoused much the same view when he stated that when a large business forces a small firm out of business it constitutes violence *in principle* just as much as if actual physical force had been used (Small, 1904).

A simple paradigm for research of violent behavior would minimally include two dimensions of violence: the mode of violent behavior and the degree of legitimacy of the behavior.[2] These dimensions can function as guidelines for research.

1. *The mode of violent behavior.* At a minimum, there are three modes of violence: physical violence, manipulation of others (involving material, social, or mental damage), and verbal attack (without threat of physical force). Any given violent act could combine any or all of the three general modes of behavior. But for analytical purposes, each may be considered separately.

(a) Physical violence includes two subtypes: (1) the actual physical behavior itself wherein someone is physically injured by forceful behavior (such as a fist fight, a murder, a war), and (2) the threat of physical violence. Often, the threat of violence precedes the actual behavior, but this is not a necessary order of events. Either form of physical violence can (and often does) occur without the other.

(b) The manipulation of others constitutes violent behavior when there is either the intent or the consequence of economic, social, or mental injury. Much manipulative violence constitutes power struggles among individuals, groups, organizations, states, or nations. Economic and political power struggles are common in the United States; each "side" is constantly attempting to manipulate others to its own advantage and to their disadvantage.

(c) Verbal violence without the threat of physical force may be the most common mode of violent behavior in America today. In fact, this behavior, in varying degrees, may be a common basis for much of the interaction in an other-directed society in which prestige is commonly gained through "one-upmanship," witticisms (often at the expense of others), and "informal" debating ability. (Informal debating frequently involves the violation of another person's social status or self-concept.)[3]

2. *Degree of legitimacy of the behavior.* The degree of legitimacy can be conceptualized as a continuum, ranging from fully legitimate on one pole to completely illegitimate on the other. For analysis, this variable may be dichotomized into two classes: illegitimate violence and legitimate violence.

(a) The average person, when asked about violence, automatically views it as negative behavior. Violence to most people means illegitimate behavior—behavior that is contrary to the mores or against the law, behavior that exceeds the tolerance limits of the society or community. Adolescent gang wars, murder, assault, rape, and childbeating are apt to be mentioned. Illegitimate violence is not limited solely to physical violence. It can occur within each of the above modes of violent behavior. A man who uses his wife as a verbal scapegoat for all of his problems during the day and a grocer's putting his competitor out of business by unlawful manipulation are both using illegitimate violence.

(b) A great deal of violent behavior in America is legitimate, i.e., is postively sanctioned. Many occupations allow for and even require violence in one mode or another—policemen, boxers, wrestlers, bouncers, soldiers, "hucksters," politicians, prison guards, judges, football players, corporation "troubleshooters," elementary school principals, salesmen, etc. Each has the mandate to use violence under certain conditions. War, possibly the most violent activity of all, has been legitimized by all of the social institutions in American society. Parents are expected legitimately to use violence on their children, i.e., spank them or scold them.

The difference between legitimate and illegitimate behavior is frequently a matter of degree. If a father uses too much violence on his child, for example, he becomes a hated childbeater. A further analytical distinction should be made between *offensive* and *defensive* legitimate violence. This distinction, which appears to be especially important in America, is part of the collective definition of the situation.

The dimension of legitimacy-illegitimacy is complicated by

consideration of the question: Legitimate *according to whom?* Legitimate according to the overall societal values? Or, legitimate according to a subgroup within a society? The various subgroups of a social system do not necessarily share the same values. Certain instances of violence are patterned evasions—patterned or institutionalized ways of avoiding the open violation of some abstract or legal norm.

For example, the use of violence by American policemen is both an occupation prerogative and necessity (Westley, 1953). There are various social pressures on policemen to produce rapid results, i.e., produce guilty persons as soon as possible. The situation appears to be one in which the goal—rapid crime-solving and culprit-catching—receives disproportionate emphasis over the legal means for reaching the goal. The public wants results, especially in cases of sensational crimes. It appears that in such cases, the people pay decidedly less attention to the means by which "guilty" persons are treated.[4] In such situations, there are social pressures on policemen to adopt the practices which are most likely to produce results quickly. These practices often involve violence. Policemen easily develop justifications and rationales for the use of violence because society indirectly gives them the mandate to be violent by turning its collective head. In various ways, policemen are led to feel that the end (catching criminals) justifies the means (violence). From their perspective, their use of violence is legitimate.

Theoretically, such behavior is illegitimate, but to a minority, possibly even the majority, of the people, it is legitimate. Probably a substantial amount of violent behavior in America constitutes a subterranean value—it is contrary to some widely accepted value but it still constitutes normative behavior to many people (Matza and Sykes, 1961). How should these behaviors be classified in the theoretical dimension of legitimacy?

VIOLENCE IN AMERICAN LIFE

Violence is not new to human experience in fiction.[5] It was an emphasis in ancient fables, fairy tales, and Shakespearean creations. The present essay is concerned, however, only with violence in America. Considerable evidence could be used to document the contention that violence is part of the American everyday scene. Only a few observations will be presented here.

Americans have developed elaborate and well-organized mechanisms to sustain violence effectively over long periods of time. The far-reaching complex organization of the military branch of the government is an obvious case; the manifest function of the military is to engage in violent behavior on a national or international level. Whether the violence theoretically constitutes "offensive" or "defensive" violence may not be a significant factor in this case, since, as Mills (1958) has pointed out, when militaries become as mammoth and complex as those in the United States and the U.S.S.R., it becomes very difficult, if not meaningless, to categorize their behaviors into the offensive-defensive dichotomy. A peculiar kind of American doublethink emphasizes that the best defensive position is a strong offense—as indicated by U. S. skirmishes in Korea, Vietnam, and the Dominican Republic—and that we must seek peace "offensively."

Witch hunting is an old American custom. The society still contains a large number of fanatics who operate to force the elimination of anything they disapprove. The themes of McCarthyism and the John Birch Society are not unlike those of the Western frontier days when self-appointed judges often took the law into their own hands. The lynching of rustlers by vigilantes and of Negroes by lawless mobs, the unconstitutional Red-chasing practices during the "Red scare" after World War I, the imprisonment of almost 100,000 American citizens of Japanese ancestry in American prison camps ("relocation camps") during World War II— all were defined as the "right" thing to do and all represent violent behavior.

The unlawful use of violence by the dominant group over minority groups has been common in American history. Traditionally, minority groups have not "fought back." However, some significant changes occurring in America today may have the consequence of increasing the frequency of violent aggressive behavior by minority-group persons in attempts to improve their situation. Simpson and Yinger (1965) point out that the traditions of violence in intergroup relations are strongest in the South. The traditions of violence there were nurtured by the slavery and plantation systems, the continuation of a frontier spirit, and the frustrations resulting from the Civil War.

Make-believe weapons for children are common today; these include toy pistols, machine guns, grenades, missiles, bomber planes, and gun-shaped teething rings. Some of the toys are complete with the noises, smoke, and smells that would accompany such weapons. With these, children can play violent games right from the start. Children learn early that it is un-American to be a "chicken." Anti-sissy and anti-pacifist sentiments are quite prevalent in the society. Action is emphasized over non-action. Carry a big stick and speak softly. One should fight for his rights. Possibly, the only kind of intellectual who is widely admired by Americans is the one who *demonstrates* power in a tangible manner.

One indicator of a society's values consists of the heroes in that society, and one common type of American hero is the "winner." In Klapp's (1962) typology of heroes, the winner lives in a world in which life is a battle of dog-eat-dog competition and in which the strong man is king. In America, the winner is viewed as the good guy. (This ideology may be necessary in a highly competitive system for, in order to justify the system, we must feel that the "right guy," the deserving person, wins out in the long run.[6] The ideology may function as a tension-reducing mechanism in that through it, much potential anomie is not realized by the participants of the system.) The deification of the winner as the right guy often means that "anything goes" so long as the right guy does it. The winner thus has the mandate to perform practically any kind of violence since he is the "good guy."[7] As Merton (1957) and others have pointed out, what counts in America is success. The means of winning are much less emphasized. The wide acceptance of the "Westerner" as a folk hero has been analyzed specifically in these terms. The adult Western has been seen as representing a "revolt against rationalism and reason" which permits catharsis for the problems of modern man (Nussbaum, 1960). Any kind of violent means can be used by the Western hero in the never-ending quest for positive goals (Homans, 1961).

Roy Francis (1965) forecasts that the themes of speed, force, and violence appear to be the primary modes of action that will shape the emerging American society. He says,

"Whatever adaptations man makes in the immediate future will be made because of and in terms of violent reaction." He feels that America has cultural commitments to violence. He emphasizes that the themes of force, speed, and violence appear in "virtually every aspect" of American public life. He points out that in fields of activity as diverse as sports and the arts, violence is increasingly the vogue. For example, baseball and golf have both increasingly become primarily "power" (thus, violent) games. In the arts, the artists, such as contemporary musical composers and contemporary painters, are increasingly applying the theme of violence to their works.

RESEARCH SUGGESTIONS

It appears that violence—both illegitimate *and* legitimate —is a relatively widespread phenomenon in America. The question is: *How* widespread? Mere cursory observation of the contemporary American scene is not enough. Systematic empirical research is needed to establish the conditions and boundaries of specific types of violence. From the standpoint of the concept of value, research data on legitimate violence are especially necessary, since values usually refer to the legitimate public life of a society. If legitimate violence is a decidedly frequent and common everyday activity in a society, this is at least an indication that the behavior is attached to *some* kind of value.

The mere frequency of an activity, however, does not necessarily mean that the behavior constitutes highly valued behavior socially. For example, American men tie their shoelaces every single day, year in and year out—a consistent, frequent activity. It does not follow, though, that shoelace-tying is an American value. We can, however, say that the habitual shoe-securing ritual is often an indirect prerequisite to several cultural goals—social mobility, occupational success, marrying the "right" person, being liked by others, etc. —and these goals do represent cultural values. Much violent behavior, then, may not appear to be a value theme, but indirectly it might be part of an overall value complex.

How does a researcher empirically prove that something is a "value" in a given society? In other words, how does one empirically verify the existence of a value? Very little systematic research has been specifically aimed at this methodological question. In fact, recently Blake and Davis (1965) have seriously questioned the worth of value as an analytical concept. They recommend that the concept of norm be emphasized instead of value. Norm can be more easily operationally defined for empirical research. But, since the majority of sociologists emphasize value as a separate concept, it may not be beneficial to drop the concept from consideration at the present time.

Williams' (1961) discussion of values includes some suggestions that could be useful in an empirical attempt to determine whether or not violence is an important American value theme. His criteria for establishing whether something is a dominant value are (1) extensiveness (What proportion of the population and its activities manifest the value?), (2) deviation (Has it been important for a long period of time?), (3) intensity with which the value is sought or maintained, and (4) prestige of the persons, objects or organizations considered to be bearers of the value. In the remainder of this essay, we shall suggest further research questions to supplement Williams' guidelines.

What are the characteristics—social class, race, sex, age —of persons who most frequently participate in *legitimate* forms of violence? Under what social structural conditions? Is legitimate violence a definite part of their everyday lives —a goal to which they aspire in a variety of conditions? Or, do they legitimately use violence primarily as a means to an end? We need to know more about the process of legitimation of violent behavior. *How* is the behavior legitimized? Certain persons appear to have a mandate to perform violently. Possibly, a few key significant others or reference groups are instrumental in legitimizing violent behavior and in giving certain persons the mandate to be violent.

Is legitimate violence usually a two-way process, with people on both sides "giving" *and* "receiving"? Numerous factors would have to be considered, but it is likely that there are some persons who are usually only on one side of the process. The concept of career, widely used in analyses of occupations and social mobility, could be applied to the sociology of violence. A simple typology of violent careers might be based on the two variables: (1) the degree to which a person has administered violence over the years, and (2) the degree to which a person has been the recipient of violence through the years. The cells of a sample typology of violent careers might look like this:

		Administration of Violence		
		Low	Medium	High
Receiving of Violence	Low	1	2	3
	Medium	4	5	6
	High	7	8	9

The typology could function as a model for empirical analysis. What are the characteristics of each type, i.e., of the persons in each cell? For example, what are the characteristics of Type 3 persons—those who have made careers of "dishing out" violence while only infrequently being on the receiving end? On the other hand, what kind of people are in Type 7—those who have had careers of being primarily recipients of violence? Which groups are most typical of American society?

In what social contexts and under what conditions does *illegitimate* violence take place? What are the social characteristics of persons who behave illegitimately with high frequency? Sociological theory leads us to expect higher rates of deviant or nonconforming behavior among social groups or categories of persons who do not have equal opportunities to achieve cultural goals. On this basis, we could expect higher rates of illegitimate violence from unsuccessful or "have-not" persons or organizations.[8]

How frequently, and under what conditions does behavior which was initially illegitimate become legitimate? Institutionalized deviant violence may be quite common in America.

Possibly the key variable in an analysis of violence in America is the mode of behavior. The discussion of either the legitimacy or the mode of behavior dimensions is of only partial worth unless both sets of variables are considered simultaneously. Combination of the two dimensions produces the following typology.

Mode of Violent Behavior	Degree of Legitimacy		
	Legitimate		Illegitimate
	Offensive	Defensive	
Physical			
a. Actual			
b. Threat			
Manipulative			
Verbal			

This could be called the Typology of Violent Acts. Research is needed to obtain descriptive and analytical data about the type of violent act. Emphasis from this perspective is initially on the behavior itself. What are the social structural conditions of each type of violent act? Emphasis on the act as the item of analysis need not and should not preclude gaining information about the persons or organizations participating in the act. It is felt, however, that the delineation of the boundaries and conditions of types of acts, regardless of the social or psychological characteristics of the actors, would yield useful and necessary propositions that otherwise might not result from a purely social psychological approach.

SUMMARY

This essay has presented an exploratory perspective for the study of violent behavior in a social or cultural setting. There is a need for empirical research to determine to what degree violence constitutes an American value theme. Some suggestions for future research consideration were raised, including a typology of violent careers and a typology of violent acts. It is hoped that these typologies will function as tentative models for future analysis.

The emphasis on violence as a possible part of American social and cultural structure is an attempt to place the general problem of violence and the mass media in a broader sociological setting. Too many of the considerations of the content of the mass media have ignored the key questions of why certain themes are focused upon by the media. The media must be analyzed in terms of their social setting in the overall society (e.g., Gans, 1957, 1964). In order to do this, knowledge is required not only of the workings of the media but also of the social and cultural structure. If the themes of the media are also themes in the society, then there would appear to be a state of relative social integration. However, if the themes of the media are *not* themes in the culture of the society, or *vice versa*, what are the consequences for the social system?

PART V

Regulation and Control: Public Participation

> I deny not but that it is of the greatest concernment
> in the church and commonwealth, to have a vigilant
> eye on how books demean themselves as well as
> men.
>
> JOHN MILTON

IN THIS "age of research" there is growing public interest in the kind of research efforts reported in the preceding section. There is even a great deal of optimism that research ultimately will provide the answers needed to cope with the problem of violence in mass communication and in society.

To some people, however, much of the research still appears to be an "ivory tower" effort. Confronted with increasingly harsh displays of violence, some critics are yet inclined to think of basic scientific inquiry on the topic as an example of "lecturing on navigation while the ship sinks." Such an extreme disposition is not readily countered by the observation that navigation today is what it is because some people were willing to study the *principles* of the subject while their individual ships went down, instead of rushing about with advice as to how to save ships that could not be saved, or were not worth saving anyway.

The question of what to do about media violence is instigated partly from a research base and partly from the friction generated from the polar views expressed about research, but mainly from the contention that the problem of violence in contemporary society is so urgent that we should move directly to measures of regulation and control instead of merely waiting for confirmed evidence about media effects.

The measures advocated tend to have three focal points: (1) Those centering on increased surveillance and classification of media material to facilitate individual selection of media content and family regulation over exposure to the media; (2) those which emphasize placing pressure on the media to the end that they will exercise self-regulation over the presentation of violent content; and (3) those which call for direct government action to stop the flow of media violence. This last alternative runs counter to precedents in American law and custom, but is, nonetheless, gaining support both inside and outside the United States. The testimony by Professor Peter Lejins before a U. S. Senate committee indicates how other nationals are amazed that Americans seem to be paralyzed by research findings and cannot see the obvious necessity for governmental action to control the media portrayal of violence.

To provide the reader with a basis for evaluating alternative strategies for the control of media violence, the selections in the next three parts describe various courses of action advocated or taken by the public, the government, and by the mass media. Several articles trace how action generated in one of these sectors has repercussions in the others. Thus control activities are highly interconnected and are separated here by broad themes into three sections for convenience of analysis only.

This three-pronged probe into matters of regulation and control begins by examining the nature of public participation in the process. These readings extend to the level of collective action the material presented in Part II. There we saw how individual opinion instigators are instrumental in bringing the issue to the public in the first place. The question now is, How does the public respond to the articulation of alarm about media violence? What can citizens do when they become concerned about media violence?

The basic answer to these questions is that aggrieved persons can register protest. To whom can such protest be directed, and by what means? The articles presented below make it clear that protest takes several forms and is channeled over many avenues.

One form of protest is to withdraw support from the mass media. Thus citizens, either individually or collectively, can attempt to boycott those forms of mass communication which persist in offending their sensibilities with violent content. The economic structure of American mass communication makes the media particularly sensitive to this kind of action. So far, however, large sectors of the American audience have not turned away from the media because they portray violence. The reasons for this are undoubtedly many and mixed. Most persons like what they get from the mass media, in part, perhaps, because they are not aware of possible alternative fare. Others do not approve of the content, but may not know what can be done about it. And, finally, there is a basic problem confronting any individual who wants to protest by withdrawing his personal support from offending media: How shall he identify the offenders? Such identification re-

quires exposure to the media and some kind of continuing
surveillance in order to know when and of what to disapprove.

Individual and collective modes of surveillance are examined in a number of selections below. In the second article,
Eve Merriam emphasizes individual responsibility and en-
courages parents to establish a "personal watch society" to
protect their children from media violence. She also notes
how parents may register protest through a growing network
of groups organized to monitor media content and to lobby
for stricter regulation of mass communication.

The articles by Twomey, Murrell, and Schwartz clearly
depict how these organizations emerge from existing voluntary associations to become active forces for evaluating, grad-
ing, labeling, and censoring mass media content. This material may be viewed as a dramatic chapter in the history
of American organizational effort, an effort that mobilizes a
serious challenge to the traditional freedom and autonomy
of American mass media. The analysis presented in these
papers bears mainly on comic books and motion pictures.
However, the elements involved are patterned in similar ways
for similar purposes for other forms of mass communication such as radio and television. In each instance a common conclusion emerges: organized, collective action by citizen groups can and does alter the content of the media
of mass communication. While this may be widely applauded
when the content deals with violence, it does raise new
questions, as yet unexplored, about the power of an organized minority to set standards that affect us all. Unless
these standards themselves are subject to changing needs,
they could institute a rigid conformity damaging to the creative requirements of society.

INTERNATIONAL OPINIONS ON AMERICAN MEDIA VIOLENCE

Peter J. Lejins

• • •

. . . I WAS asked to give some impressions which I gained at the Congress of the United Nations on the prevention of crime and the treatment of offenders last fall. . . .

• • •

In this Congress, at which the representatives of some 85 nations were gathered, the U. S. delegates found themselves pretty much alone on the issue of mass media and juvenile delinquency in two respects.

First, the U. S. Delegation, reflecting the true climate of opinion prevailing in the United States, expressed the lack of certainty about the pernicious effects of crime and brutality content of mass media, especially television, on juvenile delinquency. It seems that the rest of the world, at least as far as the countries were represented by their delegations in this Congress, is quite certain that the portrayal of crime, violence, brutality, and sadism has a bad effect on youth and is directly conducive to crime. The mention of the lack of scientific proof made by some of the U. S. delegates was met, by and large, with incredulity, perhaps one should say, with utter amazement and a certain amount of hostility.

Secondly, the clearly stated aversion on the part of the U. S. delegates toward censorship and suppression of the content of mass media which is considered undesirable is certainly not shared by the vast majority of the nations. In the session where the topic was discussed, only one or two members of the British Commonwealth sided with the views on censorship and control presented by the United States.

The rest of the world seems to solidly believe that undesirable content should be forbidden and there is absolutely noth-

---

Excerpts reprinted with the permission of Professor Lejins from his testimony before U. S. Senate Subcommittee to Investigate Juvenile Delinquency, 88th Congress, 2nd Session, Pursuant to S. Res. 274, as reported in Interim Report of Subcommittee, 1964, pp. 52–55.

ing wrong if the "bad things" are suppressed. The liberal
position of the United States was met again with surprise
and again with a considerable amount of hostility.

• • •

The representatives of very many countries seemed to express themselves in such a way as if they assumed that the
position of the United States on both counts, that is, the un-
certainty about the evil effects of the crime and violence on
TV shows and the unwillingness to control these, is explain-
able through the greed of this country in trying to make big
money on its products, which are deliberately addressed to
the base elements of human nature.

That this was not an attitude of just one or two countries
I will illustrate by giving examples from three widely separated areas of the world.

First of all, the Soviet Union:

The representatives of the delegation of the Soviet Union
and especially its head committed themselves unequivocally
from the very beginning to the recognition of the fact that
crime content and, in general, cheap content of mass media
has had effects on children in the sense of juvenile delinquency. The head of the Soviet delegation in one of his first
speeches remarked that, on the whole, the very satisfactory
delinquency situation in the Soviet Union occasionally has
its downs. One of such unfortunate episodes was the permission for some Tarzan films to be shown in the Soviet Union.

In the result, as Mr. Smirnoff put it—and I am paraphrasing his statement—some of the youngsters in the Soviet
Union also started swinging from trees and some of them
actually did swing into the upper story windows. Needless
to say, he further commented, after such films were forbidden, this nonsense stopped.

The comments of the U. S. delegates among ourselves was
that he singled out Tarzan films, which we would consider
extremely innocent, and everybody was saying, "If you only
could see some of our real crime and violence films."

In what I believe was Mr. Smirnoff's concluding speech
before the plenary session of the Congress, he made the
following statement. He expressed his amazement about the
attitude of some countries—he didn't name these, but he
meant, of course, the United States—in opposing any censor-
shop of the vile content of mass media. As Smirnoff said,

these countries do not hesitate to pass laws which promise the severest penalties for a drug peddler who sells his wares to a juvenile. What is the difference between the drug peddler who is seducing a juvenile into this horrible vice and the producer of a movie or a TV story which is as damaging to the spirit of the youngster?

One should not forget that Mr. Smirnoff's appearance before the General Assembly of the Congress on this occasion resulted in an ovation of a scope which no other nation or delegate received.

Similar comments came from the delegates from several countries of South America. One of these presented his views especially eloquently. He pointed out the importance of American aid to under-developed countries, and the respect and esteem in which the United States is held in his country because of this aid. And then he went on to point out the nature of the films which are being imported from the United States into his country. He expressed his amazement and characterized the confusion of his people by saying that they either have to think that since other things that come from the United States are progressive and good, therefore also the content of the films must be considered as proper, or, as he said, if the quality of the films is generally representative of the quality of what the United States is sending to these countries, then, of course, all the faith in the U. S. contribution is undermined.

He was the one who made an unmistakable allusion, although politely expressed, to the fact that perhaps it is the unnecessary greed on the part of this country to make profit on this cheap and base product that is responsible for such exports.

The third example of the prevailing attitude stems from an entirely different part of the world, namely, from Sweden, which would be expected in general to align itself in these matters pretty much with the United States, in the sense of an enlightened and progressive attitude. I could give many instances of the Scandinavian opinion, but I will limit myself to only one. One relatively young, very progressive and very intelligent high public official from Sweden, whom I have known now for over 10 years and have met repeatedly in various congresses, came to me one day. Instead of his usual friendly and joking attitude, he displayed anger and I would say that his face, to a certain extent, was twisted with rage. His statement to me was that his and in general Sweden's patience has come to an end, as far as American policies with regard to mass media are concerned.

I am paraphrasing him, but his words were pretty much as follows: "Don't you understand that this must be stopped, that the world is sick and tired of receiving this incredible and vicious trash from the United States? Don't you understand that the United States is undermining its own position in every other respect by insistence on this uncontrolled production of material which appeals to the basest elements in human nature?"

I was truly taken aback by this outburst.

I want it to be clearly understood that I am not necessarily in agreement with the views expressed by the representatives of these different nations. Being a social scientist trained in the United States, I am aware of the difficulties of scientific proof, and I am, of course, aware of the dangers of censorship and of governmental control in general. I am submitting these experiences, however, as facts which apparently, to a large extent, determine the attitudes of other countries toward the United States; at least did determine the attitudes of the delegates of these countries toward the United States in this particular Congress.

I would like to end this presentation by a brief reference to another group of foreign representatives who acted in a very similar fashion toward the content of American audiovisual mass media. This time it was a group of Congolese law enforcement officers who were brought to this country by the International Cooperation Administration and who for a short while were assigned to my guidance at the University of Maryland.

These three men spent their time in studying the penal and correctional institutions and practices in this country, were very much impressed by what they saw and made in general a very intelligent and cooperative impression. There was one point, however, with regard to which all three of them suddenly flared up and expressed an indignation strikingly different from their general demeanor. The graduate students of my seminar who witnessed this scene still speak from time to time of this incident.

The issue was again the content of the American audiovisual mass media. Almost all three Congolese guests suddenly addressed themselves to the membership of the seminar to do something to convey to the American people to stop the horrible procedure of exporting the kind of movies that they are getting in their country. They again indicated that the appearance of such movies undermines the faith and the respect of their people toward the United States.

GUIDELINES FOR PARENTAL
REACTION TO MEDIA

Eve Merriam

• • •

WHERE is the dividing line between the real world and the fantasy world? The problem, if it is any consolation, is not exclusively American. A group of schoolteachers in Tokyo is currently forming an anti-TV-violence committee. A poem in a Russian magazine deplores the fact that too many parents permit their children to watch unsuitable programs. In England authorities filter out the most offensive material, such as the too-raw scenes in wild Westerns coming from America. Programs deemed unsuitable for child audiences may not be shown until after nine p.m. Yet the British are by no means blameless; in Canada there are complaints that one of the worst programs children get to see is *The Saint*, a private-eye series originating in Britain.

However, in many countries around the world the most violent TV programs, films, comic books and toys are referred to simply as "American style." Can that style be changed, can nonviolent values be substituted?

Some parents think so. Believing that education against

Reprinted with the permission of the author and Marvin Josephson Associates, Inc., from "We're Teaching Our Children That Violence Is Fun," *The Ladies' Home Journal*, October, 1964, p. 52. Copyright © 1964 by Curtis Publishing Company.

violence should start as early as possible, they are refusing to buy their children toy weapons of any kind. Others are taking to heart the opinion of Senator Abraham Ribicoff of Connecticut:

> If a child is permitted to sit like a vegetable, pursuing moronic murders and ceaseless crimes, he suffers, and his parents do too, in the end. Parents must learn to say, "No, you may not listen to or look at that" as well as "Yes" or just shrugging and saying "OK."
>
> Parents must take positive steps to improve the televiewing habits of their children and themselves. And the television industry must fulfill its obligation to its viewers. It has produced programs of real significance. It has reported public affairs with insight and imagination. It can use its resources if it only has the will to do so.

There are many forms that protest can take, short of parents' picket lines around the studios. As an individual, you can express your disapproval by writing to the sponsor, in care of the station or network, to your Congressman and to the Federal Communications Commission in Washington.

You can also express your sentiments through group action. The PTA, for instance, has several regional groups that evaluate television programs. If your local PTA doesn't belong to such a group, write for information to: National Congress of Parents and Teachers, 700 North Rush Street, Chicago 11, Ill.

The American Association of University Women, 2401 Virginia Avenue, N.W., Washington 7, D.C., also evaluates the content of mass media. There are organizations devoted exclusively to broadcasting. The oldest (established in 1949) is the National Association for Better Radio and Television, 882 Victoria Avenue, Los Angeles 5, Calif.

N.A.F.B.R.A.T. publishes a quarterly newsletter, an annual survey of children's programs, and occasional pamphlets. Its president, Mrs. Clara S. Logan, often testifies at Congressional hearings.

Another national organization is The American Council for Better Broadcasts, 423 North Pinckney Street, Madison 3, Wis., Dr. Leslie Spence, executive director. Founded in 1953, A.C.B.B. monitors programs and submits its rating reports to sponsors, networks, Congressional committees and Government agencies. Like N.A.F.B.R.A.T., it publishes a news bulletin (*Better Broadcasts*, issued five times a year), an annual look-listen report, and other material.

Above all, it is important to form a personal watch society; for all of us to sit down with our children and watch what they are seeing, to check on the programs at regular intervals, and to issue our own home license as to what may or may not be seen.

Such a schedule may be demanding, but at present we have no alternative; we cannot afford to leave our children unguarded in the care of the television baby-sitter. Not, at least, until the baby-sitter comes forward with more reliable references.

NEW FORMS OF SOCIAL CONTROL
OVER MASS MEDIA CONTENT

John E. Twomey

THE GROWTH of the mass media of communication during the last decade has complicated the problem of their social control. Although no tradition of censorship exists in the United States, there appears to be a growing public attitude which favors reinterpretation of our traditional concepts regarding censorship and other forms of social control.

Such an attitude probably reflects those characteristics of the media which have become conspicuous during the last decade. The assertions often made in demands for more stringent control include the following: the mass media of today feature crime, violence, sex, and sadism; the media are as freely available to the young as to the adult; they have contributed to the 40 per cent increase in juvenile crime and delinquency since 1948.

Reprinted with the permission of the publisher from *Studies in Public Communication*, Summer, 1957, pp. 38–44; published by The University of Chicago Press.

One compentent observer (Mublen, 1949) describes this phenomenon as an American nightmare:

In psychoanalytic terms, the entertainment of a large part of the Nation's adults, and of the overwhelming majority of its youth, is directed toward *mortio* rather than *libido,* toward aggression rather than procreation, toward death rather than life. Its common denominator is violence—all the forms, techniques, systems and possibilities of violence. And almost never is there any concern with the reasons for which people act in violence—for this there is obviously little time and space in the 90 minutes of a movie, the 30 minutes of a radio play, the 60 cartoons of a comic-book story.

Margaret Mead (1955) points to the increasing vulnerability of children:

Mass communications—movies, television, paper books—bring us up against the fact that in such media it is impossible to discriminate between children and adults. We can keep children under sixteen out of theatres or movie houses, keep their allowance so low that they cannot afford to buy expensive books, and train librarians to hide books that are regarded as unfit for children. But where the child, with a turn of the dial or an easily earned quarter, can listen or look or read with no adult present to censor, this becomes impossible.

Recognizing the problems created by the mass media, many authorities have proposed censorship be instituted for the protection of the young. Walter Lippmann (1954) writes:

Censorship is no doubt a clumsy and usually a stupid and self-defeating remedy for such evils. But a continual exposure of a generation to the commercial exploitation of the enjoyment of violence and cruelty is one way to corrode the foundations of a civilized society. For my part, believing as I do in freedom of speech and thought, I see no objections in principle to censorship of the mass entertainment of the young. Until some more refined way is worked out for controlling this evil thing, the risks to our liberties are, I believe, decidedly less than the risks of unmanageable violence.

Along with the many social observers, academicians, and organizations who have deplored the emphasis on crime, violence, and sex in the mass media, government officials have also become keenly interested. Their interest has led to congressional investigations of the various communication channels. Most recently governmental bodies have been concerned with magazines, paper-bound books, and comic books, searching for evidence which would link these media to the increase in juvenile crime and delinquency.

Chief among the mass media attacked alike by private citizens, organized community-action groups and government are comic books. The campaign against the publication of these ten-cent, pulp-paper illustrated story books has assumed the proportions of a large-scale crusade.

The anti-comic book crusade in America has grown to maturity during the past decade as a result of: (1) the spread of Dr. Wertham's (1954) vehement anti-comic book propaganda, based on the findings of psychiatric research and on his own righteous conviction; (2) the provision of a strong organizational rallying point by the National Organization for Decent Literature which initiated the techniques of blacklisting "objectionable" comic books and has become, along with the Roman Catholic Legion of Decency, one of the most influential pressure groups affecting the contents of the mass media today; (3) the widespread initiation and growth among civic, religious, and women's organizations of anti-comic book crusade groups which have exerted powerful grass-roots pressures for the banning, burning and boycotting of comic books; and (4) the investigation of the comic book publishing industry, and its product's alleged social affects, by congressional investigating committees.

While the different individuals and organizations leading the anti-comic book crusade may disagree on the relative importance of the issues involved, most anti-comic book activities are predicated on the following assumptions: (1) the effects of the symbolic messages upon the readers are a direct result of the contents of the medium, i.e., the idea or theme is perceived by the media users directly as it is contained in the media; (2) because of the simplicity of the causal relationship between the content of the communication and its effect, the effect (especially upon children) is easily discernible and predictable by normal adults; (3) the subtleties of the "new obscenity" contained in comic books makes it very difficult for statutory controls to be instituted; and (4) the time and problems involved in instituting legal controls leaves as the most appropriate alternative an aroused, educated and activated "public opinion" in the form of civic, religious, and women's organizations dedicated to "cleaning-up" the mass media.

These assumptions have not gone unchallenged. Dr. Wertham's findings and basic arguments have been attacked by recognized authorities (e.g., Thrasher, 1949). Backing up these criticisms are recent social science research findings which raise serious doubts as to the validity of the "transmission-belt" theory of communication upon which the comic book crusade is based. This research, involving the social and environmental factors in perception, has revealed the prime importance of the total "need-motivation-value-belief" system of the individual to her perceptions, images, memory, and reasoning (Fearing, 1953). While this "two-way" theory of communication has gained recognition in academic circles, it has not effectively challenged the assumptions involved in the campaign. Challenges made from time to time by the American Civil Liberties Union as to the possible threat to civil liberties and freedom of the press by proposed censor legislation and the activities of blacklisting groups have been of little avail in halting the anti-comic book movement.

The anti-comic book crusade, unlike other censorial movements in America, which have briefly flourished and then vanished, has become established and is now a well-organized movement. More important, however, are the precedents which this movement established in its attempts to reverse basic attitudes toward freedom of expression.

An important precedent was the enlisting of a professionally recognized, intellectual leader in the person of Dr. Fredric Wertham, to provide the campaign with a degree of scientific rationale and legitimacy. Wertham, in addition to his professional stature, lent credibility to the movement through his book, his articles, and his testimony before legislative investigating committees of the state of New York, the U. S. House of Representatives, the U. S. Senate, and the Canadian Parliament. He was listened to when he attacked psychiatrists who "like educators, teachers and clergymen . . . were unprepared and not adjusted to the new impact of mass media on children, and as a result . . . made themselves part of the education for violence" (Wertham, 1954, p. 368). He also had an audience ready and willing to believe that the movement held no threat for civil liberties.

I have heard responsible moral leaders and educators say—both publicly and privately—that comic-book control would interfere with freedom! Evidently they think that to allow an industry to seduce children is democratic, while to prevent an industry from seducing children is undemocratic.

Another precedent set by the anti-comic book movement was the establishment, at the community level, of a vast network of self-appointed arbiters of public literary tastes and morals. Creating and sustaining the organizational base of this network has been the task of the National Organization for Decent Literature founded in 1938 by a council of bishops of the Roman Catholic hierarchy "to develop a plan for organizing a systematic campaign in all dioceses of the United States against the publication and sale of lewd magazines and brochure literature" (Lockhart and McClure, 1954, p. 304). The N.O.D.L. has only recently come to the fore as a power behind the movement for new forms of social control over popular literature.

The tactics of the N.O.D.L. have been to organize action groups among the diocesan councils of Catholic men and women throughout the United States to effect: (1) the arousal of public opinion against "objectionable" magazines, pocket-size books, and comic books; (2) the more rigorous enforcement of existing laws governing literature; (3) the preparation of monthly lists of disapproved popular literature surveyed by the organization; and (4) the visitation of newsstands and drug stores to secure the removal of blacklisted publications from sale.

The lists of disapproved publications, which are prepared by volunteer women readers, contain nearly six hundred titles listed under categories of "comic books," "pocket-size books," "digest-type novels," and "magazines." Two separate categories list "acceptable comics" and "recommended quarter books for children." Cumulative lists are distributed throughout the United States to Catholic action groups. While some non-Catholic groups in the movement are allowed access to the lists, they are not available for general publication or distribution.

Roman Catholics are urged to use the lists when purchasing periodicals for children, but their major function is to aid canvassers on "decency crusades." "Decency crusades" are instituted at parish levels to exert personalized pressure for the removal from sale of listed publications. The techniques of "decency crusades" includes the following (Archdiocesan Council of Catholic Women, n.d.):

1. Every establishment which sells comic books, pocket-size books, and magazines within the limit of your parish is to be visited. This includes corner newsstands.

2. It is recommended that your committee work in teams of two women. Each team should be assigned three dealers. It is advisable to make these visits at a time when the storekeeper or manager is not too busy to confer with you.

3. It is suggested that the members of your committee introduce themselves to the owner, manager or clerk in attendance; and, where the purpose of the ACCW DECENCY CRUSADE is not already known, a short explanation should be given, stressing the need for the protection of the morality of youth. Next, show the ACCW list of objectionable publications. Courteously request the privilege of examining the display of publications for sale.

4. Where no objectionable titles are found, the committee should commend the owner or manager. Favorable publicity should be given this dealer in your church publication.

5. Where objectionable titles are found, courteously recommend that the manager or owner remove such publications from sale. When the dealer complies, favorable publicity should be given him in your church publication.

6. Instruct your committee workers to leave silently if the owner, manager or clerk refuses cooperation. Little is ever gained by argument, but silence can often be most effective.

7. Report any refusal of cooperation to your pastor or moderator. Future action should be determined by him.

The General Federation of Women's Clubs, with a national membership of over four million women, has also taken an active role in suppressing "objectionable" literature at the community level. In the G.F.W.C. outline of project activities another tactic for social control of mass media was introduced in the form of social pressure directed at the individual purchaser and reader of various publications. The Federation recommended (G.F.W.C., n.d.):

Appoint volunteers to visit newsstands weekly with notebook in hand, to list the titles on the stands and note who does the buying.

Enlist certain classes in school to cooperate in the evaluation program and to note who buys and reads the different types of comics.

The description of these activities as "community vigilance" and "public opinion in action" by the respective members of the N.O.D.L. and the G.F.W.C. is indicative of the rationale behind the movement.

Another precedent, and one which may prove to be the most far reaching, was the position taken by the congressional subcommittee which undertook an investigation of the comic book industry.

Senator Estes Kefauver, author of the subcommittee report, stated its belief that "this Nation cannot afford the calculated risk involved in the continued mass dissemination of crime and horror comic books to children" (U. S. Congress, Senate, 1955). He then took up the crucial question of where the responsibility rests for the policing of these media.

It does not rest with government and stricter legal regulation: "The subcommittee flatly rejects all suggestions of governmental censorship as being totally out of keeping with our basic American concepts of a free press operating in a free land for a free people."

Primary responsibility for the kinds of comic books available for children rests with the comic book publishers. And that responsibility is not lightly discharged, states the report.

Standards for such products, whether in the form of a code or by the policies of individual producers, should not be aimed to eliminate only that which can be proved beyond doubt to demoralize youth. Rather the aim should be to eliminate all materials that potentially exert detrimental effects.

Vigilant parents and citizens groups are saluted for their anti-comic book campaigns of the past and recognized by the subcommittee as an essential force for pointing out potentially detrimental materials. While the subcommittee relates its "surprise that little attention has been paid by educational and welfare agencies to the potential dangers, as well as benefits, to children presented by the growth of the comic book industry," positive activities by these bodies seem precluded by the subcommittee's statement that: "The interest of our young citizens would not be served by postponing all precautionary measures until the exact kind and degree of influence exerted by comic books upon children's behavior is fully determined through careful research."

An important step taken by the subcommittee's report was the placing of responsibility for the contents of comic books on every segment of the industry. While the neighborhood newsdealer is precluded because of his weak financial position, Kefauver says of the printer: ". . . it does not seem unreasonable to expect a reputable printer to refuse to print material, the reading of which in his estimation may influence children negatively." And of the distributors: ". . . as persons engaged in an industry which plays a large part in molding the impressionable minds of youth, they should maintain constant, continuing supervision over the publications they distribute." And of the wholesaler: ". . . the wholesaler can and should make his influence felt in efforts to curtail distribution of objectionable reading materials for children."

The wide publicity given the hearings and the pronouncements of Senator Kefauver, via the report, has contributed in no small measure to legitimating the activities of extra-legal censorship organizations. In addition it has placed responsibility for the content of the published media on printers, distributors, and wholesalers. Each of these segments of the industry have been charged with the responsibility of deciding what the public should read.

These three precedents: "scientific" and professional leadership; the organization and maintenance of a nationwide network of grass roots censor groups; and the abdication of government from its traditional role as protector of freedom of the press by its condoning blacklisting activities, have been important factors in the movement to establish new forms of social control over the mass media.

Robert J. Blackely (1953) concerned with the need for adult education about the new media, views this changing attitude as a major threat to the positive advantages society has gained from the mass media.

We seem to be tending, almost by tacit agreement, to regard freedom of expression as a *private* right to be restricted like other private rights when they are abused instead of a *public* right that cannot be restricted without damage to the general welfare. True, dark irrational forces have been discovered, both in the individual and in the society, but how were they discovered? By *rational* analysis. And what is the alternative? Certainly not irrationality. True, the margins of permissible error in the modern world are narrower than used to be. But how do we avoid or minimize error? Certainly not by being ignorant of alternatives or of relevant facts. Freedom of expression from the social point of view is the right of citizens to hear all arguments and to look at all proofs and the responsibility to let others do the same.

It is not within the scope of this paper to suggest means to reverse the current trends to new social controls or to describe what the proper controls should be. Suffice to say the complexities of the total problem preclude any easy solution. It seems quite evident, however, that a solution must be found that will meet the challenge of new mass media content and yet maintain our traditional free press.

THE GREATER CINCINNATI COMMITTEE ON EVALUATION OF COMIC BOOKS

Jesse L. Murrell

THE ORIGIN of the Greater Cincinnati Committee on Evaluation of Comic Books lies back in the first Sunday of May, 1948, which was the beginning of National Family Week. Dr. Jesse L. Murrell, pastor of First Methodist Church, Covington, Kentucky, addressed his congregation on "Some Perils to the Family" and included the comic books among them. That portion of his sermon got into the Monday papers and was immediately picked up by the broadcasting stations. Mail began pouring in and the phone rang incessantly, whereupon the Kenton County Protestant Association (Council of Churches) set up a committee with Murrell as chair-

---

Excerpts from a memorandum to the editor, July, 1964. Used with the permission of the author.

man and requested it to see what, if anything, could be done about the bad comics.

The committee approached the organizations in greater Cincinnati that work with and for youth, inquiring after their degree of interest and inviting them to send representatives to a meeting. They were the University of Cincinnati, Xavier University, the Women's University Club, the Parent-Teacher Associations (public and parochial), the Boy Scouts, the Girl Scouts, the Y.M.C.A., the Y.W.C.A., the playground group, the juvenile courts, the Council of Churches, the Kenton County (Kentucky) Protestant Association, the libraries, the public and parochial schools, and the three religious faiths—Protestant, Catholic, and Jewish. This group was divided about equally between men and women and most of those who were invited attended the first meeting at the Walnut Hills Branch Library on May 25.

The beginnings of an organization were made immediately with Dr. Jesse L. Murrell as chairman. A subcommittee was appointed to find out what was being done in other communities about the comic books considered objectionable.

At the outset, a policy of cooperation with the publishers and distributors in improving the quality of comic magazines was adopted; but since this had little effect, the Committee decided that its strategy with the public would be that of education rather than censure as some advocated.

A CRITERION WAS NEEDED

The Committee realized that before review work could begin a code or criterion would be needed since only in this way could it be determined what comic books were really good or bad. Letters were sent to the publishers of comic books seeking copies of their codes, and several were received. Certain other groups across the nation that were studying this literature also had standards by which to measure it, and some of these were obtained.

In the summer of 1948, a set of criteria was formulated which was thought suitable for the purposes of the Cincinnati Committee. The criteria set up four levels on which the value of comic books could be judged: Level 1, *no objection;* Level 2, *some objection;* Level 3, *objectionable;* and Level 4, *very objectionable.* In later years Level 4 was eliminated on the ground that if a comic book was bad it was bad and further distinctions of degree were unnecessary.

The following statement was formulated to assist readers in applying the criteria to every situation encountered:

These criteria are intended to serve primarily as guides and check-points in the evaluation of comic books, rather than as complete standards which must in all cases be applied literally and rigidly. They should be used by the reviewer in the light of his best judgment regarding good taste, the intent and spirit of the story, and the context of the individual frames of the story.

A profile chart, or graphic rating scale, was also constructed to facilitate the judgment of each story and each book.

WHAT OTHERS WERE DOING ABOUT THE COMIC BOOKS

The investigation to find out what was being done about objectionable comic books in other communities discovered much activity across the nation: in fact, a veritable ground swell. It was learned that beginning with 1945 a restless mood had started to grow in those Americans who were concerned with the welfare of their children. The fledgling comic-book industry had been catapulted into a major enterprise, and many citizens had come to feel that its product was undermining the ideals and character of the oncoming generation. Boards and committees had been set up in many cities to find ways and means for handling the new threat to the nation, but they had no common pattern.

A. The American Municipal Association had released the following information through the Associated Press on May 24, 1948:

1. Working together, Indianapolis magazine distributors, city officials, and civic groups had banned 35 comic books.
2. Detroit police had forbidden the sale of 36 comic magazines at local newsstands in advance of censure that was threatened.
3. Hillsdale, Michigan, had banned the same books prohibited in Detroit. This action was taken under a Michigan statute outlawing "obscene, indecent, and immoral literature."

4. Civic leaders in Centralia, Washington, had appealed to the comic-book publishers to tone down their materials.

B. A citizens' committee of 22 members had been formed by the St. Paul City Council to see what could be done about the questionable comic books there. It was representative of a cross section of that city. Its analysis, the first in the field, placed the comic magazines in 18 categories including adventure (10.5%), crime (10.5%), detection (5%), supernatural (2.5%), supranatural (1.2%), superhuman (6%), fantastic (1.4%), jungle (4.1%), western (15.5%), true (1.2%), funnies (.5%), factual (.5%), propaganda (.3%), and religious (.4%).

C. The New Orleans City Commission became concerned about the effects of the comics upon the lives of their city's people and requested its city manager to look into the situation. His report, rendered after considerable study, contained four recommendations:

1. Voluntary cooperation and self-regulation on the part of the industry.
2. A higher degree of parental responsibility as to what their children were reading.
3. Drug store and newsstand proprietors should be requested both by the distributors, the parents and their organizations to take an interest in the problem: (a) to give better display to the more wholesome types of comic magazines; (b) to separate those made for children from those apparently designed for adults; and (c) to refuse to exhibit for sale the objectionable comics.
4. The publishers have a responsibility. If the parents of America are to let their doors remain open to 60,000,000 comic books every month, then their editors and publishers should accept their responsibilities to the home.

D. The Parent-Teacher Association of Santa Monica, California, set up a committee of five very early in this endeavor to have the comic books cleaned up. A committee to read and evaluate them, composed of women from all the Associations, met in the Board of Education Building for eight weeks before it completed its task of reviewing. The distributors cooperated by furnishing lists of the comic books sold in the area and the findings stated [the following].

1. Not all comic books are comic.
2. The newspaper comic strips and the comic books are different.
3. The number of comic books sold each week is 15,000,000; each month is 60,000,000; each year, 720,000,000. Over half of them are objectionable, and any reading is an influence on growing minds.
4. Objectionable comic books can be classed as those that emphasize violence, sadism, and immorality.

COMMITTEE STRUCTURE

The idea grew in the Cincinnati Committee that it should make independent ratings of comic books. It was convinced that if its decisions were influenced by outside interests its findings would be worthless. During the years since 1948 the personnel of the Committee has changed, but the effort has been to keep its size close to ten persons. Members have become valuable to it only after time and experience had matured them in its technical phases.

Finding money to support the Committee's work came to be a major problem in the early years. During that period the money came from Parent-Teacher Associations, women's organizations, clubs, individuals, the sale of printed lists of evaluated comic books, and from the sale of articles to *Parents' Magazine*. After two or three years there was sufficient income to finance the program adequately.

RECRUITING AND TRAINING REVIEWERS

A major problem was the recruiting and training of reviewers who would read the comic books thoroughly and record their impressions on the profile charts. They were urged to exercise care at every stage in order to be fair to all persons and organizations concerned, and to follow the criteria rather than personal bias, feelings or beliefs.

Some of the questions raised in the selection of reviewers were: From what groups in society should they be drawn? How could they be recruited? What training would they need? How much time could they be expected to contribute to this service? Could they be expected to repeat the process from month to month or from year to year? These problems were solved at least in a fashion for something over 200 reviewers who were recruited and trained.

A typical procedure in reviewing was something like this: After the reviewers had been recruited and trained, after the comic books had been procured and arranged in packets averaging five comics, they were invited to meet for final instruction and to receive their packets of comic books. They found in these packets the materials they would need in their work, including a letter recalling the entire process through which they were expected to go.

A careful selection of persons to study the work of the reviewers and to make the over-all evaluations of the comic books became the custom since this was considered the most crucial task of the Committee. Every story and picture frame was evaluated in terms of its cultural, moral, and emotional impact upon children and youths through 15 years of age and upon the levels of no objections, some objection, objectionable and very objectionable. When no feature in a comic book received anything lower than the first two ratings, the books were pronounced suitable for reading by children.

HOW THE COMMITTEE PROMOTES ITS CAUSE

Until the Committee's existence and goals were known and appreciated, it had to knock on doors here, there and everywhere, not literally but through contacts and by literature. Magazine and newspaper articles were employed extensively. Such organizations as the Parent-Teacher Associations, women's clubs, public schools, and churches afforded it vast opportunities for becoming better known.

After each round of reviews the findings were mailed to all parts of the nation, to Canada and other English-speaking countries. Similar lists of the publishers and their evaluated comic books were printed and distributed. Members of the Committee spoke or served on panels in many situations halfway across the country, and the Committee on Evaluation of Comic Books is convinced that its contribution to the im-sold in the area and the findings stated [the following].

THE COMICS MAGAZINE ASSOCIATION
OF AMERICA

By 1954 such a tide of criticism of comic books had spread across the land that the publishers organized the Comics Magazine Association of America apparently to head off a possible wave of restrictive legislation and to stop a downward trend in sales. They already had a business promotion organization but this new Association was to make the comic books more acceptable to the public. The Greater Cincinnati Committee on Evaluation of Comic Books is credited with having hastened the coming of this decision on the part of the industry.

The code of the C.M.A.A. was more liberal than the criteria which guided the Cincinnati Committee, but it did help to raise the level of comic books. While some of the publishers stayed out of the new Association its code exerted considerable influence upon their product for business, if not for moral, reasons. One inducement for the publishers to join this Association was their ability to print the code seal on the front cover of their comic books.

COMIC BOOKS EVALUATED REGULARLY

During the early years of its activity, the Committee on Evaluation of Comic Books did two reviews each year and spread its printed lists widely. *Parents' Magazine* bought them, together with covering articles, each year from the beginning until 1956 when the level of the comics had risen to the extent that comparatively little complaint was heard. Since then, the Committee has done only spot checking once or twice a year but generally has not printed its lists. However, this year, 1964, it is evaluating all the comic books that can be obtained locally in order to be sure that their trend is not slumping.

A letter from *Parents' Magazine* in 1957, answering one from the Committee that it would not be making a complete evaluation of the comic books that year for the reason that the quality of printed matter carried in the comic magazines had improved, brought a reply embodying the following observation:

We have considered your last letter for several weeks now and have finally decided that the Committee on Evaluation of Comic Books has done such a good job that it has practically put itself out of work. The comics are certainly much better now than when the Committee was first created.

THE MORALITY SEEKERS:
A STUDY OF ORGANIZED FILM
CRITICISM IN THE UNITED STATES

Jack Schwartz

THE STUDENT of film criticism and censorship in the United States is beset with a variety of often conflicting means by which civic, religious, and governmental groups attempt to "protect" the public from some alleged moral harm attributable to film content. Within governmental spheres, the censorship of films has been a very delicate issue. The Supreme Court in 1952 ruled that the freedom of motion pictures is guaranteed by the First Amendment to the Constitution, thus rescinding the Court's decision to *uphold* censorship laws in 1915. In the past decade, state and local laws providing for the censorship of movies have generally run into serious opposition from the Supreme Court. . . . The . . . Court decision supporting local pre-exhibition censorship in the case of the film *Don Juan* in Chicago gives promise of encouraging the increased activity of film censorship generally.

The increased sensitivity to sex and violence on the screen by various civic and religious groups has tended to increase the pressure on local, state, and federal government agencies to take action in regulating film content. The use of national

Unpublished paper from the Institute of Communications Research, University of Illinois, 1960 (tables renumbered from original). Used with the permission of author. The footnotes appear in the Notes and References section at the end of this book.

reviewing boards has frequently been proposed as an alternative solution to government interference. Religious groups, particularly various Protestant sects, who have hitherto been considerably less involved with an organized criticism of film content than the Catholic National Legion of Decency, are now making fairly widely publicized statements condemning the plethora of sex, sadism, crime, and immorality on the screen.

A legitimate question to ask, therefore, is: What are the existing organized groups engaged in film criticism sensitive to, since it is their advice and support which would likely be solicited if a national reviewing board were established. Also, what elements of *film content* are the existing groups sensitive to? What elements of *film content* do they find objectionable? And what relationship do the existing moral evaluations and audience classifications have on film box office? The answers which this paper will attempt to provide to these questions will be based upon the ratings, criticisms and comments of the two most popular organizations involved in film criticism in the United States: the National Legion of Decency and the Film Estimate Board of National Organizations.

Perhaps the best known, and most frequently criticized, organization involved in the *moral evaluation* of films is the National Legion of Decency. This organization, composed of Roman Catholic laymen and clergy, regularly reviews practically all domestic and foreign films exhibited in the United States. Its "principal aim . . . is to discourage the production and patronizing of films which present false moral standards which, in turn, lower traditional morality."[1] The former executive director of the Legion, Father Joseph Daly, elaborated on this position by stating that "the Legion has one clear, simple objective—to insure for the public, as legitimate recreation, a wholesome screen against which there can be no objection on moral grounds. Its strongest weapon has been an aroused public opinion, and public opinion will continue to be its most effective safeguard against salacious motion pictures."[2]

In order to guide Catholics, as well as the general public, in the moral values, or lack of them, in a given film, the Legion publishes, bi-weekly, a list of the films currently being distributed in the United States along with the "moral classification" of the film. The "scale of morality" by which each film is reviewed by the Legion is something akin to a five-point scale . . . as follows:

A-I   Morally Unobjectionable for General Patronage. . . .
A-II   Morally Unobjectionable for Adults and Adolescents.
           . . .
A-III   Morally Unobjectionable for Adults. . . .
B   Morally Objectionable in Part for All. . . .
C   Condemned. . . .

In addition to these five classifications of morality, the Legion has a "Separate Classification" given to a very small number of films which "while not morally offensive, require some analysis and explanation as a protection to the uninformed against wrong interpretations and false conclusions."[3]

The ratings of the Legion of Decency, unlike the Index of Forbidden Books, do not have the force of ecclesiastical law. It is only the diocesian clergy who "may strictly forbid the faithful of his diocese to go to a particular film. [Then] all subjects of the bishop . . . are bound under obedience to carry out the bishop's orders. The Legion of Decency issues no orders to anyone." (Dulles, 1956)

• • •

. . . In judging the effect of a particular film on the moral behavior of the audience, the Legion reviewer is concerned with the "morality of the theme and the decency of treatment." Artistic, entertainment, or technical qualities of the film are not considered. Mrs. James Looram (1955), chairman of the Legion's motion picture department, believes that the theme of the movie is what largely determines its morality. The reviewer "ought to be able to say that the movie 'is about a person who is faced with this or that problem and does this or that about it.' *It is the answer given, rather than the problem presented, that constitutes the morality of the theme. . . .*"

THE FILM ESTIMATE BOARD OF
NATIONAL ORGANIZATIONS

Civic groups have been criticizing film content ever since *The Widow Jones,* an 1896 film, was attacked for containing a kiss. The National Board of Review, originally set up to

control film content within reasonable moral bounds by the
Motion Picture Producers and Distributors of America
(MPPDA), apparently failed to live up to its expectations.
One pointed criticism of the Board's work was made in 1919
by the General Federation of Women's Clubs:

[The National Board of Review] has a stream of literature
[which] is the motion picture's industry's attempt to furnish well-
intentioned, reform-bent ladies with "harmless busy work." They
persistently and blatantly preach, "promote the good, the beautiful,
smother evil with good." Meanwhile the stream of filthy film flows.
. . . (Inglis, 1947)

At the time Will Hays was made president of the MPPDA,
the film industry made attempts to support a review board
composed of civic groups whose job it would be to criticize
the industry's own product. . . .
    . . . In the 1940's, the California branch of the industry's
Community Service Department began publishing the evaluations of individual films by the organization in a publication
called *Joint Estimates,* the name later changed to *The Green
Sheet* in 1959. The previewing committee of the Film Estimate Board, whose evaluations appear in *The Green Sheet,*
currently represents a membership of about fifteen millions.
The current membership of the previewing committee includes the American Jewish Committee, American Library
Association, Federation of Motion Picture Councils, General
Federation of Women's Clubs, National Congress of Parents
and Teachers, National Federation of Music Clubs, National
Society Daughters of the American Revolution, Protestant
Motion Picture Council, and the Schools Motion Picture Com-
mittee.

• • •

The audience classification of *The Green Sheet* and the
Legion of Decency are similar in some ways and unlike in
others. Both groups are concerned with the age levels suitable for the audiences of particular films. The Legion has its
Morally Unobjectionable for Adults, and Adults and Adolescents categories. The Film Estimate Board has the following
classifications: A-Adults, MY-Mature Young People, Y-Young
People, and F-Family. . . .
The purpose of the present paper will be to examine the
sensitivities of both the National Legion of Decency and the

Film Estimate Board by a detailed analysis of the comments which each organization makes about films released in the United States. I will also examine the relationship between the audience classification of each organization and the box-office estimates for each film rated by both organizations. And finally, a comparison will be made between the ratings of both groups when rating the same film.

RESEARCH METHODOLOGY

In analysing the sensitivities of the Legion of Decency, an examination was made of the comments made about each film reviewed since 1940. In 1940, the Legion began to explain the reasons why films were rated B-Morally Objectionable and C-Condemned. By subjecting the descriptions given to the 1694 films rated B and C between 1940 and 1960 to a content analysis it is possible to detect the elements of film content to which the Legion was, and is, particularly sensitive.

Approximately eighty different reasons for so rating B and C films are given by the Legion; however, these can be grouped into eight general categories. Occasionally, a film is objected to for more than one reason, the average number of reasons given for rating a film B or C being 1.4 per film.

The eight categories which were formed are as follows:

Category	Reasons for Rating Films B and C Included in Each Category
Sexual Suggestiveness	Suggestive or indecent costuming, dances, sequences, situations, paintings, dialogue, songs, remarks, or general atmosphere; Overemphasis on sex, prostitution, illicit love, or sensuality; Sordidness or sordid implications; Lustful kissing; Vulgarity.
Immorality	Condoning "immoral" or "illicit" actions; "Low moral tone"; Glorification of immoral characters or behavior; Frivolous treatment of purity or virtue; Offending, denying, or ignoring Christian and traditional standards of morality and decency; Lack of, or insufficient, moral compensation for an immoral act; Sympathetic portrayal or revenge; Undue sympathy for wrongdoing.

Category	*Reasons for Rating Films B and C Included in Each Category*
Divorce	Presentation of, sympathetic attitude toward, acceptability of, or justification of, divorce; Light treatment of marriage; Condoning of adultery, or adulterer; Presentation of free love, or trial marriage.
Brutality	Portrayal of excessive brutality; Sadism, morbidity; Gruesomeness.
Crime	Sympathy for crime, criminals; Condoning or glorifying the act of taking the law into one's own hands; Disrespect for lawful authority; Lack of, or insufficient, retribution for crime; Justification of murder or euthanasia; Crime minutely detailed; Preoccupation with, or sympathetic portrayal of, drug addiction; Sympathetic portrayal of duelling.
Disrespectful or Erroneous Presentation of Religion	Misrepresentation, misunderstanding, or ridiculing of Christian and/or traditional religious beliefs, practices, or persons; Disparaging, or irreverent presentations of religion, religious persons, or the name of the Deity; Credence to the presentation of superstition, spiritism, voodooism, reincarnation, or soul transmigration; Emphasis on fatalism or pessimism; Doctrine of free will portrayed erroneously.
Suicide	Presentation of, glorification of, preoccupation with, or the portrayal of the intention to commit, suicide or hara-kiri.
Miscellaneous	(Items appearing only once which are not suitable for inclusion in any of the above categories.)

The sensitivities of the Film Estimate Board are not so conveniently listed by that organization. While each organization participating in the Film Estimate Board undoubtedly has a different system of values and sensitivities, there is no way to detect this when all participating organizations agree on a given audience rating for a particular film. However, not infrequently the organizations do *not* agree and the dissenting organizations have their disagreements and reasons listed in *The Green Sheet*. . . . The disagreements, and reasons for disagreeing, of each organization were subjected to a content analysis in order to reveal each group's particular sensitivities and values.

One of the greatest concerns of the founders of the Legion of Decency was that the reaction to objectionable films rated B and C would, rather than discourage popularity for the film, increase the interest and attendance at such films *because* of the "Objectionable" label. On the other hand . . . several reviews of films in trade journals have stressed the fact that a particular film would have a small box-office in certain sections of the country *because* of the "Objectionable" label. Similar statements have been made about films seriously criticized by the Film Estimate Board. In order to obtain a better appreciation of the relation of Legion and Board ratings to box-office estimates, cross tabulations were made on Legion and Board ratings with box-office estimates given in the trade journal *Variety* for films released in the eleven-year period 1950 to 1960. A total of 2485 estimates were used where a Legion rating was available, and 1935 estimates where a Board rating was available. *Variety* reviews were omitted when the box-office estimate was not mentioned or was so nebulous and uncertain that, in effect, no clear prediction was made.

The evaluation of a *Variety* box-office estimate for a particular film was based on the inclusion of the following terms in the Variety review.

Rating Along a "Box-Office Rating Scale"	Terms Used in the *Variety* Review in Order to Rate Box-Office Estimate Along Scale at Left
5	Smash, blockbuster, sock-top, outstanding, exceptional, great
4	Above average, wide appeal, good, should cash in
3	Average, fair, routine, moderate, suitable, acceptable, passable
2	Below average, second rate, weak, poor, filler, cheapie, questionable, slim chances, meager prospect, "lower half of double bill"
1	Terrible, stinko, floppo, worst

The last analysis made, that of relating ratings by both the National Legion of Decency and the Film Estimate Board to the same films, was done by assigning a numerical value to the ratings of both organizations. In order to compare the ratings of both organizations to the same films, it was necessary to establish some scale of comparability for the different systems of ratings used by the Legion of Decency and the Film Estimate Board. Listed below is the numerical value assigned to each of the Legion and Board ratings.

Numerical Value	Film Estimate Board Classifications Used	National Legion of Decency Classifications Used
4	Young People, Family	Morally Unobjectionable for General Patronage
3	Adults and Young People, Adults-Mature Young People-and-Young People	Morally Unobjectionable for Adults and Adolescents
2	Adults and Mature Young People (only)	Morally Unobjectionable for Adults
1	Adults (only)	Morally Objectionable in Part for All, and Condemned

The Legion of Decency and Film Estimate Board ratings with the above numerical values were used to compare the ratings for all films rated by both organizations from January, 1946, to December, 1960 (N-2551 films).

RESULTS OF RESEARCH

The major reason why a film reviewed by the Legion is rated B or C is that an item appears in the film which the Legion claims is sexually suggestive. Over half of the films rated B and C were deemed objectionable on this ground. One-third were objectionable because of general immorality, while less than one-fourth of the objectionable films received the B or C classification because of the inclusion of divorce in the film's content.[4] The other objectionable categories: brutality, crime, a disrespectful or erroneous presentation of religion, and suicide, each are responsible for less than 10 per cent of the reasons for B- or C-rating films. . . .

Year-by-year trends in the proportion of total films considered objectionable or condemnable for inclusion of items in the various categories reveal some striking changes. However, the serious problem comes when one tries to interpret the trends. Are changes in objectionable content in the films due to actual changes in film content, or changes in the sensitivities of the reviewers for the Legion? Or some compounding of both? In either case, it is interesting to note that the objections to sexual suggestiveness, immorality, and brutality have shown a fairly steady increase in the proportion of B and C rated films so classified because of objectionable content in these areas. The brutality category has shown the most dramatic and sudden increase, however. For the fifteen-year period from 1940 to 1954, the average per cent of films classified B or C for this reason was less than six per year. However, the average annual per cent for the past six years, 1955–1960, has risen to 18.5. Objections because of divorce, suicide, and a disrespectful or erroneous presentation of religion have shown a gradual *decrease* since 1940. . . .

The proportion of B and C rated films to the total number of films previewed by the Legion of Decency has shown a steady increase since 1937. Seven per cent of the total films reviewed by the Legion in 1938 were rated B and C; this proportion grew steadily until a peak was reached in 1957 when over 35 per cent of all films reviewed by the Legion were rated B and C. In order to have a more quantitative index of the categories which have, or have not, contributed to the gradual increase in the proportion of B and C films to total films reviewed, a correlation was made of the year-by-year proportion of films rated B and C for the inclusion of objections in each of the objectionable categories and the year-by-year proportion of films rated B and C to total films previewed. The results . . . indicate that immorality, sexual suggestiveness, and brutality are very positively correlated with the gradual increase in the proportion of B and C films. The categories to which one may suppose Catholics to be most sensitive, divorce and suicide, show strong *negative* correlations with the gradual increase in proportion of B and C films. Caution must be used in interpreting these results to infer changes in film content, or changes in the Legion's sensitivities and values, or some combination of the two.

The box-office estimates for Legion of Decency rated films in the Morally Unobjectionable for General Patronage classification was slightly less than the estimates for films rated Morally Objectionable and Condemned. However, the difference was not statistically significant. The average box-office estimates for each Legion classification level are given in Table 1. The differences between the lowest and the highest box-office estimates are not statistically significant.

TABLE 1. Variety *Box-Office Estimates and Legion of Decency Classifications*

Legion of Decency Classification	Variety Box-Office Estimate Scale Rating						
	(Best) 5	4	3	2	(Worst) 1	Total	Average Scale Rating
Morally Unobjectionable for General Patronage	26	267	465	126	3	887	3.21
Morally Unobjectionable for Adults and Adolescents	5	63	75	37	0	180	3.20
Morally Unobjectionable for Adults	22	277	421	136	2	858	3.21
Morally Objectionable and Condemned	30	193	248	87	2	560	3.29
All Classifications	83	800	1209	386	7	2485	3.228

The box-office estimates for Film Estimate Board classifications are somewhat more widespread than the Legion classifications. The average box-office rating for all the Film Estimate Board classifications, given in Table 2, was 3.291 compared to the mean of 3.228 for the Legion classifications. This difference can probably be explained on the basis that the Film Estimate Board classifies somewhat fewer films than the Legion—this smaller number of films generally being the more popular in general exhibition theatres. The Legion of Decency reviews a larger number of films, including a considerable number shown in specialized theatres, e.g., art and foreign-language theatres. The Film Estimate Board classification of films suited for family audiences received the highest box-office estimates which were significantly different from the lowest box-office estimates recorded for films in the Board's adults only classification.

TABLE 2. Variety *Box-Office Estimates and Film Estimate Board Classifications*

Film Estimate Board Classification	Variety Box-Office Estimate Scale Rating						
	(Best) 5	4	3	2	(Worst) 1	Total	Average Scale Rating
Family, Young People	17	212	225	37	3	524	3.39
Adults and Young People, Adults-Young People and Mature People	28	280	430	107	2	847	3.27
Adults and Mature Young People	11	82	87	30	2	212	3.33
Adults	6	108	184	53	1	352	3.18
All Classifications	62	682	956	227	8	1935	3.291

A content analysis of the rating disagreements by Film Estimate Board organization representatives for the 1950–60 period revealed some generally consistent patterns for several of the participating organizations. The disagreements could generally be placed in either of two classes: either the disagreement was one of *limiting* or one of *expanding* the audience suitable for seeing the film. An example will perhaps more clearly illustrate this: let's say that the majority of participating organizations believe a film suitable for adults and mature young people; however, organizations X and Y feel that the film is suitable for a family audience. In such a case, organizations X and Y would be considered as disagreeing in the direction of expanding the audience suitable for the film. Were organizations X and Y to disagree and feel the film should be seen only by adults, then those organizations would be considered as disagreeing in the direction of limiting the audience for the film. It is interesting to note that particular members of the Board fairly persistently disagree to expand the potential audience, while other groups persistently disagree to limit the potential audience for the film. For the sake of simplicity, we'll call the groups disagreeing in the direction of expanding the audience "liberal," and the groups disagreeing in the direction of limiting the audience "conservative."

The most "conservative" Board members . . . are the Protestant Motion Picture Council, Girl Scouts, Business and Professional Women's Clubs (no longer on the Board), and the Congress of Parents and Teachers. The Protestant Motion Picture Council has disagreed with the majority rating on no less than 68 occasions, *each time* deciding to limit the audience. Other notable "conservative" Board members are the Daughters of the American Revolution and the General Federation of Women's Clubs. The more "liberal" Board members are the American Jewish Committee, American Library Association and the Daughters of the British Empire (no longer on the Board). These groups disagreed to expand the audience in 72 per cent, 71 per cent and 71 per cent of their disagreements respectively. It is also notable that the conservative organizations disagreed much more frequently with the majority estimates than the more liberal members. The three more liberal organizations—American Jewish Committee, American Library Association, and Daughters of the British Empire—disagreed with the majority an average of only twenty times each during the period under study, 1946–60. The five conservative organizations—Business and Professional Women's Clubs, Daughters of the American Revolution, General Federation of Women's Clubs, Protestant Motion Picture Council, and the National Congress of Parents and Teachers—disagreed with the majority an average of sixty-six times each.

The sensitivities of Film Estimate Board members can also be ascertained by examining the content of the comments which organizations occasionally make to the film generally, or in order to explain the reasons for their disagreement with the majority rating. The content of the films reviewed by the Board which elicited the greatest comment by Board members were on sex, brutality, crime, alcohol, and the portrayal of religion and of ethnic groups. The comments to films reviewed between 1950 and 1960 were examined. The subject of sex was mentioned in regard to 19 films, with the Protestant Motion Pictures Council, Girl Scouts, and General

Federation of Women's Club representatives most frequently taking note of this issue in film content in eight, seven, and five of the films for the three groups respectively. While brutality and crime were mentioned with regard to fifteen films each, no organization registered any exceptionally consistent sensitivity to this subject, the comments on these subjects being spread thin and evenly for all Board members. Alcohol consumption was mentioned with regard to fifteen films, and the Protestant Motion Picture Council made a complaint about this *each time*. This same group complained about the portrayal of religion or religious characters in eleven of the thirteen films in which this subject was commented upon. Sensitivity to the portrayal of ethnic groups was most frequently noted by the National Council of Jewish Women, and its successor, the American Jewish Committee. These groups reacted to the portrayal of ethnic groups in nine of the eleven films where this subject was mentioned.

The last research conducted on the National Legion of Decency and the Film Estimate Board was a study of the comparability of the ratings of both organizations when rating the same films. Using the numerical values assigned to the ratings of both groups listed previously, the average value for Legion of Decency classifications compared to Film Estimate Board scale values was as follows:

Film Estimate Board Classification	Average Scale Value for Same Film Reviewed by the Legion of Decency
4	3.47
3	2.62
2	2.05
1	1.56

As the Board rating became lower, that is as the audience rated became more adult, the Legion rating became more morally objectionable for general patronage. A similar finding occurs when the comparisons are reversed, as follows:

National Legion of Decency Classification	Average Scale Value for Same Film Reviewed by Film Estimate Board
4	3.46
3	2.47
2	2.46
1	1.88

Assuming that the numerical values assigned both organizations' ratings are comparable [as mentioned above] a comparison of both groups' ratings yields a correlation coefficient of $+.562$. Considering the large number of films rated by both organizations and used for comparison in the 1950–60 period—a total of 2551 films—the correlation seems strongly to suggest that the Legion of Decency and the Film Estimate Board have much in common when they rate the same films. . . .

SUMMARY

The National Legion of Decency and the Film Estimate Board of National Organizations are the two most active and most widely known groups involved in motion picture criticism. The Legion's ratings are based mainly upon a particular film's moral content, while the Film Estimate Board members generally base their audience classifications upon the age of the audience recommended to see the film. However, both groups have become somewhat more alike in recent years. Several years ago the Legion instituted a new audience classification which did recognize that audience age, as well as morality, was a factor in rating films. And within the past few years the Legion has begun to lend its positive support to films which it believes are excellently produced, both artistically and in regard to the film's treatment of personal and social issues. The Film Estimate Board introduced a "*mature* young people" classification several years ago, implicitly recognizing that age is inadequate, per se, in making recommendations for film audiences.

When the Legion of Decency feels a film is morally objectionable, the film is rated "B" or "C." The proportion of these films has been increasing steadily since the Legion began rating films in 1936. The bases for rating films B and C have been, in order of importance, the portrayal of sexual suggestiveness, immorality, divorce, brutality, crime, a disrespectful or erroneous presentation of religion, and suicide. The reasons under each of these seven criteria were listed, along with trends in the relative proportion for each criterion from 1940–60. The criteria of immorality, sexual suggestiveness, and brutality are positively correlated with the gradual increase in B and C films, while the proportions of films considered objectionable because of the presentation of suicide or divorce are negatively correlated with the gradual increase in proportion of B and C films. Box-office predictions for the success of particular films, based on *Variety* reviews, show slight, but statistically insignificant, differences in relation to the various Legion classifications.

A comparison of the Legion of Decency and the Film Estimate Board ratings for the same films shows that a good deal of similarity exists between both groups. A correlation of ratings by both groups for the same set of films was + .562. The relation of Board ratings to box-office estimates showed more significant differences to exist between box-office predictions and Board ratings than in the case of Legion ratings. The sensitivities of the organization representatives of the Board to particular elements of film content were determined from an analysis of comments made by individual organization representatives following the review of the film appearing in the Board's publication, *The Green Sheet*. Such an analysis indicated that certain members of the Board were more sensitive than others to such elements of film content as sex, alcohol consumption, and the portrayal of religion and religious characters, and ethnic groups. Certain organization representatives on the Board were also shown consistently to disagree with the audience classification of the majority of members on the Board. For some groups, these disagreements more often involve a recommendation to expand the potential suitable audience for the film to include more persons, while other groups disagree with the majority in the direction of limiting the potential suitable audience.

In view of the plethora of sex, violence, and immorality alleged to be all too plentiful in film content, as many groups charge, and the increasing pressure on state, local, and federal governments to decide the issue of censorship before exhibition of films, many groups and individuals have felt that a reviewing board of civic-minded persons should be used to preview films. The purpose of this paper has been to show what particular issues of film content certain active "civic-minded" groups are sensitive toward. When the general public is aware of these sensitivities, the advisability of previewing groups containing members of the National Legion of Decency and/or the Film Estimate Board can be better decided.

PART VI

Regulation and Control: Governmental Participation

> Were it left to me to decide whether we should have
> a government without newspapers, or newspapers
> without government, I should not hesitate a moment
> to prefer the latter.
>
> THOMAS JEFFERSON

AN EXTREMELY vexing question is now before us: What is
the role, what the responsibility of government for the content of the media of mass communication? More specifically,
should government measure out the quantity of violence that
will be tolerated?

Broadly viewed, there are at least two aspects to this problem—a negative aspect, control of the deleterious, and a
positive aspect, promotion of the desirable. Thus, theoretically, the machinery of government could be invoked directly
to censor media content, or it could be employed, directly
or indirectly, by the threat of investigation or the offer of
license preferences, mailing privileges, subsidies, and tax
discounts, to encourage the media to perform in accord with
standards widely conceived to serve the public interest.

Simply stated, government could carry a stick or could
offer a carrot to induce a mode of media performance. Since
there are various layers of government, from the local to the
federal, and since there are legislative, judicial, and administrative features at each level, the possible means of inter-
vening with either power or influence are many and the
question of governmental participation in media regulation
is an enormously complex one. So complex, in fact, that the
present consideration of the subject is necessarily limited to
a few selected aspects of the urge to suppress or regulate
the expression of violence by formal means.

The material in this section will not trace the intricate
history of governmental action against media content. The
interested reader may launch an inquiry into this area by
referring to Winick (1959), Paul and Schwartz (1961), and
Coons (1961). Such sources specify that, technically, censorship by government may occur in accordance with the
doctrine of prior restraint, involving prohibition of certain
expressions, or the doctrine of subsequent punishment, involving a penalty after the expression. However, the First
Amendment of the Constitution forbids the federal government to impose any system of prior restraint. Clearly, the

Founding Fathers did not envisage government as the Great Cultural Mother regulating the spheres of communication by universal decree. As a result, there has emerged an American tradition of outspoken opposition to government monitoring of opinion and expression, an opposition that rallies around the belief that while ideas may be dangerous, the suppression of them by government is fatal to a democratic society.

Despite this tradition, efforts are constantly being made at all levels of government to redefine and test the limits of free expression with respect to such controversial media content as violence, though this material has over the years received less attention than that bearing on obscenity. Naturally, for understandable political reasons, many of these efforts are responses by government officials to the actions generated by voluntary associations, as illustrated in the previous section.

With respect to media violence, the most prominent action at the federal level is found in the investigations conducted by congressional committees. Their activity—sometimes characterized as "government by raised eyebrow"—gains its importance through the power of publicity. By exposing media excesses in the portrayal of violence, they generate defensive reactions by the media to correct their offenses through self-regulation. Adverse publicity about media performance is probably a greater factor in affecting media adjustment than is the threat of legislation allowing government censorship, because no one has found a way to overcome the real difficulties in formulating legislation that would set standards for policing content in ways that would be constitutional.

The style of congressional investigation of witnesses is illustrated in the second article below. Here the fascinating testimony of William Gaines, the creator of Horror Comics, who later became the publisher of *Mad* magazine, is presented in some detail. His testimony, dealing with a comic-book cover which shows "a man with a bloody ax holding a woman's head up which has been severed from her body," created a sensational outpouring of publicity in the nation's press. This publicity was a significant factor in drawing the disparate elements of comic-book publishing into an association to engage in self-regulation designed to stem the portrayal of violence in that medium (described further in Part VII). The case represents a prime example of the power of government to induce media responsibility and alter media content through exposure and publicity.

Effective as congressional committees might be in particular cases, however, many people are not satisfied to let the question of governmental participation in the regulation and control of mass communication rest on such a wavering mechanism. Harry Ashmore, in the final article, proposes the founding of a Public Commission that "would have no power to censor, only to expose, complain, praise, and exhort —to perform, that is, on behalf of the mass media the functions the media presume to perform on behalf of all other institutions colored in any way with the public interest."

And so the great debate goes on, with fresh ideas added in each new exchange. Clearly, the First Amendment was not the last word on the subject of governmental participation in the regulation and control of mass communication.

CRIME SHOWS ON TV—A FEDERAL CRACKDOWN COMING

U. S. News & World Report

NOW THE broadcasting industry has been warned to cut down on "televised crime, violence and brutality" or face possible police action by Congress.

The warning came in a report—sharply critical of the television networks—issued on October 27 by the Senate Subcommittee on Juvenile Delinquency.

A three-year study. Findings in a three-year study declare that "violence, crime, brutality and related antisocial behavior continue to dominate the dramatic presentations which appear on the nation's television screens."

The report said that "violence and other antisocial behavior are, to an overwhelming degree, televised during time periods in which the children audience is a large one."

The Senators cited "testimony and impressive research evidence that a relationship has been conclusively established between televised crime and violence and antisocial attitudes and behavior among juvenile viewers."

The Subcommittee report asserted:

The extent to which violence and crime are currently portrayed on the nation's television screens is clearly excessive. And in the face of repeated warnings from officials directly concerned with coping with juvenile delinquency and from competent researchers that this kind of television fare can be harmful to the young viewer, the television industry generally has shown little disposition to substantially reduce the degree of violence to which it exposes the American public.

If anything, the broadcasting industry appears to have recently added a new dimension to the kinds of violence and criminality paraded across the television screens. This new trend has drawn the criticism of some of the nation's most respected critics. A columnist for *The Chicago Tribune* put the matter succinctly when he wrote:

Reprinted from *U. S. News & World Report,* published at Washington; November 9, 1964, pp. 49–50. Copyright 1964 by U. S. News & World Report, Inc.

"Television in 1963 has become something of a blur to me. It's hard to tell one sick drama from another. . . . There were stories about impotence, incest, homosexuality, adultery, euthanasia, matricide, and I'm too embarrassed to go on with the list."

Behavior influenced.   The Subcommittee did not contend that television is the only cause of juvenile delinquency, but its report said this:

It is clear that television, whose impact on the public mind is equal to or greater than that of any other medium, is a factor in molding the character, attitudes and behavior patterns of America's young people.

Senator Thomas J. Dodd (Dem.), of Connecticut, the Subcommittee chairman, pointed out that the group's first inquiry into television programing was made in 1954 "because of concern over the trend to violence."

"The results of that inquiry proved there were numerous violations of the Television Code regarding crime and brutality," the Senator said. "But the television industry, through its chief spokesman, the National Association of Broadcasters and through which its image is projected to the public, pleaded for another chance at 'self-regulation' through its 'Code of Good Practices.' "

But in 10 years, Senator Dodd went on, crime and violence shows have "increased 200 per cent" and "the NAB Code is violated with impunity."

The Senator also commented:

The industry's claim that this Code is an effective vehicle cannot be substantiated in light of the evidence of chronic violation. Network programing policies which deliberately call for the insertion of violence, crime and brutality are hardly conducive to building respect for any central authority within the industry.

The Subcommittee's hearings show that the NAB Code "has been broken hundreds of times," Senator Dodd said. The report declared: "The NAB Code lacks teeth. It is impossible to enforce. The networks themselves admit that they have the last word in programing and the content thereof."

62 million TV sets.   Senator Dodd said that, as of last January, "an estimated 62 million television sets were operating in 51.2 million American homes." He added: "This means each day more than 25 million children 12 and under look at television. These children, on the average, spend more time watching television than they do in either school or church."

"Each year," the Senator observed, "the number of television sets in American homes increases. Coupled with the general increase in population, this means that the number of children exposed to violence, crime and brutality will also increase unless there is a dramatic change. . . ."

The Subcommittee reported that, of the three major networks, only the Columbia Broadcasting System showed "any significant decline in programed violence." The report added, however; "There remains considerable room for improvement. All too many CBS dramatic shows continue to violate various sections" of the NAB Code.

The report attributed to top management of the American Broadcasting Company a "preoccupation with crime and violence." It expressed the Senators' view that the National Broadcasting Company "continued during 1963–64 to contribute all too substantially to the violence, crime and horror trend which monopolizes so much of the television fare to which the nation's children are regularly exposed."

The report listed examples of objectionable productions. Many of them have been dropped from network schedules, but continue to be shown by some stations. Among the shows listed:

• ABC's *The Untouchables*, a series in which, the report said, ABC officials "did not hesitate to override the objections of sponsor representatives to the inclusion of excessive violence."

• ABC's *Bus Stop*. Said the report: "One *Bus Stop* episode was so brutal and sex-ridden that advance complaints were registered by sponsors, the ABC continuity people and the NAB Code authorities alike. Yet that episode, titled 'A Lion Walks Among Us,' was televised to the mass public."

• CBS's *Route 66*, which the report called "particularly relevant both because of its focus on violence and sex and because of the network's role in developing the focus."

• CBS's *Gunsmoke*. The report noted that one episode, entitled "Dry Well," included "physical abuse, torture, and almost inhuman insensitivity to suffering on the part of one character," and that the characterizations portrayed included "a fiendish old man, a killer, an unfaithful wife and an amoral son."

• NBC's *The Lieutenant.* The report described a two-minute sequence during which "there were 25 blows struck, including kicks to the groin, the stomach and the kidneys and two attempts to stomp on one participant's face. . . ."

• NBC's *The Virginian.* The report's comment: "One episode, about which there were several substantial complaints, was entitled 'Man of Violence.' In just this one show there were 13 individual killings, 9 by shooting, 2 by knives and gun butts, 1 by torture and 1 by smothering."

The Subcommittee urged that the networks themselves take corrective action. The Senators proposed:

1. Joint development by the networks of prime-time programs specifically designed for youngsters.

2. Agreement between the Federal Communications Commission and the industry on "realistic standards for programing in the public interest."

3. Mandatory action against violators of the NAB Code. The Code's seal of approval never yet has been removed from a broadcaster despite repeated violations, the report said.

4. A community polling system in which viewers can express their opinions on local programming "and make them felt where the licensee is concerned."

5. A co-ordinated plan to develop more information about the impact of television on juvenile behavior.

Will Congress act?   Senator Dodd made it clear that the actions of the industry itself will determine whether legislation aimed at curbing TV crime and violence is introduced. He said:

"Effective self-policing is the desirable approach to this problem which poses so clear a threat to our present and our future.

But the patience of Congress, though considerable, is not endless. The public's demand for concrete results grows more intense, and indeed it should.

"I LIKE THE IDEA OF SADISM . . ."

In one section of its report on TV, the Senate Subcommittee on Juvenile Delinquency listed these comments by some TV executives on various programs under their guidance.

■ "I wish we could come up with a different device than running the man down with a car, as we have done this now in three different shows. I like the idea of sadism, but I hope we can come up with another approach to it." (Note to a script writer)

■ "This scene is the roughest I have ever seen and I don't know if we can get away with it, but let's leave it in. Have a feeling you may have to kill the girls off the camera." (Note to a producer)

■ "I don't believe that we should subject the American people as a whole to childish themes in the entertainment we put on just because children happen to be up at 10:00 viewing them. I consider this an adult western; I consider this an adult theme." (Statement to the Subcommittee, about a show including torture, a fiendish old man, a killer, an unfaithful wife, an amoral son)

■ "I have no firsthand knowledge about whose suggestion it was. I know only that I was told to put sex and violence in my show." (Statement to the Subcommittee)

■ "I did not find it objectionable . . . I think there were scenes of physical violence within the program. But I would not call the program a violent program." (Statement to the Subcommittee about a Christmas Eve show including 13 killings—9 by shooting, 2 by knives and gun butts, 1 by torture, 1 by smothering—plus 5 fights and 3 assaults)

CONGRESSIONAL INTERROGATION
OF THE CREATOR OF HORROR COMICS

U. S. Senate

THE CHAIRMAN: You may proceed in your own manner.

MR. GAINES: Gentlemen, I would like to make a short statement. I am here as an individual publisher.

MR. HANNOCH: Will you give your name and address, for the record?

Excerpts from the testimony of William M. Gaines, Publisher, Entertaining Comics Group, New York, N.Y., in U. S. Congress. Senate. Committee on the Judiciary. Subcommittee to Investigate Juvenile Delinquency, *Juvenile Delinquency (comic books)*; hearings pursuant to S. 190, April 21, 22, and June 4, 1954 (83:2, 1954), pp. 97–109.

MR. GAINES: My name is William Gaines. My business address is 225 Lafayette Street, New York City. I am a publisher of the Entertaining Comics Group.

I am a graduate of the school of education of New York University. I have the qualifications to teach in secondary schools, high schools.

What then am I doing before this committee? I am a comic-book publisher. My group is known as EC, Entertaining Comics.

I am here as a voluntary witness. I asked for and was given this chance to be heard.

Two decades ago my late father was instrumental in starting the comic magazine industry. He edited the first few issues of the first modern comic magazine, *Famous Funnies*. My father was proud of the industry he helped found. He was bringing enjoyment to millions of people.

The heritage he left is the vast comic-book industry which employs thousands of writers, artists, engravers, and printers.

It has weaned hundreds of thousands of children from pictures to the printed word. It has stirred their imagination, given them an outlet for their problems and frustrations, but most important, given them millions of hours of entertainment.

My father before me was proud of the comics he published. My father saw in the comic book a vast field of visual education. He was a pioneer.

Sometimes he was ahead of his time. He published *Picture Stories from Science*, *Picture Stories from World History*, and *Picture Stories from American History*.

He published *Picture Stories from the Bible*.

I would like to offer these in evidence.

• • •

Since 1942 we have sold more than 5 million copies of *Picture Stories from the Bible* in the United States. It is widely used by churches and schools to make religion more real and vivid.

Picture Stories from the Bible is published throughout the world in dozens of translations. But it is nothing more nor nothing less than a comic magazine.

I publish comic magazines in addition to *Picture Stories from the Bible*. For example, I publish horror comics. I was the first publisher in these United States to publish horror comics. I am responsible, I started them.

Some may not like them. That is a matter of personal taste. It would be just as difficult to explain the harmless thrill of a horror story to a Dr. Wertham as it would be to explain the sublimity of love to a frigid old maid.

My father was proud of the comics he published, and I am proud of the comics I publish. We use the best writers, the finest artists; we spare nothing to make each magazine, each story, each page, a work of art.

As evidence of this, I might point out that we have the highest sales in individual distribution. I don't mean highest sales in comparison to comics of another type. I mean highest sales in comparison to other horror comics. The magazine is one of the few remaining—the comic magazine is one of the few remaining pleasures that a person may buy for a dime today. Pleasure is what we sell, entertainment, reading enjoyment. Entertaining reading has never harmed anyone. Men of good will, free men, should be very grateful for one sentence in the statement made by Federal Judge John M. Woolsey when he lifted the ban on *Ulysses*. Judge Woolsey said:

> It is only with the normal person that the law is concerned.

May I repeat, he said, "It is only with the normal person that the law is concerned." Our American children are for the most part normal children. They are bright children, but those who want to prohibit comic magazines seem to see dirty, sneaky, perverted monsters who use the comics as a blueprint for action.

Perverted little monsters are few and far between. They don't read comics. The chances are most of them are in schools for retarded children.

What are we afraid of? Are we afraid of our own children? Do we forget that they are citizens, too, and entitled to select what to read or do? We think our children are so evil, simple minded, that it takes a story of murder to set them to murder, a story of robbery to set them to robbery?

Jimmy Walker once remarked that he never knew a girl to be ruined by a book. Nobody has ever been ruined by a comic.

As has already been pointed out by previous testimony, a

little, healthy, normal child has never been made worse for reading comic magazines.

The basic personality of a child is established before he reaches the age of comic-book reading. I don't believe anything that has ever been written can make a child over-aggressive or delinquent.

The roots of such characteristics are much deeper. The truth is that delinquency is the product of the real environment in which the child lives and not of the fiction he reads.

There are many problems that reach our children today. They are tied up with insecurity. No pill can cure them. No law will legislate them out of being. The problems are economic and social and they are complex.

Our people need understanding; they need to have affection, decent homes, decent food.

Do the comics encourage delinquency? Dr. David Abrahamsen has written:

Comic books do not lead into crime, although they have been widely blamed for it. I find comic books many times helpful for children in that through them they can get rid of many of their aggressions and harmful fantasies. I can never remember having seen one boy or girl who had committed a crime or who became neurotic or psychotic because he or she read comic books.

I would like to discuss, if you bear with me a moment more, something which Dr. Wertham provoked me into. Dr. Wertham, I am happy to say, I have just caught in a half-truth, and I am very indignant about it. He said there is a magazine now on the stands preaching racial intolerance. The magazine he is referring to is my magazine. What he said, as much as he said, was true. There do appear in this magazine such materials as "Spik," "Dirty Mexican," but Dr. Wertham did not tell you what the plot of the story was.

This is one of a series of stories designed to show the evils of race prejudice and mob violence, in this case against Mexican Catholics.

Previous stories in this same magazine have dealt with anti-Semitism, and anti-Negro feelings, evils of dope addiction and development of juvenile delinquents.

This is one of the most brilliantly written stories that I have ever had the pleasure to publish. I was very proud of it, and to find it being used in such a nefarious way made me quite angry.

I am sure Dr. Wertham can read, and he must have read the story, to have counted what he said he counted.

I would like to read one more thing to you.

Senator Hennings asked Dr. Peck a question. I will be perfectly frank with you, I have forgotten what he asked him, but this is the answer because I made a notation as he went along.

No one has to read a comic book to read horror stories.

Anyone, any child, any adult, can find much more extreme descriptions of violence in the daily newspaper. You can find plenty of examples in today's newspaper. In today's edition of the *Daily News,* which more people will have access to than they will to any comic magazine, there are head-line stories like this:

Finds he has killed wife with gun.
Man in Texas woke up to find he had killed his wife with gun. She had bullet in head and he had a revolver in his hand.

The next one:

Cop pleads in cocktail poisoning.
Twenty-year-old youth helps poison the mother and father of a friend.
Court orders young hanging. Man who killed his wife will be hung in June for his almost-perfect murder.

Let us look at today's edition of the *Herald Tribune.*

On the front page a criminal describes how another criminal told him about a murder he had done. In the same paper the story of a man whose ex-wife beat him on the head with a claw hammer and slashed him with a butcher knife.

In the same paper, story of a lawyer who killed himself.

In another, a story of that man who shot his wife while having a nightmare.

Another, a story of a gang who collected an arsenal of guns and knives. These are very many stories of violence and crime in the *Herald Tribune* today.

I am not saying it is wrong, but when you attack comics, when you talk about banning them as they do in some cities, you are only a step away from banning crimes in the news-papers.

Here is something interesting which I think most of us don't know. Crime news is being made in some places. The United Nations UNESCO report, which I believe is the only place that it is printed, shows that crime news is not permitted to appear in newspapers in Russia or Communist China, or other Communist-held territories.

We print our crime news. We don't think that the crime news or any news should be banned because it is bad for children.

Once you start to censor you must censor everything. You must censor comic books, radio, television, and newspapers.

Then you must censor what people may say. Then you will have turned this country into Spain or Russia.

MR. BEASER: Mr. Gaines, let me ask you one thing with reference to Dr. Wertham's testimony.

You used the pages of your comic book to send across a message, in this case it was against racial prejudice; is that it?

MR. GAINES: That is right.

MR. BEASER: You think, therefore, you can get across a message to the kids through the medium of your magazine that would lessen racial prejudice; is that it?

MR. GAINES: By specific effort and spelling it out very carefully so that the point won't be missed by any of the readers, and I regret to admit that it still is missed by some readers, as well as Dr. Wertham—we have, I think, achieved some degree of success in combating anti-Semitism, anti-Negro feeling, and so forth.

MR. BEASER: Yet why do you say you cannot at the same time and in the same manner use the pages of your magazine to get a message which would affect children adversely, that is, to have an effect upon their doing these deeds of violence or sadism, whatever is depicted?

MR. GAINES: Because no message is being given to them. In other words, when we write a story with a message, it is deliberately written in such a way that the message, as I say, is spelled out carefully in the captions. The preaching, if you want to call it, is spelled out carefully in the captions, plus the fact that our readers by this time know that in each issue of shock suspense stories, the second of the stories will be this type of story.

MR. BEASER: A message can be gotten across without

spelling out in that detail. For example, take this case that was presented this morning of the child who is in a foster home who became a werewolf, and foster parents. . . .

MR. GAINES: That was one of our stories.

MR. BEASER: A child who killed her mother. Do you think that would have any effect at all on a child who is in a foster placement, who is with foster parents, who has fears? Do you not think that child in reading the story would have some of the normal fears which a child has, some of the normal desires tightened, increased?

MR. GAINES: I honestly can say I don't think so. No message has been spelled out there. We were not trying to prove anything with that story. None of the captions said anything like "If you are unhappy with your stepmother, shoot her."

MR. BEASER: No, but here you have a child who is in a foster home who has been treated very well, who has fears and doubts about the foster parent. The child would normally identify herself in this case with a child in a similar situation and there a child in a similar situation turns out to have foster parents who became werewolves.

Do you not think that would increase the child's anxiety?

MR. GAINES: Most foster children, I am sure, are not in homes such as were described in those stories. Those were pretty miserable homes.

MR. HANNOCH: You mean the houses that had vampires in them, those were not nice homes?

MR. GAINES: Yes.

MR. HANNOCH: Do you know any place where there is any such thing?

MR. GAINES: As vampires?

MR. HANNOCH: Yes.

MR. GAINES: No, sir; this is fantasy. The point I am trying to make is that I am sure no foster children are kept locked up in their room for months on end except in those rare cases that you hear about where there is something wrong with the parents such as the foster child in one of these stories was, and on the other hand, I am sure that no foster child finds himself with a drunken father and a mother who is having an affair with someone else.

MR. BEASER: Yet you do hear of the fact that an awful lot of delinquency comes from homes that are broken. You hear of drunkenness in those same homes.

Do you not think those children who read those comics identify themselves with the poor home situation, with maybe the drunken father or mother who is going out, and identify themselves and see themselves portrayed there?

MR. GAINES: It has been my experience in writing these stories for the last 6 or 7 years that whenever we have tested them out on kids, or teen-agers, or adults, no one ever associates himself with someone who is going to be put upon. They always associate themselves with the one who is doing the putting upon.

THE CHAIRMAN: You do test them out on children, do you?

MR. GAINES: Yes.

MR. BEASER: How do you do that?

SENATOR HENNINGS: Is that one of your series, the pictures of the two in electric chair, the little girl down in the corner?

MR. GAINES: Yes.

SENATOR HENNINGS: As we understood from what we heard of that story, the little girl is not being put upon there, is she? She is triumphant apparently, that is insofar as we heard the relation of the story this morning.

MR. GAINES: If I may explain, the reader does not know that until the last panel, which is one of the things we try to do in our stories, is have an O. Henry ending for each story.

SENATOR HENNINGS: I understand you to use the phrase "put upon," and that there was no reader identification— with one who was put upon, but the converse.

MR. GAINES: That is right, sir.

SENATOR HENNINGS: Now, in that one, what would be your judgment or conclusion as to the identification of the reader with that little girl who has, to use the phrase, framed her mother and shot her father?

MR. GAINES: In that story, if you read it from the beginning, because you can't pull things out of context—

SENATOR HENNINGS: That is right, you cannot do that.

MR. GAINES: You will see that a child leads a miserable life in the 6 or 7 pages. It is only on the last page she emerges triumphant.

SENATOR HENNINGS: As a result of murder and perjury, she emerges as triumphant?

MR. GAINES: That is right.

MR. HANNOCH: Is that the O. Henry finish?

MR. GAINES: Yes.

MR. HANNOCH: In other words, everybody reading that would think this girl would go to jail. So the O. Henry finish changes that, makes her a wonderful looking girl?

MR. GAINES: No one knows she did it until the last panel.

MR. HANNOCH: You think it does them a lot of good to read these things?

MR. GAINES: I don't think it does them a bit of good, but I don't think it does them a bit of harm, either.

THE CHAIRMAN: What would be your procedure to test the story out on a child or children?

MR. GAINES: I give them the story to read and I ask them if they enjoyed it, and if they guessed the ending. If they said they enjoyed it and didn't guess the ending, I figure it is a good story, entertaining.

THE CHAIRMAN: What children do you use to make these tests with?

MR. GAINES: Friends, relatives.

SENATOR HENNINGS: Do you have any children of your own, Mr. Gaines?

MR. GAINES: No, sir.

SENATOR HENNINGS: Do you use any of the children of your own family, any nieces, nephews?

MR. GAINES: My family has no children, but if they had, I would use them.

THE CHAIRMAN: You do test them out on children of your friends, do you?

MR. GAINES: Yes.

MR. BEASER: Mr. Gaines, in your using tests, I don't think you are using it in the same way that we are here. You are not trying to test the effect on the child, you are trying to test the readability and whether it would sell?

MR. GAINES: Certainly.

MR. BEASER: That is a different kind of test than the possible effect on the child. Then you have not conducted any tests as to the effects of these upon children?

MR. GAINES: No, sir.

MR. BEASER: Were you here this morning when Dr. Peck testified?

MR. GAINES: I was.

MR. BEASER: Did you listen to his testimony as to the possible effect of these comics upon an emotionally maladjusted child?

MR. GAINES: I heard it.

MR. BEASER: You disagree with it?

MR. GAINES: I disagree with it.

Frankly, I could have brought many, many quotes from psychiatrists and child-welfare experts and so forth pleading the cause of the comic magazine. I did not do so because I figured this would all be covered thoroughly before I got here. And it would just end up in a big melee of pitting experts against experts.

MR. BEASER: Let me get the limits as far as what you put into your magazine. Is the sole test of what you would put into your magazine whether it sells? Is there any limit you can think of that you would not put in a magazine because you thought a child should not see or read about it?

MR. GAINES: No, I wouldn't say that there is any limit for the reason you outlined. My only limits are bounds of good taste, what I consider good taste.

MR. BEASER: Then you think a child cannot in any way, in any way, shape, or manner, be hurt by anything that a child [he] reads or sees?

MR. GAINES: I don't believe so.

MR. BEASER: There would be no limit actually to what you put in the magazines?

MR. GAINES: Only within the bounds of good taste.

MR. BEASER: Your own good taste and salability?

MR. GAINES: Yes.

SENATOR KEFAUVER: Here is your May 22 issue. This seems to be a man with a bloody ax holding a woman's head up which has been severed from her body. Do you think that is in good taste?

MR. GAINES: Yes, sir; I do, for the cover of a horror comic. A cover in bad taste, for example, might be defined as holding the head a little higher so that the neck could be seen dripping blood from it and moving the body over a little further so that the neck of the body could be seen to be bloody.

SENATOR KEFAUVER: You have blood coming out of her mouth.

MR. GAINES: A little.

SENATOR KEFAUVER: Here is blood on the ax. I think most adults are shocked by that.

THE CHAIRMAN: Here is another one I want to show him.

SENATOR KEFAUVER: This is the July one. It seems to be a man with a woman in a boat and he is choking her to death here with crowbar. Is that in good taste?

FIGURE 1. *Cover of controversial horror comic book. The response to this cover by the Senate investigating committee and by the press was instrumental in bringing about self-regulation activities by the comic book industry.*

MR. GAINES: I think so.

MR. HANNOCH: How could it be worse?

SENATOR HENNINGS: Mr. Chairman, if counsel will bear with me, I don't think it is really the function of our committee to argue with this gentleman. I believe that he has given us about the sum and substance of his philosophy, but I would like to ask you one question, sir.

THE CHAIRMAN: You may proceed.

SENATOR HENNINGS: You have indicated by what—I hope you will forgive me if I suggest—seems to be a bit of self-righteousness, that your motivation was bringing "enjoyment"—is that the word you used?

MR. GAINES: Yes, sir.

SENATOR HENNINGS: To the readers of these publications. You do not mean to disassociate the profit motive entirely, do you?

MR. GAINES: Certainly not.

SENATOR HENNINGS: Without asking you to delineate as between the two, we might say there is a combination of both, is there not?

MR. GAINES: No question about it.

• • •

SENATOR KEFAUVER: Mr. Gaines, I had heard that your father really did not have horror and crime comics. When he had the business he printed things that were really funny, and stories of the Bible, but you are the one that started out this crime and horror business.

MR. GAINES: I did not start crime; I started horror.

SENATOR KEFAUVER: Who started crime?

MR. GAINES: I really don't know.

• • •

MR. BEASER: Just to settle the point which came up before, Mr. Gaines, who is it that gets the idea for this, for one of your stories, you, your editor, the artist, the writer? Where does it come from?

MR. GAINES: Principally from my editors and myself.

MR. BEASER: Not from the artists?

MR. GAINES: No.

MR. BEASER: He just does what he is told?

MR. GAINES: He just follows the story and illustrates it.

MR. BEASER: He is told what to do and how to illustrate it?

MR. GAINES: No, our artists are superior artists. They don't have to be given detailed descriptions.

MR. BEASER: He has to be told what it is?

MR. GAINES: It is lettered in before he draws it.

MR. BEASER: He knows the story pietty much, so he knows what he can fit in?

MR. GAINES: Yes.

MR. BEASER: You said that you had a circulation of 5 million Bible storybooks.

MR. GAINES: Yes.

MR. BEASER: How many years is this?

MR. GAINES: Twelve years, since 1942.

MR. BEASER: In other words, in little over 3½ months you sell more of your crime and horror than you sell of the Bible stories?

MR. GAINES: Quite a bit more.

MR. BEASER: They seem to go better?

MR. GAINES: This is a 65-cent book. The crime-and-horror book is a 10-cent book. There is a difference.

MR. BEASER: No further questions, Mr. Chairman.

THE CHAIRMAN: Thank you very much, Mr. Gaines.

MR. GAINES: Thank you, sir.

A PUBLIC COMMISSION ON MASS COMMUNICATION AS AN ALTERNATIVE TO GOVERNMENT INTERVENTION

Harry S. Ashmore

• • •

NOT LONG ago a discouraged member of the Federal Communications Commission, Kenneth A. Cox, publicly described

Excerpts reprinted with the permission of the publisher from Harry S. Ashmore, "Cause, Effect, and Cure," in *Mass Communication,* An Occasional Paper on the Role of Mass Media in the Free Society, Published by the Center for the Study of Democratic Institutions, 1966, pp. 30–38.

the current run of television programs as ranking "somewhere between undistinguished and calamitous." Lawrence Laurent in the *Washington Post* observed that Commissioner Cox probably wouldn't have been so kind had he spoken after the advent of *Batman*, the sensation of the 1965–66 mid-season. This ABC serialization based on an old comicbook character was launched with a publicity campaign which touted it as "camp"—a current vogue word borrowed from the homosexual, meaning in this case that the program is so bad by all normal standards it is somehow "good," or at least smart. Thus, Mr. Laurent wrote, "the poorest kind of published trash becomes the basis for a worse television series. The excuse for propelling it into the public's airwaves is that it is a kind of grisly joke that a tiny in-group is playing on the people."

Batman provides a particularly revealing measure of television's low estate. The series' executive producer, William Dozier, greets criticism by pointing to the ratings and noting: "It's entertaining a lot of people, and we're in the entertainment business. . . ."

• • •

The indispensable fountainhead of these riches is the limited number of broadcasting licenses granted by the Federal Communications Commission under an act of Congress requiring the licensees to operate in the "public interest, convenience, and necessity." This gives a public utilities cast to broadcasting, and regulation is never questioned so long as the FCC employs its powers to set engineering requirements, police technical performance, and make such determinations as that requiring the industry to standardize on one of several competing systems of color television. However, on the very rare occasions when the Commission has moved into the area of programming, it has run into cries of censorship, invocations of the First Amendment, and appeals to the democratic gods—to such an extent that the agency has had inordinate difficulty with relatively simple matters like obscenity and political fair practice. And, by some legerdemain of public relations, these free speech arguments are carried over to thwart every effort to deal with such purely commercial matters as the frequency of advertising.

Over the years, valiant individual commissioners from time to time have cited poor programming and demanded improvement, offered tangible reforms such as formulas for the allocation of prime time to public service, and even suggested that maybe the government ought to share in the vast profits being derived from the "public air." In every significant test, however, the broadcasters' interest has prevailed. On the few occasions when the FCC as a whole has stiffened its neck, the station owners, network proprietors, and their fuglemen in the advertising industry have had no difficulty in persuading Congress to override.

There can be no doubt that great financial resources, plus the celebrity-making power of the medium, contribute to the the broadcasters' ability to checkmate every Washington effort to correct their most evident abuses. But, unlike the other special interests that seek support and/or immunity from Washington, broadcasting enjoys another overwhelming advantage that so far has made it impossible to muster any effective force for governmental reform—the stubborn, democratic fact that the great majority of viewers like their television the way it is.

• • •

. . . Every effort to bring government authority effectively to bear on broadcasting has failed in the United States—even when the effort has been as wide of First Amendment proscriptions against censorship as the effort to prevent stations from turning up the volume during commercials. Hal Humphrey of the *Los Angeles Times* has recounted the dismal history of organized public efforts to save quality programs when their audience ratings fell below an arbitrary number of the Nielsen scale. After failing to impress the networks with a barrage of thousands of letters, these mail campaigns have been directed at the FCC with similar lack of result. Humphrey cites a particularly flagrant case:

Baskets of mail from irate Los Angeles viewers landed before FCC commissioners after a local hothead with a "hate-talk" show on Channel 11 displayed a gun on camera during the Watts riot. It was an inflammatory act and the most crass kind of irresponsibility. But last week the august FCC, which said it was "particularly concerned" with that show, still managed to give Channel 11 an unqualified three-year renewal of its license, and with no recommendation for changing its programming. . . .

If the FCC commissioners are protecting the public interest here, they prove it in strange ways. The FCC is supposedly not functioning on the basis of a Nielsen rating, as the networks do, but apparently it has little regard for the voice of the people when a large commercial TV channel (part of the Metromedia chain in this case) is involved. . . . What can the parent-teacher groups and other concerned organizations do to impress networks and the FCC, if the latter won't read their mail?

Yet the coin does have another side, and the thought of what might happen if government did undertake affirmative intervention in television programming still tends to bring down the blood pressure of libertarians outraged by the sins committed under the presumed shelter of the First Amendment. Ever since Franklin Roosevelt discovered that a radio fireside chat enabled him to go directly to the people and short-circuit the dissident voices of the press, broadcasting has become an increasingly important tool in the hands of politicians. Lyndon Johnson's relentless exploitation of the media has led Ben H. Bagdikian to complain in *Columbia Journalism Review* that the President practices "common, ordinary press agentry." When such an effort is combined with the weight of high public office there is a real threat to Thomas Jefferson's free market-place of ideas. Here is the testimony of Fred Friendly, then of CBS, on the aftermath of his network's critical coverage of some aspects of the war in Vietnam:

I found myself days later under the fingers of two of the highest men in government, being lectured about, "Did I not think about what was right for the United States?" . . . As the power and strength of broadcast journalism increase, the desire of people to use and manage and ever so delicately control you increases and increases and increases.

Mr. Friendly's complaint can be regarded as another measure of the shifting locus of power in the communications industry. Many an editor has felt the manipulating finger of officialdom, but if he chose to resist he had not only the First Amendment but an honored tradition of independence to sustain him. A broadcaster in similar straits is not likely to forget that he is dependent upon a renewable government license, and the dominant tradition in his depersonalized industry is that the customer is always right. Moreover, the news and public affairs side of broadcasting is under special internal pressure because, despite the lucrative return from regular newscasts, this is the only form of broadcasting that operates at a net loss. "Networks can't make news pay, even when the regular programs are sold out to sponsors," says Jesse Zousmer, director of ABC's news division. All of this adds up to a high degree of vulnerability when a television newsman goes up against a President who, as Joseph Alsop has said of Mr. Johnson, has undertaken "attempts at news control . . . so much more aggressive, comprehensive, and, one must add, repugnant to American tradition, than any such attempts by other presidents."

Aside from the unresolved constitutional questions inherent in the relationship between government and the communications media, the problems raised here cut straight through to the fundamental issues of our time. Free speech, with its inescapable corollary of free communications, provides a far more significant distinction between West and East than the economic differences that have survived extensive renovation of capitalist and Communist theory and practice. An independent source of criticism and untrammeled creative endeavor is essential to a pluralist society, as it is anathema to a collective, unitary society. Thus, even in the face of extreme provocation, only the most desperate of those who have been conditioned by the Western tradition are disposed to join in the cry of young Mr. Al-Gailani of Iraq: "One thing surely must be done about the American press and American TV and American movies. They must be censored! They must be controlled by the government!"

This is the ultimate reason, I suggest, that those who set themselves up as critics of the media tend to go around in worn circles. The dilemma was defined in the most ambitious and competent analysis of these issues I know, an analysis undertaken twenty years ago by the Commission on Freedom of the Press, chaired by Robert M. Hutchins, then Chancellor of the University of Chicago. The Commission concluded that while the government could not, and should not, act in the critical area that borders on censorship, the public could not continue to rely on the media to set their own standards and police their own performance. The proposed answer was the establishment of an independent agency, without powers of legal enforcement but armed with great prestige, to appraise and report annually on the performance of mass communication—in those pre-TV days defined to include newspapers, radio, motion pictures, magazines, and books.

The Commission's report, published under the title *A Free and Responsible Press*, was greeted by a storm of protest from the media, and as a result its supporters failed to arouse enough financial aid to carry through its recommendations. Yet, almost everyone who thinks seriously about the state of our communications system in terms of the public interest sooner or later comes back to some version of the basic idea. . . . Jack Gould, in his report on the new study of educational TV, concluded that "it is regrettable that the Carnegie Corporation did not go all-out and set up a National Commission on Television. Such a body could make periodic assessments of all forms of the medium, a variation of a British royal commission. . . ." And Hal Humphrey, putting a pox on both the broadcasters and the FCC, wrote in the *Los Angeles Times:*

> The late President Kennedy was talking about an arts and cultural committee of private citizens who could talk directly to people like TV presidents on their own level. This idea seems to have died with Kennedy, but something like it soon must be revived and fulminated before the public voice in the communications and arts fields is stifled forever. It takes an organized lobby in Washington to get your case heard. . . .

The Commission report did produce one not insignificant by-product. Its publication aroused an immediate response among the group of outstanding young journalists assembled at Harvard under the fellowship program of the Nieman Foundation. Louis Lyons, then curator of the Foundation, has recounted the initial reaction in the introduction to the anthology, *Reporting the News:*

> Responsible was the key word, and freedom and responsibility were linked: only a responsible press could remain free. Responsibility of the press is a concept introduced by the Hutchins Commission, or at least given currency by its report. The publishers who scoffed at it as an academic notion in 1947 have long since adopted it into their vocabulary. I am sure many of them think they invented it. It became at once the basic theme of *Nieman Reports,* and has threaded through the reviews, critiques, and articles occupying seventy-two issues.

• • •

. . . I have spent a good deal of time exploring the possibility of establishing the proposed critical agency in association with a university. In a circuit of the Ivy League, and excursions elsewhere, I have found a good deal of sympathy, but no tangible support. There are, of course, good conventional reasons why a university should be reluctant to join in such an unconventional enterprise. But perhaps more compelling is the understandable prudence of administrators who know that the undertaking is inherently controversial, and certain to involve powerful men who have the means to talk back in loud and penetrating voices. One weary university president told me sadly, "Of course it ought to be done, and I'll be glad to sit as an individual on such a commission. But I've just got too damned much trouble on my hands already to think of giving you house-room on this campus."

• • •

I have never understood why the idea of collective judgment regularly rendered has aroused so much apprehension among those who agree that stringent criticism of the media is very much in order. . . . The proposed commission would have no power to censor, only to expose, complain, praise, and exhort—to perform, that is, on behalf of the mass media the functions the media presume to perform on behalf of all other institutions colored in any way with the public interest. The formal trappings of the commission, including an annual report, would be intended only to give it sufficient prestige to meet powerful adversaries on fairly equal terms, and guarantee that its findings could not simply be ignored—as, for example, most of the well-intentioned critiques of *Nieman Reports* have been.

It has always seemed to me that the unseemly reaction of the media to the original Hutchins Commission in itself provided a compelling argument on behalf of the proposal. Many publishers and broadcasters uttered outraged protests against "official" intervention in the free press, when, of course, the proposal is the precise reverse of this. There was the equally preposterous argument that the members of the Commission were disqualified because they were not professional journalists—a complaint that not only implied that such distinguished and broadly experienced men were incapable of judging the quality of what they read, see, and hear, but ignored the fact that the Commission was supported by a professional staff and in the course of its deliberations had spent many hours discussing the special problems of the media with leading proprietors and practitioners.

Indeed, the professional associations themselves have long provided the best evidence to support the Commission's premise that effective criticism can only come from those who are outside the media's immediate orbit, and wholly independent of it. I was a member of the American Society of Newspaper Editors when *A Free and Responsible Press* was published, and saw the august membership huddle rumps together, horns out, in the immemorial manner of, say, the National Association of Manufacturers faced by a threat of regulated prices. When, in the ASNE *Bulletin*, I suggested that there might be some merit in the Commission report I was roundly denounced for fouling my own nest. We had reached a point where you couldn't tell the ASNE from the American Newspaper Publishers Association without a program.

This blind reaction to the Hutchins Commission served to reduce the Commission's proposal to a sort of shibboleth; the test of loyalty was to denounce it out of hand, and in a curious way it became the special target of sensitive and frustrated men who privately recognize the media's grave deficiencies but feel constrained publicly to deny their existence. The experience of the past twenty years provides ample evidence to refute the specious arguments of the early days. Even those who still contend that the media are doing the best they can rarely argue that the best is good enough. With the entry of the great, bland behemoth of television the stultifying tendencies cited by the Commission have been accentuated; with three giant broadcasting corporations dominating the bulk of the programming available to Americans, the existence of centralized control, conformity, and vulgarization of public taste has become inescapably self-evident. We are confronted by a communications system that already comes very close to providing a circus to accompany the bread promised to all by the Great Society.

The pursuit of excellence has become a fashionable undertaking, or at least a fashionable phrase. But in a modern society no man can pursue excellence undeterred and uninfluenced by the image-building, taste-setting, attention-diverting system of communications that reaches out to him wherever he may be. In making the case for the commission to the universities I have argued that academic self-interest does not deny but rather demands concern and support; teachers have access to their students' minds for only a few hours out of a lifetime, but the media reach them always and forever; and the values and standards of *academe* cannot long stand inviolate if they are at odds with those that prevail in the market-place.

No one has ever argued that there is a perfect solution to an issue that is not only critical in its own right but symbolizes, and in a sense summarizes, those that now divide the world. The flyleaf of *A Free and Responsible Press* bears this quotation from John Adams, dated 1815:

> If there is ever to be an amelioration of the condition of mankind, philosophers, theologians, legislators, politicians and moralists will find that the regulation of the press is the most difficult, dangerous and important problem they have to resolve. Mankind cannot now be governed without it, nor at present with it.

The problem has not been resolved, and I do not believe the most sanguine philosophers, theologians, legislators, politicians, and moralists can argue that it has become less urgent. It is in this light that the proposal for a commission on the mass media deserves the serious consideration it has never had. At the very least it stands as an inescapable challenge to all those who profess concern with the low state of the media along with devotion to the tradition of the free and independent press. I have heard much argument that this is a good idea whose time has not yet come, but I have seen no evidence that this is so, and heard of no alternative.

PART VII
Regulation and Control:
Media Participation

> To those few broadcasters and their professional
> associates who would evade the nation's needs by
> crying, "Censorship! Oh, where will it end?" I ask,
> "Responsibility! When will it begin?"
>
> NEWTON MINOW

THIS BOOK might have ended with the material in the previous section. Government frequently has the last word. Its agencies are often turned to as the final arbiter of controversy and as the ultimate author of solutions to pressing social problems. However, while government has direct powers to deal with the plentiful array of real violence in society, it is, in the United States, restricted by law and custom from having the last word about the portrayal of violence in the mass media.

True, within these restrictions government does influence the content of mass communication. The principal means of influence, as we have seen, is the collection and exposure of the media to the cutting-edge of public complaint and the threat to initiate more formal, punitive action. The result is a loosely defined system of exposure and threat that links the public to the media through government. Sociologically, this is something less than a regime of law and may be viewed as a changing blend of public and private interests common in many sectors of American life and perhaps inherent in any complex, diverse, democratic society. It is a highly flexible arrangement, with neither side wishing to run the risk of completely clarifying its responsibility for limiting media content. Each side derives from the situation some positive power, and each must adjust itself to and manipulate the margin of doubt. Prodded by the public, government agencies prod the media. But the pressure is cyclical, with sharp peaks of protest and broad valleys of indifference, and the system often seems to perpetuate either dead-center mediocrity or an evasion of responsibility.

Some critics, therefore, while reluctant to get the government into the business of mass communication, would like to see the power of federal regulatory agencies extended to encompass a greater, continuing responsibility for the end product of mass communications. Short of total governmental intervention, how might this be done? Federal responsibility, it is contended, could be exercised by the official formulation of standards regulating the portrayal of violence and other controversial content (e.g., giving media codes the sanctions of law), by imposing on the media an obligation to study the programmatic needs of their constituencies, and by insisting that the media regularly defend their performance with reports to the government that will receive unrelenting publicity. Such proposals, at this juncture in the history of the problem of media violence, are purely hypothetical and surely controversial. Accordingly, responsibility for media content is located more realistically if this book concludes not with the intervention of government but with the response of the mass media themselves.

This section, therefore, describes how the media of mass communication are engaged with the regulation and control of violence. That they are so engaged is a direct product of the pressure mounted both by the public and by the government. The implication is clear: the form, the scope, and the continuity of their future efforts will depend more on the clarity, the consensus, and the force of public opinion than it will on innovations internal to the media themselves. This also means that the responsibility for violent content in mass communication rests not alone with the media, but resides instead in the *relationship* between the media and their audience.

Media sensitivity to this relationship is reflected in a number of ways. The tastes of the audience are constantly being assessed, with emphasis on the interests of a numerical majority, not only by what "sells" or what is tolerated, but also through the measurement of preferences by various rating schemes and polling devices. The media are also responsive to suggestions, although there are limits to their willingness to accommodate them (one mother is reported to have written to the Federal Communications Commission that she knew what to do about all this violence on television —"Why don't you let those fellows use live bullets?").

Most important, however, is media response to persistent criticism of media content, particularly when it stems from organized sources linked to political power. These pressures draw the agents of a given medium together in an association to engage in "self-regulation." The selections presented below illustrate two key functions of self-regulation as currently practiced by American media: (1) censorship of content to accord with codes developed by the industry, and (2) the practice of public relations designed primarily to assure the public that self-regulation is working and to suggest modes for continued public participation in the process of regulation and control.

Self-regulation is not unique to the industry of mass communication. Many other industries as well as professions and other occupations form associations to engage in similar activity. However, the media would appear to have a particular advantage over their counterparts in fulfilling one of the peculiar functions of self-regulation. Given their vast, built-in resources for launching public-relations campaigns, it is conceivable that the media can do a more thorough and expert job of image-building and self-justification than can others engaged in self-regulation. They can indeed disarm their critics through cooptation by opening mass media channels to the special needs of the critics. Thus it is not unusual for religious and civic organizations which have been in the forefront in criticizing the performance of violence on the media to find suddenly that they have generous access to media channels for their own special "public-interest" messages.

The larger point implied here is that to assess objectively the workings of self-regulation, it is necessary to work behind the image-building process of media public relations and even to go beyond the testimony of former critics such as the "watch-dog" committees of voluntary associations. Indeed, such an appraisal must consider not only the presence of widely heralded media codes and current changes in them (e.g., the first two articles below on the new motion picture code), but also the manner of their use and the effects of their application.

The administration of codes involves a "gatekeeper" function where someone is designated to screen mass media output through a sieve of public relations, moral, political, marketing, and other specifications (see, e.g., Gerbner, 1959; Gerbner and Tannenbaum, 1960). Occupants of this key position bear such titles as Network Editor, Continuity Acceptance Director, Code Administrator, or Review Board Chairman. The formal specifications guiding their activities are embodied in the codes formulated by the various media. But codes must be interpreted and applied to specific materials, and informal working assumptions and arrangements naturally emerge.

Some indication of how codes are administered may be seen from the articles on comic books and network television in this section. Further research of this activity is needed to understand its full implications, including possible merits and costs were this system somehow to come under closer governmental supervision.

Self-regulation has evolved to sense the public tastes and tolerance for media content and to blunt the criticism of media performance. It places highly specific powers in the hands of a few to decide the limits of what the many shall experience through mass communication. Before this mechanism is discarded in the interests of absolute free expression, or before it is brought under more stable and impartial auspices in the interests of controlling the flow of media violence, its workings in its present setting should be thoroughly explored and pondered.

The concluding material of this book barely sketches some dimensions of this challenge. For those who want to do something now about violence in mass communication, this ending marks the critical beginning point.

NEW MOVIE STANDARDS:
GENERAL FILM CODE,
NOT SPECIFIC BANS

Louis Chapin

"WHAT WE now have in family magazines should be available on the screen."

In these words Jack J. Valenti, president of the Motion Picture Association of America, summed up the main intention of the trade association's new code of self-regulation, updating standards originally set 36 years ago. In the more formal phraseology of the declaration itself, announced to the press at MPAA's New York headquarters, "This revised code is designed to keep in closer harmony with the mores, the culture, the moral sense, and the expectations of our society."

Central to the revision, which has been under active discussion for several years, is a new emphasis on the way doubtful subjects are treated on the screen, coupled with an "expansion of creative freedom" through the use of general guidelines rather than the old code's specific prohibitions.

INFORMATION PLEDGED

As Mr. Valenti put it: "Judgment is the key word. It's not the specific action that's most important, but why it's done, how it's done—and need it be done? The new code sets standards; within these standards the creative being can operate."

At the same time the member producers and distributors (consisting of the eight major American companies) have more strongly committed themselves to supplying information to parents, "the arbiters of family conduct, so they can choose which motion pictures their children should see." As part of this effort, some pictures given the MPAA seal of approval will be identified in all advertising and displays as "Suggested for Mature Audiences."

STANDARDS LISTED

The new standards, which will be applied in issuing approval by Geoffrey Shurlock, the code's administrator, are as follows:

The basic dignity and value of human life shall be respected and upheld. Restraint shall be exercised in portraying the taking of life.

Evil, sin, crime and wrongdoing shall not be justified.

Special restraint shall be exercised in portraying criminal or antisocial activities in which minors participate or are involved.

Detailed and protracted acts of brutality, cruelty, physical violence, torture, and abuse shall not be presented.

Indecent or undue exposure of the human body shall not be presented.

Illicit sex relationships shall not be justified. Intimate sex scenes violating common standards of decency shall not be portrayed. Restraint and care shall be exercised in presentations dealing with sex aberrations.

Obscene speech, gestures, or movements shall not be presented. Undue profanity shall not be permitted.

Religion shall not be demeaned.

Words or symbols contemptuous of racial, religious, or national groups, shall not be used so as to incite hatred.

Excessive cruelty to animals shall not be portrayed, and animals will be treated humanely.

APPEAL PROVIDED

When any film is refused approval by the administrator, its producer may appeal to a new "motion picture code board," to consist of the MPAA president as chairman, nine other directors of the association, six exhibitors nominated by the National Association of Theater Owners, and four producers nominated by the Screen Producers' Guild.

Questions by reporters pinpointed certain examples. Would *The Pawnbroker*, for instance, be acceptable under the new procedure? Probably it would, with a "Suggested for Mature Audiences" proviso.

But most of the questioning turned Mr. Valenti back to the uses of reasonableness and "common sense."

"We're not going to satisfy everybody," he admitted. "But the longer I'm in this job, the more I'm convinced you're not dealing with specifics, but with guidelines. That's why a law is all wrong.

"I think Geoff [Mr. Shurlock] attacks these problems in a pragmatic-idealist way. And I believe in it."

MAGAZINE COMMENTARY ON
NEW MOVIE CODE

Newsweek

HOLLYWOOD'S major studios, whose movies have long flouted the industry's own 36-year-old self-censorship code, put a new, more liberal code into effect last week; having flooded the river, they raised the bridge. "This is still self-restraint, self-regulation and self-discipline," cautioned Jack Valenti, president of the Motion Picture Association of America that presides over the code. "We want to make it clear that expansion of the artist's freedom doesn't mean tolerance of license."

In an era of crumbling legal restraints on film content, the code's most significant innovation (or largest loophole) was a provision for labeling certain films "Suggested for Mature Audiences" (or simply "SMA" if the advertisement is small). This transfers the potential guilt to parents, and the new code made no bones about it. "Parents have the primary responsibility to guide their children," it said.

Instead of the exhaustive and evidently exhausted list of prohibitions in the old code (no "lustful embraces" or "sex perversion or any inference of it"), the new code comes out

Reprinted with the permission of the publisher from "Hollywood: Three-and-a-half Square," *Newsweek*, October 3, 1966, p. 22.

foursquare against justification of evil, sin, crime, wrong-doing or illicit sex relationships, and three-and-a-half square against "indecent or undue exposure of the human body," "undue profanity" and "excessive cruelty to animals."

Due Profanity? Could there be due profanity, due nudity or moderate cruelty to animals? Absolutely. *The Pawnbroker* was first denied approval under the old code because of two scenes showing a woman's bare breasts, then granted an "exemption" because the scenes were found artistically justi-fiable. The new code is intended to eliminate the need for such exemptions.

Hollywood attaches such solemn importance to self-cen-sorship in the hope it will preclude harsher measures by Federal, state, local or religious authorities. Yet the new code, like the old, is a glittering diadem of hypocrisy that Hollywood places on its own head. Whenever the major studios have a picture that cannot qualify for code approval, they release it anyway through subsidiary companies that are not members of the MPAA—nor signatories to any moral ententes.

THE ROLE OF THE
CODE ADMINISTRATOR

Comics Magazine Association of America

DURING my sixteen months as Code Administrator, I have had occasion to discuss the program of the Comics Code Authority with civic-minded groups all over the country. This has been for me a stimulating experience, for in any public-service post, we must know what the public wants. But I have a special interest in meeting with you who are law-

Address by the Code Administrator, Comics Magazine Association of America, at the Annual Meeting of the Association of Towns of the State of New York, February 9, 1956. Used with the permission of the Comics Magazine Association of America, Inc.

enforcement officers, since our work has so much in common. The statutes you enforce may be far more numerous and consequential than the forty-one provisions of the Comics Magazine Code. But our roles are somewhat similar. We both have our codes or sets of rules. We must see to it that they are applied equitably and fairly, in the manner most conducive to the welfare of all.

Your Code, of course is hardly a new one. It reaches back to the time when the first rules of government were formulated. By contrast, the Code I administer is of recent origin. It was designed to meet the needs of a relatively new field. Some fifteen years ago comic books were almost nonexistent. But from then on the format became very popular and the industry developed fast. In September, 1954, its responsible leaders realized that certain comic magazines, having attracted criticism, were jeopardizing the industry's future. To put a stop to this and guarantee uniform good practice, they organized the Comics Magazine Association of America, Inc. The membership included printers, engravers and distributors, as well as all but two of the nation's comic-book publishers.

At that time they also adopted a Code. Its specific provisions were designed to prevent the recurrence of the types of material previously criticized. Its general objective was to keep all future comic books, regardless of type, up to recognized standards for decent, wholesome reading matter. Although this was a voluntary program, the Association pledged itself to strict adherence. This meant that I, as Code Administrator, was given strong independent powers to see that all the rules were followed. This has not always been easy. Up to now my office has examined some 15,000 individual stories. Even with the best intentions of all concerned, 15,000 stories can mean a lot of interpretive problems. But regardless of difficulties, the Code has been enforced, and the public everywhere is voicing approval.

But if the comic-book Code is new, its basic principles are not. They are, in fact, much the same as those underlying your own professional activities. Fundamental to both is a concern with the nation's youth. In your work to preserve order in the community much effort is directed toward the welfare of children. You want them to live secure and happy now, and to enjoy their full democratic heritage when they

grow up. But you are also realists. You know that this heritage is not something we can hand them on a platter at
age 21. It actually demands the development of high ideals
and good social attitudes throughout the entire span of childhood and adolescence. Realizing this, you have always been
among the first to champion whatever helped get young people started in the right direction. At the Code Authority we
too have this very much in mind.

We both know how vital it is that children acquire a
healthy respect for all legitimate authority. You yourselves
further this aim not only by your splendid public service as
officers but by actively sponsoring various youth programs.
The Code for Comic Books serves to reinforce such efforts.
It demands that all stories show those in positions of respect
as deserving of admiration.

Some months ago I received a letter from John E. Carton,
President of the National Conference of Police Associations.
He asked that my office see to it that comic books never show
policemen and the police profession "ridiculed, disparaged
or degraded." I assured him that any such presentation would
clearly violate the Code and would never receive approval.
That pledge has been kept. Never will you find in Comic
Books bearing our Seal of Approval any story in which a
lawbreaker makes a police officer look foolish. The heroes in
our new-look detective fiction are either officers themselves
or work with them in close harmony. J. Edgar Hoover recently asserted that "law enforcement has not yet attained
the measure of public support it justly deserves." This is the
kind of unfortunate situation we must all strive to correct.
But at least in comic books with the Seal that support is
given.

Yet you as peace officers would, I believe, agree that it is
not enough to set up excellent models for young people to
imitate. The temptation may still be strong when wrong-
doing promises rich rewards or is made to seem too easy. The
Comic Book Code takes this into account. It clearly rules out
the glamorizing of law breakers, that is, picturing them as
successful, living in comfort, unsuspected by the authorities.
They must never, in the Code's actual words, "occupy a position which creates a desire for emulation." On the other
hand, there must be no exposition of criminal methods, no
blueprints or unique details, no unusual devices for conceal-

ment. At the same time, the Code rules out all ads for switch-blade knives, gun facsimiles and other objectionable items. And finally the Code bans all stories that might be considered lurid, sadistic, or excessively violent.

But even with such emphasis upon respect for public officials and worthy institutions, results will be negligible unless young people first develop the proper concept of family life. Naturally this cannot be learned exclusively from books of any kind. But we can and do see to it that in comic books with the seal "respect for parents, the moral code and for honorable behavior shall be fostered." In a recent article in the *Reader's Digest*, A. J. Cronin discusses the trouble in today's world. "Parental authority," he says, "has become a joke; discipline is a forgotten word." In the comic books we approve, every attempt is made to uphold high ideals of family life. Divorce is not treated humorously or represented as desirable. Violent love scenes are never permitted. Dress must be modest, and there must be nothing suggestive in illustrations. To sum up, in the words of the Code, "stories shall emphasize the value of the home and the sanctity of marriage."

We have said a great deal about the kinds of material we will and we will not approve. How do we go about it? In general, this self-regulation process is a preventive measure. I mention this because I know that you, as police officials, appreciate fully the value of eliminating problems in advance. My office examines comic books in their preliminary stage, several months before they appear on the stands. The books are sent to us in the form of a large black and white art board. We screen them page by page, panel by panel, to see that they comply with the Code. We carefully review covers, art work, captions, dialogue and advertisements. If there is anything out of line with the Code, the book is returned to the publisher for revision. When everything does comply, the book is stamped as acceptable. The publisher is then authorized to place the coveted white seal of our Office on the upper right corner of the cover. The Seal reads: "Approved By The Comics Code Authority." A comic book bearing that Seal is a comic book with standards.

When we talk about removing objectionable material, the impression is sometimes created that all of our efforts are negative. Actually, the Association and the Code Authority are also very much interested in encouraging new and progressive developments in the field. As you may have heard, the government made excellent use of comic books for instructional purposes during World War II. They were then utilized not only for training service personnel but for conveying information about our country to people of other nations. City governments, too, as well as large industrial firms, have used this type of presentation. The City of Rochester, for instance, has a clear, concise comic-type booklet explaining its water system, and New York City's Fire Department is now distributing thousands of its new comic book showing how to prevent and control fires. Just last month the Roswell, New Mexico, Police Department issued two comic books designed to help young people observe safety rules when they ride bicycles or drive cars.

Comic books with the Seal are, of course, primarily designed for entertainment. But in many of these there is also educational material. One example in particular might interest you. You may have read recently a statement of James H. Bobo, General Counsel for the Senate Subcommittee to Investigate Juvenile Delinquency, on the subject of children leaving school. He stated that the thousands of youngsters who leave school and then stay idle constitute a group "particularly vulnerable to delinquency." Combatting such trends are comic-book pages prepared in conjunction with public-service groups like the National Social Welfare Agency. Such pages point up the advantages to be gained by boys and girls who complete their education and prepare for worthwhile careers. This may be only a step, but the direction is surely right.

The public, taking note of all such positive elements, has responded favorably to the work of the Code Authority. Letters of commendation reach my office daily from parents, teachers, civic, religious and veterans leaders, and the young readers themselves. Not long ago, I received a letter from Senator William Langer, of the Kefauver Committee, offering his "congratulations on a job well done." This meant a great deal to us, as also did the resolutions passed by many interested groups. Last fall, for instance, Governor Harriman called a conference in Albany to study juvenile problems. Its final report on Mass Media included highly gratifying comments on the success of the comic-book industry's self-regulatory efforts. Equally favorable has been the action taken by the American Legion and the American Legion Auxiliary at their national conventions in Florida, by the New York City Federation of Women's Clubs and by the National Society for the Prevention of Juvenile Delinquency.

But despite such welcome recognition, more, much more remains to be done if the program is to receive the universal support it must have to be fully successful. The interim report of the Kefauver Committee issued last March outlines two conditions absolutely essential for effective self-regulation. The Committee states, first of all, that "there must be wide public education of the code and the meaning it has for the public when making purchases." In other words, all of us who know what has been done, and what is being done, to improve comic books, must get together to spread the word. We must talk to parents, to teachers, to all who have an interest in our youth. We must pass along our knowledge to those who buy comic books and to those who sell them.

The Committee's second observation is "the public must be sold this idea of restricting purchases of comics to those carrying the seal of approval." In this field, as elsewhere, the law of supply and demand continues in effect. Only if the public buys good comics can good comics remain in circulation.

I have no hesitation about asking for your help, because I feel that you realize fully the importance of offering our young people reading matter that is above reproach. You know what problems may be created for you both professionally and as family men by objectionable material. This self-regulation program is a great experiment. It may well prove to be the proverbial "stitch in time" that forestalls many future difficulties. But its continued success depends upon concerted effort. So work with us. Tell the public about our Code. Tell parents and their youngsters about the Seal. For our part, we guarantee that comic books approved by us at the Comics Code Authority will always offer youthful readers fine, wholesome entertainment.

APPLYING THE COMIC BOOK CODE

Comics Magazine Association of America

WAR AND WESTERN COMICS

MOST OF THE revisions in books in these categories are to reduce violence. We do not accept bludgeoning and many corrections involve removal of a gun used as a bludgeon. Also, we seldom accept a situation where a man is killed by gunfire and showing the trajectory of the bullet into a vital part of the body. The business of shooting a gun out of an enemy's hand, rather than either killing or wounding him, which is used extensively both in comics and television, is in a large measure due to Code corrections. We will not accept knife play.

In a number of cases we have used the Code directive, "Criminals shall not be presented so as to be rendered glamorous, etc." Now "Billy the Kid" and other outlaws are depicted as having committed minor indiscretions but ·not real crimes and while they are wanted by law men, they are really not criminals.

One story showed a sheriff allowing a criminal to escape because the outlaw had saved the sheriff's life in a gunfight. We had the story changed to show that the sheriff did not know his savior was an outlaw.

Mugging is never allowed, garrotting, grabbing a man by his collar or tie in a way that might choke him is always deleted.

Sadistic behavior, often indicated by the very common directive "work him over," is not acceptable.

ROMANCE

The revisions most often required in romance books are "delete cleavage," "raise neckline," and "reduce bosom." Now

---

Memorandum to the editor, August 24, 1960, from a staff member, Comics Magazine Association of America. Used with the permission of the Comics Magazine Association of America, Inc.

and again an embrace will be considered too impassioned and occasionally we will insist that a beach scene be turned from night to day. Formerly we had a number of situations where a young man and woman were shown alone in a house or apartment and we had a chaperon written or drawn into the story. This seldom happens anymore.

Our present problems involve stories about teenagers in which they are shown as becoming interested in "gang" boys or girls. Of course, they always take a moral course in the end, but we watch out for too detailed expositions of the behavior of gang members depicted as horrible examples.

In these stories we play down quarrelsome parents and slum conditions used as explanations of anti-social behavior in the children.

Innuendo is a problem in Romance books and we are very careful to eliminate it. The most common form of innuendo is to show a girl completely bowed down with guilt and remorse and yet the story indicates only that some boy kissed her. When we find this kind of situation, we remove some of the guilt and remorse because we won't show her as having done anything to be truly guilty about. Another revision we have often made is in a story depicting a girl as cruel, grasping and rude, but reforming completely in the last panel and getting the boy. The revisions in a story such as this are usually to delete or minimize her nastiness or make her misunderstood.

We prefer making her good enough to deserve the boy rather than to show her as bad enough to lose the boy and have an unhappy ending, because we have found that most of the unhappy endings are morbidly emotional.

FANTASY

Pre-code stories often dealt with ghouls, werewolves, tombs, death, etc., and some were pretty gruesome. At the time the Code Authority came into existence the publishers agreed to discontinue this type of book and have kept their word.

At present the trend in fantasy books is to monsters. In most cases the monsters are from space and they are enormous, but seldom do serious harm. The revisions asked for in these books are to eliminate snaky tentacles, to blunt talons, and see that innocent people are not shown as being harmed.

The device most often used to indicate that though a monster is stalking through a town and uprooting buildings no one is hurt, is to say: "Lucky it is a holiday and no one is in the building," or, "It's fortunate that the people were warned in time to get out."

One aspect of fantasy and crime (usually outer space crime) stories is to see that the "punishment fits the crime." There is a tendency to show a person guilty of a minor offense being doomed to perpetual punishment. In these cases we insist that loopholes be left for escape after fitting punishment.

CENSOR AND SENSIBILITY:
A CONTENT ANALYSIS OF THE
TELEVISION CENSOR'S COMMENTS

Charles Winick

THE CONTEMPORARY confusion over censorship is nowhere better illustrated than in the large number of thoughtful Americans who are unalterably opposed to censorship of art but who are in favor of censorship of mass media. The current debate over censorship of mass media can best be understood in the light of the considerable history of the problem.

Men of good will have been preoccupied with the consideration of how much social control needs to be imposed on the free expression of ideas. Plato pointed to a need for a "royal lie" in order to help establish the state, and justified such a lie because the state itself was the embodiment of truth and justice. Plato even expelled poets from his ideal state be-

Reprinted with the permission of the author and the editor from *Journal of Broadcasting*, Spring, 1961, pp. 117–135 (footnotes omitted).

cause no one could predict what they would say. Spinoza, though his own work was heavily censored and he was a champion of free speech, recommended that the sovereign could properly insist on those beliefs which a reasonable person could hold. Our era may appropriately be called Hobbesian, because it was Hobbes who detailed how the state should maintain some control of people's opinions in order to maintain the peace which Hobbes saw as the major purpose of the state. Just as Hobbes wanted to avoid the tumult occasioned by different viewpoints, so modern censorship has developed as a kind of commonly held mass sensibility writ large, trying to anticipate and forestall the tumult which might arise from certain kinds of expression.

Other countries also have their areas of special concern, which are hedged about with taboos. Some films and other artistic representations of the Dreyfus case, like the distinguished American film, *Zola*, starring Paul Muni, have never been shown in France. The film version of *A Farewell to Arms* was protested by Italian veterans of World War I who found the original novel and its film version "degrading."

Ever since an actual 1907 automobile theft was attributed to the thief having seen the film *The Great Automobile Robbery*, there has been growing discussion about the extent to which mass media require censorship or self-regulation. As a result of this incident, Chicago, in 1907, passed the first film censorship legislation. Movie censorship boards still operate in some states and cities. However, the major regulation of the content of movies has been conducted by the industry itself since 1930, through the Motion Picture Association's Production Code Administration, which is a central editing and advising office to which producers submit scripts. Each approved film is given a seal of approval. Similar industry-wide editing is performed by the comic magazine trade association, established in 1954 after public and legislative expressions of disapproval of comic content. The power of voluntary codes in mass media is of particular concern today for several reasons. Both the proponents and foes of media regulations have been becoming much more vocal in the last decade than they ever have been. The proponents of regulation feel that Communist attacks on America are easier to make because of the content of mass media. Respected intellectuals like Walter Lippmann have endorsed

"censorship of the mass entertainment of the young." Legislative investigative groups have often attributed part of the
post-World War II increase in juvenile delinquency to mass
media. Similar charges have been made by voluntary organizations which have intensified their grass roots campaigns
to "clean up" the popular arts. The power of these voluntary
groups can be inferred from the role of a woman's club in
fomenting the outcry over Fatty Arbuckle in 1922, and thus
leading to the self-regulation of motion pictures. The Legion
of Decency was formed after protests by voluntary organizations as a result of the 1934 cycle of gangster films.

Almost simultaneously with this spurt of interest in a
stricter censorship, there has been a parallel increase in the
activity of those opposed to censorship. A series of court decisions since 1952 has substantially undercut the censorship
power of the Post Office Department and of state obscenity
laws. The civil liberties groups which have consistently called
censorship a conspiracy in restraint of trade of ideas have
stepped up the tempo of their attacks, focusing the selective
indignation of Americans on the censorship issue. Social
scientists have generally felt that their knowledge of the
effects of media is not substantial enough to permit recommendation of what ought to be proscribed, even assuming
the existence of a censorship apparatus.

Censorship is such a negatively loaded concept that few
media censors or monitoring agencies have discussed their
activities in any detail. A close-up examination of how self-
regulation of media actually takes place might help to cast
light on those shibboleths or institutions of our society whose
lengthened shadows are reflected in the censor's changes and
could clarify the kind of use which is being made of the
censors' power. Rather than debate censorship in the abstract, an examination of how it actually works might serve
to make more real the concept of censorship.

Television was selected as the mass communications industry to be examined for two reasons. There are practically
no studies either of the industry or of the broadcasters themselves, whereas power and managerial patterns in other
media have been analyzed. Another reason was the extent
to which television has become the central mass medium
of our time, with children spending an average of 15 to 20
hours a week with television.

BROADCASTING SELF-REGULATION

Broadcasting, like comic books and movies, engages in self-regulation. Broadcasting in the United States is largely supported by the sale of time to advertisers, often through advertising agencies, by stations which are licensed by the Federal Communications Commission to conduct television broadcasting on assigned frequencies. Broadcasting is the only mass medium in which *access* to the audience is sold and the audience itself does not pay for access to the specific program. The F.C.C. does not supervise the specific content of radio and television programs, and any censorship activity on its part is prohibited by the Communications Act.

The first codification of what should and should not go into radio programs was adopted in 1934, and an industry-wide code was adopted in 1937. It included a detailed statement dealing with program and advertising content. An industry-wide voluntary television code was established by the National Association of Broadcasters in 1952. Approximately two-thirds (387) of the country's television stations subscribe to the code.

Although it is possible that any horizontal industry code is illegal, the Supreme Court has never decided a case involving a code. The codes for motion pictures, radio, and television differ somewhat. The motion picture code could be said to have a moral and near-theological tone. There was provision for a $25,000 fine for violation of the code which has never been levied. The motion picture code uses the principle of "compensating moral values," which permits the presentation of otherwise unacceptable material if the wrong-doing is accompanied by appropriate suffering. The radio code is more general than the film regulations. The radio code highlights radio's commercial overtones and its interest in avoidance of external control. The television code differs from the radio code because of the extent to which it emphasizes the station licensee's active responsibility toward his audience. The television code is much more detailed than the radio code. Neither the radio nor television code uses moral language, provides for a fine for violations, or has the principle of "compensating moral values." Although each motion picture must get a specific seal of acceptance, subscribing radio and television stations get a seal which the station keeps.

In terms of actual program practice radio probably was more emancipated than television. Radio came of age in the 1930's, when there was a feeling of urgency about many social problems and a feeling that they might be solved. Radio also had a cadre of professional writers who had developed a feeling of identification with their profession. The nature of the problems of the television era has made many people feel that not much can be done about them. There is today almost a revulsion from problems and a sharp trend toward romantic and fairy-tale entertainments like the Cinderella story, *My Fair Lady*.

METHOD

One of the three major television networks was asked to permit an examination of the work of its program-screening department, which not only implements the voluntary industry code but also acts to implement network program "ground rules." Since over nine-tenths of the country's television stations are affiliated with one of the three networks, the pattern of decision on program content made by network executives would appear to be a paradigm of the most emancipated broadcaster's practice. The network provided access to its files, and it was decided to examine all monthly reports of the program-screening group for the years from 1954 through 1956. The enormous workload of this group can be inferred from the over 8,000 hours of programming which it screens and edits in an average year.

These reports include discussions of deletions and changes made during the preceding month from television programs before they go on the air, based on analysis of scripts, recordings, kinescopes, or observation of rehearsals. The discussion of each deletion is likely to be relatively thorough and may range from a few lines to a few pages. The reports also include representative comments from the three million communications which the network gets in an average year from its audiences.

The reports include only a very small fraction of the deletions and changes made during the preceding month. They include, however, a discussion of those deletions and comments which were considered important or interesting or typical enough to be communicated to the production personnel who receive the reports. The contents of these reports may thus be regarded as representative barometers.

An analysis of these reports should provide a paradigm of the day-to-day work of broadcasting screeners. In order to determine how representative the contents of these reports are, the results of this analysis for one year were compared with an analysis of every change made in all network programs during a typical week—the first week of April 1957—and the degree of correlation was .96. Possibly the only category of change or deletion which is not adequately represented is that of scientific inaccuracies, which are so individual and so unique that they have little generalizability. The number of actual changes, cautions or deletions for any individual half-hour program may range from none to nine.

All the monthly screening reports of the network for the calendar years 1954–1956 were examined. Each year's reports were studied separately and each report analyzed individually. The reports were given to three different analysts who had training and experience in media-content analysis. Each judge independently placed each comment, change, or deletion, into one of fourteen categories which had been previously established on the basis of inspection of the material by a fourth judge. The categories are: advertising, animals, anti-social, crudity, legal, liquor, medical, political, racial-ethnic, religion, sex, spoofing the serious, special interests, and violence. It was felt that an adequate impression of the actual content of the comments could be obtained by analysis of the detailed comments for the year 1956, the last year studied.

Quantifying the screening group's comments necessarily does violence to the extended discussions and gradations of meaning in the reports. The listing of these comments should not give the impression that the screening group is exclusively concerned with these or any other discrete parts of a radio or television program: it is just as concerned with the larger themes of program material.

In order to simplify analysis of the network comments, ascription of value judgments to these comments has been eliminated. For example, whenever possible the use of words like "vulgarity" in the categorization below does not concede that any cited instance actually conveys vulgarity, but only that this content category was discussed in a specific report.

DELETIONS AND COMMENTS FOR 1956

The comments which follow may not be restricted to the specific materials cited in Table 1 and may refer to other programs and situations. The deletions and comments are arranged alphabetically for the fourteen categories. The breakdown within each category indicates the details of each category of change occurring in the year. The "number" column indicates the number of times that the specific kind of deletion or comment occurs.

Advertising (Table 1a): The informal restrictions on print media advertising are generally more detailed than are similar restrictions for television advertising. The television sponsor may, however, have the right to suggest script changes, which a print media advertiser could not do to a magazine story. The network demands written proof of every advertising claim before a commercial is approved. A substantial number of commercials are rejected each year for reasons like those noted in Table 1a. The National Association of Broadcasters and the Federal Trade Commission both have staffs which monitor commercials. The maximum length of commercials is fixed by Code regulations. It is the "back-to-back" sequence of commercials at a station break which often gives the impression that the commercials consume an inordinate amount of time. Another reason for the public's sensitization to frequency of commercials is that television stations are permitted to have all their programs sponsored, although the public has various erroneous impressions about there being certain proportions of time which are required to be free of commercials.

Animals (Table 1b): Television is traditionally so cautious about presenting animals that there is an apocryphal industry wheeze about a scene in which a dog was to bark at a bear. A man in a bear suit was used in order to avoid possible difficulties with the humane society. There would appear to be little disagreement that animals should not be treated brutally on television shows.

Anti-social (Table 1c): Anti-social content is that which implicitly attacks institutions or established customs, or the

TABLE 1. *Number of Deletions, by Category, 1956*

Number of Deletions or Comments	Content of Deletions or Comments
	a: Advertising
5	Reportedly excessive claims for product
3	Possible crudeness of commercial
2	Anxiety may be provoked by commercial
1	Association of flag with product
1	Unpaid commercial mention
1	Attack on competing brands
1	Representation of violence in movie commercial
—	
14	(11.1% of total)
	b: Animals
1	Use of rabbit on magic show
1	Dog knocked unconscious in Western
1	Scenes of details of cattle-branding
1	Jungle film showing animals in pain
1	Electrocution of animals in old film
—	
5	(4.0% of total)
	c: Anti-social
2	Ineffectual teacher in old film
1	Implied encouragement of teen-agers smoking
1	Conveying impression that divorce is easy
1	Confidence games detailed in film
1	Hero's motives not clearly drawn in children's series
1	Supernatural as focus of program
1	Married couple presented as quarreling often
—	
8	(6.4% of total)
	d: Crudity
1	Crude language about sailors
1	Actors working at their neckties in vulgar manner
1	Actors' hands kept in pockets
1	Use of vulgar language by guest comedian
—	
4	(3.2% of total)

TABLE I. (*Continued*)

Number of Deletions or Comments	Content of Deletions or Comments
	e: Legal
1	Use of designations like "Oscar" without appropriate clearance
1	Burlesque of movies, literary works, radio and television series may impinge on others' legal rights
1	Implied endorsement by F.B.I.
—	
3	(2.4% of total)
	f: Liquor
1	Animals drinking rum
1	Tipsiness shown in circus show for children
1	Social drinking as a device merely to pass time
—	
3	(2.4% of total)
	g: Medical
2	Representation of pain during childbirth
1	Propriety of psychiatric sketch on comedy show
1	Misuse of hypnosis
1	Caesarian section shown
—	
5	(4.0% of total)
	h: Political
2	Possible left-wing propaganda in old film
1	Joke about a senator
—	
3	(2.4% of total)
	i: Racial and ethnic
1	Representation of Irish as alcoholic
1	Italians called "Wops"
1	Negro stereotype
1	Down-the-nose reference to Japanese & Mexicans
1	Reference to "dumb Polocks"
1	Latins misrepresented
1	Exaggerated reference to gangster's Italian name
1	Chinese laundry stereotype
1	Satire on British speech
1	Television guest made ethnic slurs
1	Series appears to advocate colonialism
—	
11	(8.7% of total)

TABLE I. (*Continued*)

Number of Deletions or Comments	Content of Deletions or Comments
	j: Religion
3	Use of "damn" and "hell"
1	Minister presented in unfavorable light
——	
4	(3.2% of total)
	k: Sex
12	Comments or scenes concerned with sex
5	Fornication and seduction references
3	Sexy costumes
2	Display of body
2	Homosexual situation
1	Reference to "Ladies' Night at Turkish Bath"
——	
25	(19.9% of total)
	l: Special interests
1	Use of leather jacket for hoodlum protested by tanners and jacket manufacturers
1	Plumbers presented as crooked
1	Smoking cigarette often shown as cause of asphyxiation
1	Implication that dentists have no feelings
1	Police not handling sick people expeditiously
1	Implied criticism of chiropractors by showing character who could not get M.D. degree and became a chiropractor
1	Motorcyclists presented as delinquents
1	Maligning journalists
1	Too many special interest "weeks"
1	News photographers misrepresented
——	
10	(8.0% of total)
	m: Spoofing the serious
17	References to mental illness as "crazy," "nuts," "cracked," and similar slang terms
1	Children breaking into mail box
——	
18	(14.3% of total)

TABLE 1. (*Continued*)

Number of Deletions or Comments	Content of Deletions or Comments
	n: Violence
4	Details of murder or assault
3	Sadistic descriptions
2	Children's show has details of crime
2	Details of horror situations
1	Science fiction film ghastly
—	
12	(10.3% of total)

government, or which appears to praise some socially disapproved activity. Program content which will affect younger viewers as a possible disparagement of authority is especially studied.

One reason for the degree of concern over such content is the fear that parts of the audience will emulate anti-social behavior like pickpocketing, or that it may learn some techniques of crime or destructive behavior. Against such possibilities, it must be remembered that almost all television crimes are solved, whereas only about 35 per cent of the crimes known to the police are solved.

The glorification of police in American popular culture is greater than in that of any other country. No other country has any analogue for the veneration accorded F.B.I. chief J. Edgar Hoover. Even the glamorous private detective in television turns his quarry over to the police.

Crudity (Table 1d): Every attempt is made to cut both language and visual crudity from television programs. Crudity is especially likely to be a matter of concern in presentations of bodily functions, in old films, and in the appearance of personalities who were trained in the less inhibited school of the night club.

Legal (Table 1e): Although there were relatively few comments on legal matters, such matters are closely watched by a network. In some states a station is even legally liable for defamatory remarks made by someone appearing on a network program.

If a situation resembles a current news situation or has

relevance to some ongoing legal action, there may on occasion be a disclaimer of similarity to any reality situations.

Another legal area of concern is in the representation of lawyers. The power of complaints from lawyers can be inferred from the threatening connotations of the phrase "lawyer's letter." Lawyers are very sensitive to how they are represented on television, perhaps as one reflection of their long history of being attacked.

Liquor (Table 1f): Most of the comments in Table 1f represent letters from the audience, especially from a few midwest states. Dry groups have been powerful enough to keep liquor advertising off television and no network or station has carried such advertising, although some have tried and then changed their plans. The dries are very sensitive to the representation of what they regard as too much social drinking on the screen.

Medical (Table 1g): Medical matters are likely to be questioned by editors or viewers primarily because of the extreme realism which television makes possible. The relatively large number of television medical programs during this period would probably have yielded more comments if close attention were not paid to medical content. Physicians are almost never presented unflatteringly on television.

Political (Table 1h): The relatively infrequent treatment of controversial political matters by television, except during a political campaign, can be inferred from the small number of comments on political matters. The decision to avoid controversial material of a political nature may be made before a dramatic program ever reaches the script stage. In 1956, for example, two different television producers were reported to be thinking of doing *The Male Animal*, a play the plot of which hinges on a professor's right to read a letter by Bartolomeo Vanzetti at a public meeting. Both producers were reported to have rejected the play because of the dependence of the plot on the letter.

Racial and ethnic (Table 1i) The racial and ethnic stereotypes which flourished in cartoons and motion pictures for decades are almost never seen on television. Negroes have been presented on the network without any special identification for some years. Contemporary television programs generally avoid presenting stereotyped minority groups, and may even err in the other extreme by presenting minority groups only minimally. American Indians represent the only minority group which did not protest its representation on television. Even they have recently begun protesting the stereotype of the Indian with long black braided hair, a band around his forehead and a feather stuck at the back, buckskin breeches with fringe, and painted fierce face.

Religion (Table 1j): Religious matters are likely to be scrutinized very closely by members of the television audience. Although network religious programs are likely to have very small audiences, the appearance of religious content in other programs is likely to elicit audience comments if the content is perceived as inappropriate. Mail response to errors of omission or commission on religion is perhaps comparatively greater than to any of the thirteen other areas.

The differences between faiths are not likely to be emphasized in television programs, and even repeating some of the almost Voltairean comments on religion of men like George Washington and Thomas Jefferson might possibly develop a storm of protest. It is difficult to imagine a broadcaster who might, for example, have a discussion based on the United States treaty with Tripoli which was signed by George Washington in 1795. This treaty states that "the free government of the United States is not, in any sense, founded on the Christian religion."

A problem in presenting ministers in dramatic productions is the audience's frequent tendency to assume that any one minister is a representative of all the ministers of his faith. Another problem at least historically related to religion is that Federal laws still provide for a fine for profanity in broadcasts. Although there have been some ghost stories on television, the possible objections of some religious groups may have caused the cancelation of other contemplated ghost programs.

Sex (Table 1k): Deletions because of some kind of sexual content were more numerous than any other kind for each year studied. Inasmuch as the network editor is especially alert to "blue" material, such content is carefully examined. The quiet disappearance of the "television neckline" of the early 1950's suggests how effective self-policing has been. Just what constitutes obscenity is a very debatable and complicated subject on which there is no judicial agreement. Practically nothing is intrinsically obscene; the dimension of obscenity is provided by the cultural matrix. Even in Catholic moral theology on the definition of the obscene, ". . . very little readily comes to hand. This may come as a surprise, especially to those who have thought that the Catholic Church has succeeded in reducing life and thought to a precise set of neat axioms."

Sex taboos differ from one medium to another, and even on different formats within one medium. In sex, as in other dimensions of freedom of expression, the theatre is the most emancipated medium. It will be remembered that the Broadway theatre was the only medium which was never accused of engaging in "blacklisting," and Actors' Equity was the only large employee group in any entertainment industry which established an anti-blacklisting committee. There is a general chronology of adaptation followed by plays which are later shown in other media: the movie adaptation of a play usually comes from two to five years after the play's first appearance, and television adaptations may run about ten years later. Feature films released for television are likely to be shown an average of fifteen years after they were made. Thus it is logical to expect that this time lag will have some effect on the degree of freedom with which sexual matters are discussed and presented on television, as compared with the other media.

Special interests (Table 1l): Television's enormous coverage makes it likely that representatives of almost every occupational or special interest group will be watching a network program. Representatives of a trade or profession often are especially sensitive to a presentation of their group which they regard as unflattering or derogatory. Sometimes the special interests represent non-commercial groups, like the organization for the aid of the blind which requested the minimization of cliches like "blind drunk" and "blind as a bat." Since it is often necessary to present some groups as behaving in a non-laudatory way, a television producer may be offending some group or other every time he shows a "heavy." Almost all of the groups referred to in Table 1l complained to the network about how they had been presented on television.

Spoofing the serious (Table 1m): The network editor is concerned where the spoofing of a serious subject is likely to be offensive or in bad taste, particularly when mental illness is referred to flippantly. Audiences may complain if they feel that an institution or situation is treated too humorously on either a dramatic or comedy show.

The insatiable demands of television for new material have made it into a kind of Medusa for satirists or comedians, who are likely to have a meteoric rise and equally dazzling decline. No television comedian has survived professionally for long enough to have developed and modified his approach and style within a television framework.

Violence (Table II): The word "violence" is listed without qualifications, although in many of the instances cited in Table II the "violence" is alleged or implied. The network report may be calling attention to an instance of actual violence which is excised or to a letter from a viewer in order to suggest that the viewer is inaccurately regarding an expression of conflict as violence. The difficulty of defining violence in operational terms makes the editor's task very difficult.

Perhaps the favorite observation of critics of television is that it unduly emphasizes violence. Conflict and violence are, of course, widely found in contemporary life, and it has been argued that television would be remiss if it did not mirror this aspect of reality.

The vast predominance of young people and young adults as central protagonists of television drama and the general absence of older persons as important *dramatis personae* may be related to the emphasis on activity and violence. This emphasis has been questioned on the ground of it being an implied attack on the value of older people and thus not consonant with the geriatric emphasis of our culture. Of course, some of this emphasis is a reflection of the special time requirements of television drama, in which a great deal may have to be presented in a half hour, so that the action develops in an unavoidably staccato manner and with little opportunity to give the reasons for different kinds of behavior.

TOTAL DELETIONS, COMMENTS AND CHANGES

The detailed comments for 1956 were shown in Table 1 above. The total breakdown of deletions, comments and changes by category during the 1954–1956 period is given in Table 2.

The degree to which any of the fourteen categories of deletions, changes or comments were more or less important in each year from 1954 through 1956 should provide clues to the extent to which the work of the network screeners has different emphases from one year to the other. Even if there were any bias in the screeners' selection of changes for their monthly reports, it may be assumed that the bias

TABLE 2.   *Total Comments for 1954–1956*

Subject Category	Total Number of Comments	Percentage of Total
Sex	110	20.7%
Violence	65	12.2
Advertising	60	11.3
Racial-ethnic	47	8.8
Spoofing serious	44	8.2
Anti-social	44	8.2
Special interests	38	7.1
Religion	28	5.3
Crudity	27	5.1
Liquor	23	4.3
Medical	17	3.2
Animals	16	3.0
Legal	8	1.5
Political	6	1.1
Totals	532	100.0%

is in the direction of presenting change from month to month and from year to year. If there are realignments in the degree of importance of any of these dimensions over the three years studied, such realignments would be reflected in the number of comments in each category and thus in the comparative rank of each category for that year. In order to clarify these realignments the categories were ranked within each year on the basis of the number of comments within each category. The Spearman rank correlation coefficient was computed for the years 1954–1955, 1955–1956 and

1954–1956. The rank correlation between 1954 and 1955 is
.78; between 1954 and 1956 it is .76; and between 1955 and
1956 it is .69. Each of these categories is significant at better
than the one per cent level of significance.

The lowest degree of correlation should be between the
individual years 1954 and 1956, if the greatest differences
are associated with the greatest distance in time. The degree
of correlation, however, is greater between 1954 and 1956
(.76) than between 1955 and 1956 (.69), suggesting that
changes in emphasis are not a direction function of changes
in time. Additionally, the coefficient of concordance was computed for 1954–1955–1956 as an independent recheck on the
Spearman rank correlation. It was found to be .79, indicating a close overall agreement among the comparative ranks
of the categories from year to year. Snedecor's F was computed (.43) as a measure of significance of the coefficient of
concordance and confirmed that there was no significant degree of variation in rank in the years studied.

There would appear to be considerable stability in the
content areas within which monitoring occurs, on the basis
of the Spearman rank correlation analysis by pairs of years
and the coefficient of concordance for all three years. The
major emphases of this network's program examination thus
appears to be significantly stable. This suggests that the
broadcasting code itself and the requirements of the medium
and of our culture remain fairly constant in terms of ad-
missible program content. It is, of course, possible—but un-
likely—that the relatively high degree of homogeneity of
content change between 1954 and 1956 may represent the
tail end or beginning of a period with a more accelerated
rate of change.

In spite of the considerable stability of the fourteen categories' relative importance, a substantial overall decrease
in the number of comments and deletions was reported from
one year to the next. This probably reflects the increasing
internalization of the norms of the program-screening group
by producers and writers of the network.

CONCLUSION

The detailing of the typical deletions and comments above
must be considered against the network's total program out-

put. The comments and deletions in these reports, of course, represent a small representative fraction of the changes, emendations, and audience comments to many thousands of programs screened by the monitoring group during the three years studied. In the face of the pressures involved in screening such a huge volume of program output it would appear that the screening group has a very difficult job which it is executing with reasonable permissiveness. Within the framework of the television code, its deletions and changes are not often arguable, except by those who feel that all censorship is undesirable and that the television code should be scrapped. The matter-of-fact work of the network censors does not seem to represent the sort of interference with free expression around which the "great debate" on censorship has raged. We can only speculate on the extent to which television may have lost freedom and vitality because its creative personnel knew that there would be a network censor scrutinizing their work. A content analysis of the censor's work cannot measure this kind of intangible, however important it may be.

It appears visionary to expect that the censor's function will disappear in the immediate future. The qualities which make a television writer or producer distinguished are not necessarily those which make him alert to material offensive to some parts of the audience. Specially trained personnel to exercise editorial responsibility would appear to be a necessity, so long as sponsors pay for programs, and the concept of media responsibility for its output remains a "given" of our culture. The development of non-network toll television and of new program format may conceivably alter the nature of the censor's functions or ultimately lead to the disappearance of the function.

PART VIII

Epilogue

ISSUES AND PERSPECTIVES:
A PUBLIC CONFRONTATION

GOVERNOR ROCKEFELLER: We are now ready to go to the last part of the session, a panel which is represented by men of unique experience in a field which is of tremendous importance to all of us. There is no greater challenge, I think, to our society today than the question of the portrayal of violence in the mass media. This is something that is interesting, and has caused all of us to consider and wonder and study the question.

There is concern among the public and professionals alike regarding the nature and degree of violence in the mass media. The issue has become surrounded with some emotion, and has been widely discussed.

Yet this concern and these discussions have instilled no firm conclusions in the public mind. A child growing up today sees or reads hundreds or perhaps thousands of specific incidents of violence in the print, broadcast and entertainment media.

Does this have some effect on behavior in childhood or later life?

We have gathered here today informed persons from across the country to discuss this subject. I am deeply grateful to all the members of the panel. Without further delay, then, I will turn the meeting over to Dr. Otto Larsen, the chairman of the panel.

DR. LARSEN: Thank you, Governor Rockefeller. Given our topic, I suppose the first words I should utter would be *bam, biff, pow, zow, zingo, smack,* and *whack.* However, let me rather express my gratitude for being invited to come across the country to participate in this important conference on crime. You have hammered out a consensus about an impressive array of new programs designed to cope with pressing social problems.

Excerpts, edited by the participants, from the transcript, of a panel presentation on "Violence in Mass Media" at Governor Nelson Rockefeller's Conference on Crime, New York, April 22, 1966. Used with the permission of panel participants.

But now we turn to the last topic on the conference schedule, and here the search for solutions has hardly begun.
Perhaps it is because there is no clear consensus on what
the problem is. It's undoubtedly wise to place a topic like
this at the end of a conference, particularly a conference
like this that has been marked by so much harmony.

For years I have read and freely borrowed from the published work of Dr. Klapper, Dr. Berkowitz and Dr. Wertham.
I have even tried to imagine, in print recently, what a con-
frontation would be like when men with their backgrounds
got together to talk about the topic before us now. The
four of us include in our professional interest a common
curiosity and concern about violence in the mass media and
elsewhere, and its impact on man and its meaning for society. In our professional work, each member of this panel
has approached the subject with a different set of tools.

Dr. Klapper has been concerned mainly with survey research and statistical analysis of interview and questionnaire data.

Dr. Berkowitz has been concerned mainly with controlled
experiments in laboratory situations.

Dr. Wertham has been concerned mainly with clinical
case studies.

Given the complexity of this problem, I think it's fortunate
that we are equipped with so many instruments in the search
for truth. But this also means that when you come to professionals and ask, "What effect does media violence have?"
you are going to get a variety of answers.

While this might be reflected in today's discussion, our
main effort, I trust, will be to give you our best estimate of
the meaning and significance of violence in the mass media.

It is tempting to indict the mass media for many of our
ills, including those associated with violence. Given certain
facts, this is quite understandable. It is a fact, for example,
that all over the world more and more people are spending
more and more time in exposure to the mass media, particularly to television. In the United States over 90 per cent
of the homes have at least one television set, and the average
set is on something over six hours a day. Children between
the ages of six and fourteen spend as much time in front of
the television as they do in school.

Now most of us would think that such concentrated exposure must mean something. And it might mean something different today than at an earlier time, if you take it one step further—if you agree that a big part of the media menu is a large dose of violence, showing persons inflicting injury on one another. So if you add this violent content to the heavy pattern of exposure, what are the consequences?

Do you get more crime, more violent crime, more violent behavior, as some assert?

And if you do, what can be done about it, given our preference for a free press in a free society?

Are there workable alternatives to censorship? Is there something beyond industry's self-regulation, but short of government censorship, that would work and that could satisfy us?

As professionals, we might advocate caution in developing new controls until more is known about the effects. But many citizens do not want to wait and risk possible damage that could flow from the sea of media violence.

This conference has issued many calls for education to improve public understanding. We always seem to end up at that point. And, of course, the mass media have a responsibility and an opportunity to enhance public understanding of critical issues. But the public must also come to understand the media—what they can and what they cannot do.

All of us—public, mass communicators, researchers—face a kind of two-world question. Out there in the real world there is real violence, lots of it. Then there is a mass media world, which both reports the violence of the real world and portrays a fantasy violence of its own.

What is the linkage between these two worlds? Under what conditions does the media world change the real world, alter it, influence it? With respect to violence, do we expect the media to reflect the real world or to be better than the real world?

These are questions that could come out for discussion here today. We are dealing with a many-faceted problem. When we look at the role of the mass media, I am sure we will recognize that it is merely one feature, but a potentially important and highly visible feature, of this problem. We are fortunate in having with us three panel members who have done a great deal of work in thinking and writing about violence and mass communication. Each of them will make a brief presentation, and then there will be opportunities for discussion.

Our first speaker is Dr. Joseph Klapper, who is Director of Social Research for the Columbia Broadcasting System— the author, among other publications, of a book widely used in universities called *The Effects of Mass Communication*.

That, in a special sense, is our topic today. I am pleased to present first, Dr. Klapper.

DR. KLAPPER: This concern about the depictions of violence in mass media and their effect on people's behavior— particularly children's behavior—is nothing new, nor is it anything which is uniquely tied to television. It has existed literally since the publication of the *Tales of King Arthur,* and has been discussed in relation to print, including classics, and of course the Penny Dreadfuls, and more recently the comic books, and newspapers and magazines. It has been discussed in relation to radio and movies, and it is being discussed now in relation to television.

One of the ways that this problem may be examined is by survey techniques. But survey techniques do not consist exclusively of looking at questionnaires and analyzing statistics. They also involve or can involve comparing people.

Various social scientists, both in this country and abroad, have compared children who were exposed to violence in the media and those who were not. The conclusion to which they came was that they found no more aggressive, maladjusted—I am quoting—"no more aggressive, maladjusted or delinquent behavior among the viewers than among the nonviewers."

This is not to say that the violence didn't have any effect at all. Some of it did frighten some children, but the fright appeared to be transient, and in any case certainly did not lead to aggressive and violent behavior.

It was also found, and I think this is rather significant, that what we as adults tend to think of as violence is a rather crude and meaningless term in reference to what children perceive. Thus it was found, to everyone's surprise, that *verbal violence*, arguments between adults, was more disturbing to the children than was the physical violence—not always, but in many instances.

It was found that violence in *stereotyped form*, such as in detective stories and westerns where everybody knew what was going to happen, had little or no effect on children, whereas violence in unusual vehicles, which the children did not know well, was more frightening. By way of curious example, the most frightening thing that the researchers encountered was *Jane Eyre,* which one would hardly think of as dangerous material.

But, and I repeat, the essential point is that the researchers found no more criminal violence or aggressive behavior among the viewers than among the nonviewers.

Now there are some studies which indicate that there are certain differences between persons who watch a lot of violent material and those who do not watch a lot of violent material. Some of these studies have revealed that the children who like the violent material tend to have a somewhat lower IQ and that they tend to be somewhat less well adjusted generally. I want to fasten momentarily on the lower IQ, because one thing is certain, and that is that neither television nor comic books nor any other medium lowers anyone's IQ. Accordingly, then, we are led to consider the theory that perhaps these differences exist before the child's media experiences, and lead him to the media experiences, rather than vice versa.

Actually, there is a considerable amount of evidence in support of this view. A recent study, for example, divided children not into viewers and nonviewers, or readers and nonreaders, but rather into those who had satisfactory relationships with their peer groups and those who didn't. The researchers found that the violent material was much more liked among those who did not have good relations with their peer group. Further, and to my mind more importantly, the researchers found that among the children who did have good peer group relationships, the violent material tended to have little effect and tended to get translated into rather innocuous group games. Among those who did not have good relationships with their peer group, the violent material tended to be used to stimulate eerie, unhealthy fantasies of one sort or another.

Basically similar findings have been consistently made in reference to mass media in areas quite apart from violence —for example, in reference to the effect of propaganda and in reference to the effects of political campaigns. I can sum up these findings by saying that the media appear to have,

as their most important effect, a *reinforcement* tendency.
They tend to reinforce the opinions, tastes and behavioral
patterns which the audience member, child or adult, pos-
sesses when he comes to that television console or comic
book, or whatever. It is this kind of finding which has led
Wilbur Schramm to say that what the child brings to the
medium is perhaps much more important than what the
medium brings to the child.

This is in no sense a whitewash. For the media tend to
reinforce whatever the tendencies of the child may be, with
a complete disregard of whether these tendencies are socially wholesome or unwholesome.

These considerations suggest that the starting point for
any efforts to ameliorate the situation should be so located
as to deal with those forces which make the child what he
is when he comes to the media. I refer primarily to those
forces which influence the child when he is extremely young:
his family, above all; his play groups and other peer groups;
schools, and so on down the line. And I suggest that while
it is legitimate, desirable and wholly understandable to seek
the cooperation, in fact to demand the cooperation, of the
media in this pursuit, the major focus of any program designed to reduce violent behavior should not be upon the
media, but rather upon the children who are brought to the
media.

In the course of these remarks I have deliberately avoided
making any reference to how much violence there is in the
media. I am sure we can all agree that there is a great deal
of it, not only in our media, but also in those of other
countries.

I submit, then, that while the cooperation of the media
should be sought in this matter, the major fruitful efforts
will come from dealing with the child and rendering him
better able to face the media and all other aspects of life.

DR. LARSEN: Our next speaker is Dr. Leonard Berkowitz
from the Department of Psychology of the University of Wisconsin. He is the author of the book entitled *Aggression, A
Social-Psychological Analysis* and the editor of several vol-
umes on "Advances in Experimental Social-Psychology."

DR. BERKOWITZ: I think everyone should be warned that I
come from a very different research tradition than Dr. Klapper to my right, and we are indeed in danger of getting into

a violent argument. Perhaps we had better put Governor Rockefeller in between.

Our findings are based on laboratory research in which we place college students in certain specified situations and see how they act. It is important to remember that our subjects are usually quite inhibited people. That may sound strange, with the drug-taking, panty raids and so forth that supposedly go on in colleges, but college students, at least in laboratory situations, are generally well behaved and quite inhibited. They don't go around punching each other in the nose.

The point that I want to make is this. Even though they are really not juvenile delinquents, we have found over and over again in our experiments that these students can be made to act aggressively after watching filmed violence.

There is no necessary contradiction between what Dr. Klapper just said and our persistent findings—and I might say other researchers around the country and in Canada have obtained essentially similar results. What Dr. Klapper's survey research suggests is that the effect of observed violence may not be long lasting. Persistent juvenile delinquents are not formed as a result of watching filmed violence. Our research indicates, nevertheless, that there may be a definite but quite temporary, transient effect of this type of witnessed event. It may not last more than a few minutes, but it does seem to be quite dramatic and reliable.

This is a very complicated issue and I am in danger of greatly oversimplifying, but let me draw an analogy. Some people have contended that media violence may have socially beneficial consequences. Viewers supposedly could have their pent-up aggressive urges drained by watching other people beat each other up.

For me at least, it is quite interesting that nobody has ever maintained that sexual desires can readily be satisfied through watching a couple make love. If aggressive urges are drained through seeing aggression, why aren't sexual urges lessened by watching sexual activity? As far as sex is concerned, just the opposite probably occurs; observed sex leads to increased sexual tendencies within the observer. I think the analogy should hold; just as a person might become temporarily sexually excited by watching people make love or by going to a burlesque show, so people may become somewhat aggressively excited through watching aggression for a period of time.

Now a person who goes to a burlesque show does not necessarily come out and assault the first woman he meets. For one thing, he probably has strong inhibitions against this form a disapproved behavior. This also is the case when most of us watch filmed aggression. A person may come away from the TV screen or film theatre with strong inhibitions against aggression so that he does not display any aggressive tendencies. If these inhibitions are weak, however, even if only temporarily, openly aggressive behavior may be revealed.

Our experimental research has demonstrated that the observer's attitude toward the scene he witnesses is an important consideration in this regard. If the observer thinks the filmed violence he sees is bad, morally improper, relatively strong restraints against aggression are often aroused. He may then lean over backwards to avoid acting aggressively. But, should the observer believe that the filmed aggression is good or proper, there is a somewhat greater likelihood that he, himself, will act aggressively, for a few minutes at least, after seeing the film.

Putting this as an abstract proposition, our research shows that the individual's aggressive behavior is very greatly affected by the stimuli in the situation. If someone is ready to act aggressively for one reason or another, and he encounters a stimulus that in his mind is associated with aggression, he will have a greater likelihood of acting aggressively than if he had not met up with that aggressive stimulus.

As one specific illustration of this in our research, we have found that when we place a rifle or a revolver in front of subjects who have been deliberately angered, they display stronger aggression than they would have if the weapon were not in front of them. The rifle evidently serves as a stimulus which draws out stronger aggression than would otherwise have been exhibited.

One final observation. Our experimental research indicates that the effects of observed violence depend upon at least three types of factors. One, how ready the observer is to act aggressively. Two, his inhibitions against aggression, which are affected by his attitudes toward the observed violence. Three, we also have to consider the qualities of the person who is available to be attacked. Some people apparently are more likely to be attacked than others. This is in part a matter of fear of retaliation. A person who is big, strong and threatening obviously is not in great danger of being punched by most of us. This is not all. We also have found in our laboratory research that those people who are associated or connected with the victim of the observed violence generally receive the strongest attacks.

We have here all sort of reasons why Dr. Klapper's survey results haven't found any apparent evidence for effects of film violence. Suppose a child watches aggression on the screen. Does he regard what he sees as good or bad aggression? What is the strength of his inhibitions against aggression at that moment? He goes out of the theatre or his living room. Does he meet anybody that he connects with the observed violence? If not, he may not display any aggression himself. On the other hand, should an angry and comparatively uninhibited youngster happen to see somebody he associates with the victim of the observed violence, somebody who reminds him of the victim, this unfortunate person, at least for a very short period of time, is more likely to be attacked than he would have been if the boy had not seen the television program.

Well, with this great oversimplification, I will stop being the target and quit.

DR. LARSEN: As I said at the outset, each of us is employing different tools in dealing with this problem, and now we move to still another approach.

I don't suppose our next speaker needs introduction to New York audiences. Indeed, even to national audiences he needs no introduction, because he has been very prominent in drawing attention to this as a public issue—through his publications, through his other work.

You may be familiar with some of his books, *The Seduction of the Innocent, Show of Violence,* and a 1966 volume entitled, *A Sign for Cain, An Exploration of Human Violence.*

I am pleased to present Dr. Fredric Wertham.

DR. WERTHAM: The subject of violence, whether it be in war or crime or LSD or juvenile delinquency or mass media, is always controversial. I don't think we should shy away from controversy, this being a serious subject.

We live in an era of complacency about violence. That

does not mean that we can indulge in any vast generalizations, but rather that we have to consider every specific manifestation of violence and study it, even if it may seem insignificant.

In our world, violence abounds. Since the end of World War II there have been forty wars. In New York City on an average day we have more than one murder, four rapes, twenty-two holdups, forty-one assaults, and so on.

Now two undisputable facts stand out in this field. First of all, younger and younger children commit more and more brutal acts. I have seen many of these children and examined them, and I have done so for many years. I can see the curve of the increase.

The second fact, which to my mind is undisputable, is that there is an endless profusion of violent images in our mass media: the crime comic books, the television, the bubble-gum cards and all other kinds of media,

Now this goes from the glorification of violence in television shows at the time of the children's viewing time, up to the movies with the technocrat sadism of James Bond.

In the United States and in West Germany at present, more and more movies and programs publicize war. Many of these programs are just what I call war commercials. Violence is a predominant element in our whole civilization now, and the huge entertainment industry has been built around that.

What are the effects of this mass violence on immature people, on youth, and on children?

Three so-called scientific methods have been used to study these effects. I say the ordinary layman doesn't need any science to realize, without knowing all the details of the exact mechanisms involved, that it can't be good for a child, or have no effect on him, if you give him a profusion of slugging, killing, torture, bleeding, branding and so on. This is true even with children from the most normal families, and with the most normal makeups.

The first research method used is the questionnaire method, which sometimes goes by the elegant name of the structured interview method. You ask and you get an answer. I would like to say this method is entirely unreliable. Whole books have been written about that. You ask a child, "Do you believe in God?"

And he says, "Yes."

You ask the next child. He says, "No."

Then you ask the third child, "Do you believe in God?"

He says, "Sometimes."

So then you have scientific research and statistics and you make three groups: Believer, Non-believer and Undecided. It's like market research. I don't think that's good.

One book which Dr. Klapper mentioned, he said they studied 2,000 children. May I say in all humility they do not study 2,000 children. To study a child, you study a child. If you ask a child a few questions and get some answers and then put them into statistics, you haven't studied that human being. The children may not even know themselves what effect something has on them.

Now the second method is the experimental method in laboratories, of which you heard Dr. Berkowitz speak. Now undoubtedly, and especially in his work, which is among the best in this field, it can give us useful hints—better even than the questionnaire methods, which may also give us some hints. But the whole approach in the laboratory is un-lifelike.

After all, young people are not rats or white mice. They are human beings. They have an unconscious. They have imagination. What the laboratory technique has to leave out is, to my mind and in my experience, the most important point, and that is this: we are not so much interested when a child sees a movie or television show in what happens to him that day or even that night. We are interested in what happens three, four, five years later. In other words, we are interested in the long-range sleeper effects.

As far as I can see, the only method that can come near to giving us valid results is what is called the clinical method. What does that consist of?

Very briefly, you examine the child. You study not only this particular television show, but all kinds of other factors —his family, his health. You give him tests. You have group or playroom observation and most important of all, you must have follow-up studies. You can't examine a child when he is seven years old and make all kinds of generalizations.

How is he going to be at twelve?

For many years my associates and I have been trying to do that on hundreds of children, and we have found that there is a cumulative effect in all this enormous amount of violence, and that this violence is a contributing factor to all kinds of childhood troubles.

I must say I feel like a fool in stating this, because it is obvious. How can a human being see all this blood and all this torture and not be in some way affected?

I use the words contributing factor because very often in the literature on the subject they speak of primary causes and basic causes and direct causes. Well, in mental life, to my mind, there is no such thing. All contributing factors are causal factors, and all causal factors are contributing factors. There is not one thing that makes a man vote or kill or marry or whatever people do. There are many, many different factors that enter into that. The best we can do, and that is difficult enough, is to try and disentangle these different motives.

Of course, the effects are very different on different children. We cannot tell beforehand which child will be more affected or which child will be less. But I can tell you briefly what two most important effects are which we have proved by actual case studies. We have found first of all that the over-all effect in many children, and not by any means all, is a blunting of sensibility. These children become hard. They don't see any more that a child suffers. And they have learned a devaluation of human life. Death means much less to them than it should.

Now many children have been accustomed to regard violence as a natural, correct response—I don't think I have to tell that here to a group which knows about law enforcement in New York City.

What happens is that the exhibition of violence is close to an invitation to violence, and showing the means of violence is close to seduction.

Juveniles want to identify themselves—not only with their parents, not only with their teachers, not only with great figures—but with a group in the widest sense. That is part of their orientation. That is part of their moral frame of reference, which they need. That is affected because children see now that the group evidently approves this display of violence and feels that this is all right.

I have found, for instance, that children and adolescents and young people who watch these Vietnam war films and then see the Westerns look at both in practically the same way. I mean, you see a Western and six or seven people bite the dust, and then you see a Vietnam film, and so on, with Viet Congs being killed. And the image that we give these children is that Lyndon Johnson is the fastest gun in the West.

There are two kinds of experts who work in this field, apart from the methods they use, and I am speaking now about psychology. There are some who we call I.D. experts. That means, industry-directed. They are interested in the industry. And there are other experts who are interested in children; we call them C.D. experts, and their attitude is very different.

I can tell you in one sentence that some of the I.D. experts have the industry at heart, and they always blame the children: "The children were wrong before they saw that violence, the children are wrong."

We have the children at heart and we blame the industry.

This is quite a serious matter for those of us, like myself, who began speaking up about this subject quite a number of years ago. I will tell you what happened to me. You probably heard about Mr. Nader, who challenged the safety of automobiles. And you probably read in the papers that detectives were after him. They tried to intimidate him, and they promised him a job. They asked everybody who knew him what his sex life and what his social life was. All this happened to me. All this was done to me by the violence publishers. They had two detectives after me for six weeks. They called everybody who knew me. They tried to find out what car I drive.

They want to find out something about either me or Mr. Nader or somebody else and then they try to intimidate you.

I think that's a very serious interference with democracy.

I am talking about the scientific investigation of mass media. But I cannot agree that it is a very complex and difficult subject. If you turn on the television tonight and you see countless murders, that is not complicated. Mass media and life are not two entirely separate worlds. The stories imitate life, and life imitates the story. If we really want to prevent violence and crime, which of course this Conference wants to do, we must be attentive both to the representation of violence and to the violence of life.

DR. KLAPPER: Dr. Wertham says that one should not draw distinctions between contributory causes and direct causes. I cannot accept that, and would like to talk about it for a moment.

In this connection, let me repeat that the surveys which I have mentioned found no difference in criminal or violent behavior among persons who view this material—and the same is true with reference to comic books—and persons who don't.

This is extremely important, for if the kids who are not exposed to media violence exhibit the same rate of this undesirable behavior, as do those who are exposed, then either exposure has no effect at all, or, if it does have a contributory effect, then the unexposed find some other contributory cause which is just as efficient as the mass media.

I am not making any play for violence. I am only suggesting that to look at contributory causes—to look at indirect causes—can, at times, be very nonparsimonious of work, funds and effort. It is my feeling that if a child is sufficiently on the brink that witnessing depictions of violence on television or in the films or in a comic book will cause him to go out and commit violence, then the removal of those sources will achieve nothing; the child will be similarly influenced by descriptions of crimes in the newspaper, by overheard remarks, or by any of a million other sources.

I have a different sort of argument, but not a violent argument, with Dr. Berkowitz. I accept Dr. Berkowitz's experiments, but I have certain questions about his interpretation of his findings. These questions bear mainly on what he means by aggression.

I think we really ought to define what we each mean by aggression. Dr. Wertham and I have been somewhat aggressive towards each other this afternoon, but neither of us is going to shoot the other. And I believe very strongly that the kind of aggression manifested in the experiments of Dr. Berkowitz and his colleagues has nothing to do with the kind of aggression that this conference has been called to discuss and about which people are concerned. In a nutshell, we are concerned about crime and interpersonal violence, not about somebody simply feeling aggressive. Feelings of aggression are a normal part of human life, and an adaptive reaction to one's environment, and their expression in socially approved ways is not our concern. Crime and injury to persons are our concern.

I want also to say in reference to Dr. Berkowitz's experiments, that if the only effect of violence in films is to make people feel somewhat more aggressive for fifteen minutes, and if this aggression is implemented only by those who don't have any inhibitions, and who within the fifteen minutes are stimulated by seeing a rifle or someone they don't like who, into the bargain, is a person whom society considers it for some reasons not improper to attack, and if the film viewer, still within the same fifteen minutes, attacks him, well, if that's all that the media can do, I think I have been wasting my time for the last ten or fifteen years studying the possibilities of the media having very harmful effects.

DR. LARSEN: With children spending more time in front of television than they have with any other medium, isn't it possible that there could be a creative effect here? If something is to be reinforcing, it must come from somewhere. If the mass media now take so much time, away from other things, isn't it reasonable to expect some effect that you have not yet detected?

What is being reinforced? Where does it come from?

DR. KLAPPER: There have been to date no worthwhile studies of the cumulative effects of exposure to violence on television or anywhere else. Vast technical difficulties are involved in researching such a thing. In the course of ten or fifteen years, there are millions of influences upon an individual, media influence and millions of other influences, and to attempt to determine the actual effects of each of these influences, or what effects would not have occurred if a given influence were absent—all this involves a research undertaking which is massive, and in certain ways perhaps impossible. Certainly it has been impossible of accomplishment to date. So we don't know a great deal about the cumulative effects of exposure, and everybody interested in this subject, both in the industry and outside it, has been trying for years to find some effective way of studying it. And no one has as yet found the way.

Now in reference to another point raised by Dr. Larsen, the media are extremely effective, as revealed by research, in creating opinions on new issues—issues in reference to which no opinions as yet exist.

One pertinent study has indicated that children will obtain ideas from the mass media about how people in other social classes in other countries live and act. But they will not be affected by mass media portrayals of how people in their own social class live and act, because they know very well how they live and act.

I do not think that media can possibly be the first or major influence upon a child in reference to whether he adopts a non-violence oriented or a violence-oriented view of life. I think, rather, that the child's family, the kind of social sanctions or family sanctions that are administered, are much more likely to be the first major influence in that area. I point out to you that a child's life does not consist exclusively of watching violence on television. He does a million other things, he watches a lot of non-violent material, and he is in contact with other people. I cannot accept the proposition that television is more influential than a family.

DR. BERKOWITZ: I agree with Dr. Klapper that television is just one of many, many influences, and I think that's possibly one of the reasons why I still believe that the effect is very short-lived.

I might also suggest that even if the effect is very short-lived, if it lasts fifteen minutes, five minutes or half an hour —if twenty million people see a scene, one person may be hurt who otherwise might not be hurt because of an aggressive scene on television. In other words, it may not be a very long lasting effect, and it may be a very tiny effect, but it still affects someone.

Just one final observation with regard to our experimental procedure. Most of the laboratory experiments nowadays actually involve not reported feelings but physical actions in which our college-student subjects believe they are physically attacking somebody.

DR. LARSEN: How do we get from the laboratory to the real live situation that Dr. Wertham talked about? How do you take your knowledge to the next step?

DR. BERKOWITZ: I suppose I must confess that I have, generally, been theoretically oriented, and haven't faced up to the practical issues. I think that there are implications in the research that we have been doing.

For example, as I understand it, every police department is familiar with crimes that seem to follow immediately upon reports of other cases of violence; reports of a gory murder which seems to produce other attacks.

Kennedy's assassination led to attacks on, or at least threats of attacks on, Prime Minister Wilson, as a case in point.

I think essentially we are dealing with the same phenomenon of an observed scene which serves as a stimulus to maybe one, two, three crackpots, setting into motion previously acquired aggressiveness habits.

I think the parallel exists, but how to go from our very limited laboratory situation to these real-life problems, I couldn't say. I do, nevertheless, believe, if I can make the extrapolation, that aggressive stimuli whether on the screen, whether in terms of rifles in people's homes, increase the probability that somebody will act aggressively who otherwise might not have done so.

DR. LARSEN: Dr. Wertham, we turn to you.

May I ask you just one question that troubled me?

You said that one of the major outcomes, you believe, of the portrayal of violence is the blunting of sensitivity. I would like to ask you, how about the blunting of sensitivity to violence itself, and would you consider this a positive contribution?

DR. WERTHAM: I don't quite understand that.

DR. LARSEN: You said there is a blunting of sensitivity as a result of exposure to the media, correct?

DR. WERTHAM: Yes, disregard for violence, in that they don't realize any more that pain is pain, that this girl gets really hurt.

I can tell you very simply. Formerly, people would identify themselves with the victim. Somebody gets hit and you read it, in a story or something, and you identify yourself with the victim and you feel it's something bad. Now they identify themselves with the person who is doing the killing, or the hitting. This is the great Superman. He does it. That's elegant.

You slap a girl. That shows what a good man you are. They identify themselves not with the victim. That's what I call blunting of sensitivity.

I would like to say a very few words with regard to what Dr. Klapper said, merely by way of clarification. In the first place, I have no intention to offend anybody in saying he is

an industry-directed person. We all are to some extent industry-directed. To some extent we live in a society where
we have to deal with big industries, and where we work,
have income. We are influenced by the industries that are
around us, and it requires a very special effort to really
identify oneself with these children, with these young people.

Then he has an argument which is very difficult. He says
that if the child wouldn't find it in television, he would find
it somewhere else. Where can you find these thousands of
murders and homicides that these kids have seen? Where
else can they find it? Not in life, not even in the newspapers.

Then I think he said—I don't want to speak too contro-
versially—that there is no massive research. My associates
and I have worked for years. We have done massive research.
We have examined hundreds of children, where we found
exactly what I told you today.

Then he used the expression that television is not a first
or major influence. This I have heard innumerable times.
I am not speaking about Dr. Klapper, but I am speaking
about many other books and studies, alas. They say it's not
the first or major cause. Nobody can say what is the first or
major cause. We are not talking about that. It's an evasion.

If you say a first or major cause, or a crucial cause, that
means you open the door for all kinds of excuses.

We say it has something to do with it, and I give you an
example. In a recent copy of the *Annals of the Academy of
Political and Social Science*, where Dr. Larsen's article appeared, I found this sentence which criticized, incidentally,
my humble self.

The article says, "Comic books are apt to reinforce delinquent tendencies and to teach new and better ways of being
delinquent. But then the basic issue is the delinquent tendency, not the comics."

I don't understand that. What more can you do? If you
reinforce something and if you teach a child new methods
of how to steal and how to do all kinds of things, they say
that's not important. They say the important thing is the
delinquent tendency.

Dr. Klapper said that he cannot accept that TV is more
important than the family. It's all up to the family. How
could Dr. Wertham talk about television and comic books?
If the child comes from a good family, everything is fine.

Let me tell you, that was so fifty years ago when many people lived in the country.

Nowadays, there are influences which the family cannot control. The families have been unable to control the comic books. They have been unable to control television. It can't be done.

DR. LARSEN: I would like to have a question from the floor for Dr. Berkowitz.

MR. CHEIN: My name is Isador Chein, Professor of Psychology from the New York University.

On this issue I sympathize with Dr. Klapper. I would like to ask Dr. Berkowitz, isn't it correct that college students are notoriously inclined to the expectations of the experiments so that they have a way of producing what the experiment wants? Isn't it also true that when you say that physical acts of violence are involved, that it's a rather important qualifier in your statement, to wit, that they believe that they are physically injuring somebody? Isn't it more correct to say that you believe that they believe?

DR. BERKOWITZ: Our subjects, who are paid for participating in the research, get their rewards, and then we go through some very intensive open-end interviews to determine to what extent these college students are concerned about giving us what we want. This is very standard practice. The subjects, by the way, are debriefed; that is, the experiment is explained to them afterwards. We are completely honest with them. We try to get them to be completely honest with us and we are quite convinced that these subjects, one, do not suspect what it is that we want; and two, are not attempting to act in order to please us or to put their best foot forward. That is all I can say.

Obviously this isn't clinical, but it is our definite belief that the subjects are not play-acting.

MRS. JOHN JERMON: I speak now as the mother of five children, rather than as a representative of the National Council of Jewish Women.

We all know that inhibitions are developed over the years of life. Consequently, as Dr. Wertham so aptly pointed out, continuous exposure to violence makes it part of the norm rather than the abnormal. I think that we are approaching this entirely wrong.

If there is such concern, why spend money and time in

trying to find out the extent of the damage? No matter how little it is, if there is going to be the smallest amount of damage, put that money, put that time, put that effort towards creative activity, as Dr. Larsen pointed out—towards creating programs. We talked about educating the public, educating the children. Everyone knows that a spoonful of sugar makes the medicine go down. Why cannot our cultural artists, our creative people, bring before the people, before the children the sort of education that we want our children to grow up with? Put those efforts to good use then, if there is the slightest effect at all.

DR. KLAPPER: This is really an extremely complicated matter. In the first place, you have to make a distinction, I think, between programs which are designed for child viewers, and programs which are not designed exclusively for child viewers.

In reference to programs designed exclusively or primarily for child viewers, there is, to the best of my knowledge, no pursuit of violence. I don't mean that it never occurs, but rather that there is a consistent effort on the part of most good program producers to avoid it.

Then there are all the other programs, which are designed for a family audience, or for adults. Of course children may see some of these, and they may see violence depicted or even see it in news programs. You cannot seriously suggest that all violence should be removed from the medium, which after all deals with life in a world which is violent.

As Dr. Wertham has said, there is a great deal of violence in this world. He mentioned, and I repeat, that this is not only fictional violence, but real violence. For that matter, if you will stop talking and thinking of television for a moment, you will find extreme and extensive violence in practically all of the plays of Shakespeare—and in the Bible, in the King Arthur stories; in, oh, say, *Treasure Island;* in Mother Goose, in the nursery rhymes. Violence abounds.

I would like to say one other thing. You said that violence is becoming normative.

I very much doubt that your family normally engages in violence. Depictions of violence may be visible on your television screen, and maybe there is too much of it. But I don't think violence is becoming normative.

DR. LARSEN: Mass communication may—and I think we

have had some indications that it does—influence audiences. But audiences can influence mass communication. The media are sensitive to the expressions of complaint from the audience. Content can be changed, and it has been changed, and will be changed. And part of our problem, which we haven't touched upon today, is how to make that two-way communication system continuously representative of the great variety of public tastes, needs, and preferences.

GOVERNOR ROCKEFELLER: I would like to first thank this panel. I only regret that the time factor is such that we really can't go further, because I think this is a productive discussion, and I really am very excited. Things are beginning to come out on this.

I couldn't help thinking while these last two speakers were speaking about the children watching some of these programs. Sometimes it is the parents who select the program, not the children. Sometimes the children watch the parents' program, and maybe the parents are a little more interested in something that has more violence.

But I think this gets us back to the theme that has been going on through the discussions for the last two days, namely, *public participation*.

As I said in the opening, until the citizens of this State or country collectively and individually make the war on crime their war, and their responsibility in all its phases, I don't think we really are going to be completely successful. And I think that we get back here again to this question of the present panel, the question of how much responsibility do we have as citizens?

I know a little bit about the television industry, and I am confident that they are responsive, at least, to what they think public interest is. And they are trying to give the public programs it wants to look at, because those programs are advertising media. The sponsors of the programs sell their products as a result of the popularity of the program.

So here we have another case where the *public* is an important element in the solution of this problem.

Notes and References

VIOLENCE AS AN AMERICAN VALUE THEME

Walter M. Gerson

1 This approach to violent behavior is similar to the conflict approach to social phenomena. For example, Rose defines social conflict as "activity intended to hurt others physically or mentally or to deprive others of liberty (or property) and as activity designed to prevent one from being so intentionally hurt or deprived by others." See Arnold Rose, *Sociology: The Study of Human Relations* (New York: Alfred A. Knopf, 1965), p. 635. The possibility of emphasizing social conflict rather than violence in the present essay was seriously considered. The emphasis on social conflict would have allowed for a great deal more integration with sociological theory, past and present. However, to most sociologists, conflict refers to *intergroup* conflicts. Since the present essay centers around the normative or value structure of the society, the intent is to keep all "levels" of social behavior, including interpersonal relations, "open" for possible analysis. It was felt that the concept of "violence" might better accomplish this initial aim than the more restrictive concept of "social conflict."

2 Other dimensions of violence may also be relevant. For example, is the behavior anticipated (planned for) or is it an unanticipated (unplanned for) consequence of the social situation? Various psychological theories have attempted to explain the reasons for aggressive behavior. One limitation to the applicability of these theories is that they have, for the most part, been developed in an effort to explain individual behavior, whereas we are concerned with behavior on *all* levels of social interaction. Further, not all violent behavior as we have conceptualized it constitutes aggressive or hostile behavior. There is no necessary correlation between the two variables.

3 Violence in America sometimes functions as a means for testing out others in social situations and, hence, a means of defining a previously undefined or vague situation. Adult persons, as well as children, often "test out" newcomers or strangers by violent behavior. The specific *form* of violence used in testing others out may vary. Male children sometimes test out a new boy in the neighborhood by fighting or wrestling with him (physical violence). Girls, on the other hand, seldom resort to physical violence. They, like adults, tend to engage in verbal or manipulative violence in testing out the new person. "One-upmanship" or other verbal potential violences may have the same consequence: the new person is typed, and, once a person is categorized as a social type, others can interact with him with some degree of ease. Violence can be a means of defining the situation for interactors, then.

4 This is the case *unless* the mass media or some group makes a special point to draw public attention to the methods used by the law enforcement people.

5 For example, murder mysteries and detective stories have been popular for over a century, ever since *Graham's*, the world's first mass circulation magazine, published Edgar Allan Poe's "The Murders in the Rue Morgue" in 1841.

297

6 Chinoy's findings concerning automobile workers are consistent with this hypothesis. See Ely Chinoy, *Automobile Workers and the American Dream* (Garden City, N.Y.: Doubleday, 1955).

7 The widespread popularity of James Bond might be explained in such a manner. Bond, being a "good guy," has the legitimate right to commit violence at any time he so desires.

8 In order to put this hypothesis to the test, it probably would be necessary to delineate the have-not or unsuccessful categories in terms of the specific goal under consideration, whatever it might be.

THE MORALITY SEEKERS: A STUDY OF ORGANIZED FILM CRITICISM IN THE UNITED STATES

Jack Schwartz

1 *How to Judge the Morality of Motion Pictures:* A Popular Guide to Right Standards in Motion Picture Entertainment, Authorized by the Episcopal Committee on Motion Pictures for the Legion of Decency (Washington: National Catholic Welfare Conference, n.d.), p. 4.

2 Quoted in John C. Ford and Gerald Kelly, S.J., "The Legion of Decency," *Theological Studies*, September, 1957, p. 228. The extent of this "public" would presumably embrace all mankind according to the Encyclical Letter of Pope Pius XII, "Miranda Prorsus," which states that radio, motion pictures, and television, more than the written word, aid mental culture and spiritual growth, contributing to" . . . the right training and shaping of the civil society of our times. And since this purpose is essentially connected with the advancement of the civilization of all people, the Catholic Church—which, by the charge committed to it, embraces the whole human race—desires to turn it to the extension and furthering of benefits worthy of the name— to serve truth and virtue." Encyclical issued September 8, 1957, quoted in *The 1958 National Catholic Almanac* (Paterson, N.J.: St. Anthony's Guild, 1957), p. 115.

3 *Feature Motion Pictures Reviewed by the New York Office of the National Legion of Decency, October 1959–October 1960* (New York: National Legion of Decency, 1960), p. 9.

4 This would disagree with Paul Blanshard in *American Freedom and Catholic Power*, 2nd edition (Boston: Beacon Press, 1958), p. 233, where he states that "about one-third of the 'objectionable in part' films were given this low rating because of 'light treatment of marriage and divorce.' "

REFERENCES TO SOURCES CITED IN READINGS

ALBERT, R. S., "The Role of Mass Media and the Effect of Aggressive Film Content Upon Children's Aggressive Responses and Identification Choices," *Genetic Psychology Monographs*, 55 (1957), pp. 221–285.

ARCHDIOCESAN COUNCIL OF CATHOLIC WOMEN, CHICAGO, *ACCW Decency Crusade*, Instruction and Procedure Sheet, n.d.

BAILYN, LOTTE, "Mass Media and Children: A Study of Exposure Habits and Cognitive Effects," *Psychological Monographs*, 73 (1959), pp. 1–48.

BANDURA, ALBERT, and ALETHA C. HUSTON, Identification as a Process of Incidental Learning," *Journal of Abnormal and Social Psychology*, 63 (1961), pp. 311–318.

BANDURA, ALBERT, and RICHARD H. WALTERS, *Social Learning and Personality Development*, New York: Holt, Rinehart and Winston, 1963.

BANDURA, ALBERT, DOROTHEA ROSS, and SHEILA A. ROSS, "Imitation of Film-Mediated Aggressive Models," *Journal of Abnormal and Social Psychology*, 66 (1963), pp. 3–11.

BANDURA, ALBERT, DOROTHEA ROSS, and SHEILA A. ROSS, "Transmission of Aggression through Imitation of Aggressive Models," *Journal of Abnormal and Social Psychology*, 63 (1961), pp. 575–582.

BERELSON, BERNARD, "Forward," to Gary A. Steiner, *The People Look at Television*, New York: Alfred A. Knopf, 1963.

BERKOWITZ, LEONARD, "The Effects of Observing Violence," *Scientific American*, 210 (February, 1964), pp. 35–41.

BERKOWITZ, LEONARD, and EDNA RAWLING, "Effects of Film Violence on Inhibitions against Subsequent Aggression," *Journal of Abnormal and Social Psychology*, 66 (1963), pp. 405–412.

BERKOWITZ, LEONARD, R. CORWIN, and M. HIERONIMUS, "Film Violence and Subsequent Aggressive Tendencies,' *Public Opinion Quarterly*, 27 (1962), pp. 217–229.

BLAKE, JUDITH, and KINGSLEY DAVIS, "Norms, Values, and Sanctions," in R. E. L. Faris (Ed.), *Handbook of Modern Sociology*, Chicago: Rand McNally, 1965, pp. 456–484.

BLAKELY, ROBERT J., "The Citizen and the Mass Media," in Nelson B. Henry (Ed.), *Mass Media and Education*, Chicago: University of Chicago Press, 1953.

COONS, JOHN E. (Ed.), *Freedom and Responsibility in Broadcasting*, Evanston, Ill. Northwestern University Press, 1961.

DULLES, AVERY, "The Legion of Decency," *America*, 95 (1956), pp. 240–242.

DYSINGER, W. S. and C. A. RUCKMIK, *The Emotional Responses of Children to the Motion Picture Situation*, New York: Macmillan, 1933.

EMERY, F. E., "Psychological Effects of the Western Film: A Study in Television Viewing; II, The Experimental Study," *Human Relations*, 12 (1959), pp. 215–232.

FEARING, FRANKLIN, "Social Impact of the Mass Media of Communication," in Nelson B. Henry (Ed.), *Mass Media and Education*, Chicago: University of Chicago Press, 1953.

FESHBACH, S., "The Stimulating Versus Cathartic Effects of a Vicarious Aggressive Activity," *Journal of Abnormal and Social Psychology*, 63 (1961), pp. 381–385.

FRANCIS, ROY, "Kapow!! An Argument and a Forecast," *Social Problems*, 12 (Winter, 1965), pp. 328–335.

FURU, T., *Television and Children's Life*, Radio and Television Cultural Research Institute, Japan Broadcasting Corporation, 1962.

GANS, HERBERT J., "The Creator-Audience Relationship in the Mass Media: An Analysis of Movie-Making," in Bernard Rosenberg and David Manning White (Eds.), *Mass Culture*, New York: The Free Press, 1957, pp. 315–324.

GANS, HERBERT J., "The Rise of the Problem-Film: An Analysis of Changes in Hollywood Films and the American Audience," *Social Problems*, 11 (Spring, 1964), pp. 327–336.

GENERAL FEDERATION OF WOMEN'S CLUBS, *Unity in the Community*, n.d.

GERBNER, GEORGE, "Mental Illness on TV: A Case Study in Changing Patterns of Network Censorship," *Journal of Broadcasting*, 3 (Fall, 1959), pp. 293–303.

GERBNER, GEORGE and PERCY H. TANNENBAUM, "Regulation of Mental Illness Content in Motion Pictures and Television," *Gazette*, 6 (1960), pp. 365–385.

GERSON, WALTER M., "Alienation in Mass Society," *Sociology and Social Research*, 49 (January, 1965), pp. 143–152.

GOLDWATER, JOHN, *Americana in Four Colors*, New York: Comics Magazine Association of America, 1964.

HIMMELWEIT, HILDE T., A. N. OPPENHEIM, and PAMELA VINCE, *Television and the Child*, London: Oxford University Press, 1958.

HOMANS, PETER, "Puritanism Revisited: An Analysis of the Contemporary Screen-Image Western," *Studies in Public Communication*, 3 (Summer, 1961), pp. 73–84.

INGLIS, RUTH A., *Freedom of the Movies*, Chicago: University of Chicago Press, 1947.

KLAPP, ORRIN E., *Heroes, Villains, and Fools*, Englewood Cliffs, N.J.: Prentice-Hall, 1962.

KLAPPER, JOSEPH T., *The Effects of Mass Communication*, New York: The Free Press, 1960.

LACY, DAN, *Freedom and Communications*, Urbana, Ill.: University of Illinois Press, 1965.

LARSEN, OTTO N., "Social Effects of Mass Communication," in R. E. L. Faris (Ed.), *Handbook of Modern Sociology*, Chicago: Rand McNally, 1964, pp. 348–381.

LIPPMANN, WALTER, "The Young Criminals," *New York Herald Tribune*, September 7, 1954.

LOCKHART, WILLIAM B., and ROBERT C. McCLURE, "Literature, the Law of Obscenity, and the Constitution," *Minnesota Law Review*, 38 (March, 1954).

LOORAM, MRS. JAMES, Speech at the convention of the International Federation of Catholic Alumni, cited in Harold C. Gardiner,

Catholic Viewpoint on Censorship, Garden City, N.Y.: Hanover House, 1958.

LOVAAS, O. IVAR, "Effect of Exposure to Symbolic Aggression on Aggressive Behavior," *Child Development*, 32 (1961), pp. 37–44.

MACCOBY, E. E., and W. C. WILSON, "Identification and Observational Learning From Films," *Journal of Abnormal and Social Psychology*, 55 (1957), pp. 76–87.

MACCOBY, E. E., W. C. WILSON, and R. V. BURTON, "Differential Movie-Viewing Behavior of Male and Female Viewers," *Journal of Personality*, 26 (1958), pp. 259–267.

MATZA, DAVID, and GRESHAM SYKES, "Juvenile Delinquency and Subterranean Values," *American Sociological Review*, 26 (October, 1961), pp. 712–719.

MEAD, MARGARET, "Sex and Censorship in Contemporary Society," *New York World Writing* No. 3, New York: New American Library of World Literature, 1955.

MERTON, ROBERT, *Social Theory and Social Structure*, New York: The Free Press, 1957.

MILLS, C. WRIGHT, *The Causes of World War Three*, New York: Simon and Schuster, 1958.

MUHLEN, NORBERT, "Comic Books and Other Horrors," *Commentary*, 7 (January, 1949), pp. 80–87.

MUNSEN, PAUL H., and ELDRED RUTHERFORD, "Effects of Aggressive Cartoons on Children's Aggressive Play," *Journal of Abnormal and Social Psychology*, 62 (1961), pp. 461–464.

NUSSBAUM, MARTIN, "Sociological Symbolism of the 'Adult Western'" *Social Forces*, 39 (October, 1960), pp. 25–28.

OLSON, PHILIP (Ed.), *America as a Mass Society*, New York: The Free Press, 1963.

PAUL, JAMES C. N., and MURRY L. SCHWARTZ, Federal Censorship: *Obscenity in the Mail*, New York: The Free Press, 1961.

ROSE, ARNOLD M., "Reactions Against the Mass Society," *Sociological Quarterly*, 3 (October, 1962), pp. 316–330.

SCHRAMM, WILBUR, JACK LYLE and E. B. PARKER, *Television in the Lives of Our Children*, Stanford, Calif.: Stanford University Press, 1961.

SIEGEL, ALBERTA E., "Film-mediated Fantasy Aggression and Strength of Aggressive Drive," *Child Development*, 27 (1956), pp. 355–378.

SIMPSON, GEORGE E., and J. MILTON YINGER, *Racial and Cultural Minorities*, New York: Harper & Row, 1965.

SMALL, ALBION W., "The Sociology of Conflict," *American Journal of Sociology*, 9 (January, 1904), pp. 490–525.

SMYTHE, DALLAS W., "Dimensions of Violence," *Audio-Visual Communications Review*, 3 Winter, 1955), pp. 58–63.

STANTON, FRANK, "Parallel Paths," in Norman Jacobs (Ed.), *Culture for the Millions?* Princeton, N.J.: D. Van Nostrand, 1961, pp. 85–91.

THRASHER, FREDERIC M., "The Comics and Delinquency: Cause or Scapegoat," *Journal of Educational Sociology*, 23 (1949), pp. 195–205.

U. S. CONGRESS, SENATE, *Comic Books and Juvenile Delinquency*,

Interim of the Subcommittee to Investigate Juvenile Delinquency to the Committee on the Judiciary, 84th Congress, 1st Session, Washington: Government Printing Office, 1955.

WALTERS, RICHARD H., and E. L. THOMAS, "Enhancement of Punitiveness by Visual and Audiovisual Displays," *Canadian Journal of Psychology,* 16 (1963), pp. 244–255.

WALTERS, RICHARD H., E. L. THOMAS, and C. W. ACKER, "Enhancement of Punitive Behavior by Audiovisual Displays," *Science,* 136 (1962), pp. 872–873.

WALTERS, RICHARD H., MARION LEAT, and LOUIS MEZEI, "Inhibition and Disinhibition of Responses through Empathetic Learning," *Canadian Journal of Psychology,* 17 (1963), pp. 235–243.

WERTHAM, FREDRIC, "It's Still Murder," *Saturday Review,* April 9, 1956.

WERTHAM, FREDRIC, "Mass Media and Sex Deviation," in Ralph Slovenko (Ed.), *Sexual Behavior and the Law,* Springfield, Ill.: Charles C Thomas, 1965, pp. 829–849.

WERTHAM, FREDRIC, "The Scientific Study of Mass Media Effects," *American Journal of Psychiatry,* 119 (October, 1962), pp. 306–311.

WERTHAM, FREDRIC, *Seduction of the Innocent,* New York: Holt, Rinehart and Winston, 1954.

WERTHAM, FREDRIC, *A Sign for Cain: An Exploration of Human Violence,* New York: Macmillan, 1966.

WESTLEY, WILLIAM A., "Violence and the Police," *American Sociological Review,* 26 (October, 1961), pp. 34–41.

WILENSKY, HAROLD L., "Mass Society and Mass Culture: Interdependence or Independence," *American Sociological Review,* 29 (April, 1964), pp. 173–197.

WILLIAMS, ROBIN M., JR., *American Society,* New York: Alfred A. Knopf, 1961.

WINICK, CHARLES, "Censor and Sensibility: A Content Analysis of the Television Censor's Comments," *Journal of Broadcasting,* 5 (Spring, 1961), pp. 117–135.

WINICK, CHARLES, *Taste and the Censor in Television,* New York: Fund For the Republic, 1959.

WRIGHT, CHARLES R., *Mass Communication,* New York: Random House, 1959.

INDEX

INDEX OF NAMES

INDEX OF SUBJECTS

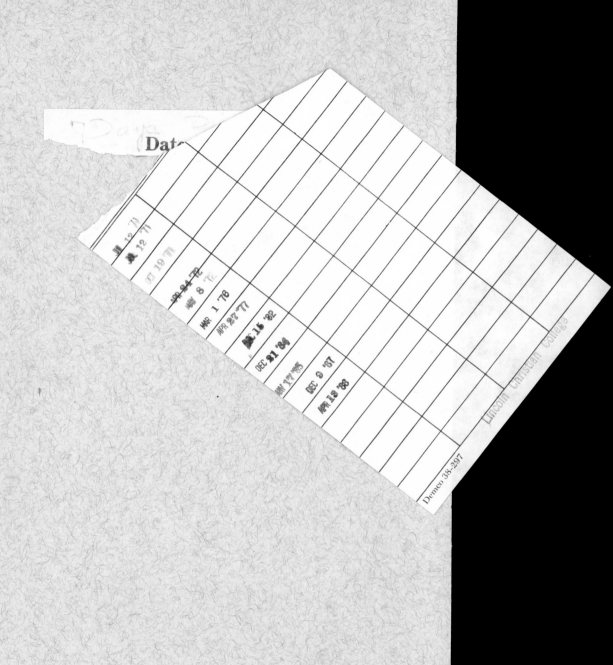